DOROTHY EINON'S
COMPLETE BOOK OF
CHILDCARE
& DEVELOPMENT

DOROTHY EINON'S
COMPLETE BOOK OF
CHILDCARE
& DEVELOPMENT

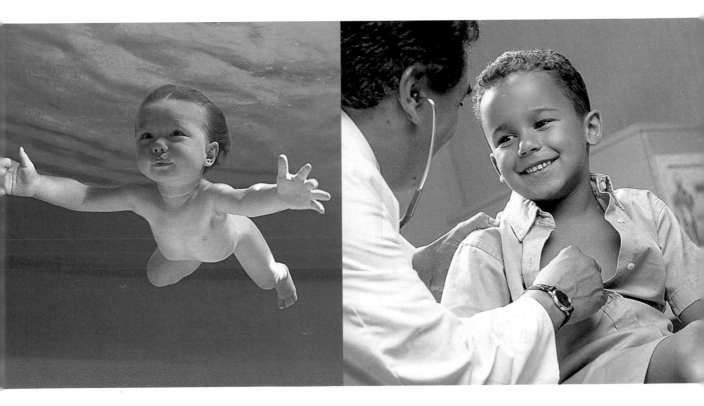

Raising happy, healthy and
confident children

Dr Dorothy Einon

In memory of Frederick and Catherine Ridgway and Francis and Dorothy Budge whose skills – and faults – made me what I am.

Copyright © 2001 Marshall Editions
Conceived, edited and designed by Marshall Editions
The Old Brewery, 6 Blundell Street
London N7 9BH

This edition published in 2003 by Apple Press Ltd
Sheridan House, 112-116A Western Road
Hove, East Sussex BN3 1DD
www.apple-press.com

ISBN 1-84092-453-5

Project Editor Sylvia Goulding
Project Art Editor Hugh Schermuly
Designer Nick Buzzard
Picture Researcher Sarah Stewart-Richardson
Managing Editor Anne Yelland
Managing Art Editor Helen Spencer
Editorial Director Ellen Dupont
Art Director Dave Goodman
Editorial Assistant Gillian Thompson
Proofreader Marion Dent
Indexer Dorothy Frame
DTP Editor Lesley Gilbert
Production Nikki Ingram, Angela Couchman

Originated in Singapore by PICA
Printed and bound in Portugal by Printer Portuguesa

Jacket picture credits
Front Jacket: l Gettyone Stone, cl, cr, r and b Mike Good
Back Jacket: l Mike Good, cl Gettyone Stone/Tim Brown,
cr Bubbles, r Mike Good

Note: Every effort has been taken to ensure that all information in this book is correct and compatible with national standards generally accepted at the time of publication. This book is not intended to replace consultation with your doctor, healthcare or education professional or to replace professional first aid training. The authors and publisher disclaim any liability for loss, injury or damage incurred as a consequence, directly or indirectly, of the use and application of the contents of this book.

Note: The terms "he" and "she", used on alternate spreads, refer to children of both sexes, unless a topic or sequence of photographs applies only to a boy or girl.

Foreword

When I was small my grandfather would take my cousin and I to help him with his prize chrysanthemums. I remember feeling important, because that is how he made me feel. Most of all I remember him turning to me and then to my cousin, shaking his head and saying "A head of dark curls and one of blond hair. Now who could ever say which is the most beautiful?"

Almost anyone can raise children, just as almost anyone can grow a few flowers. But to raise prize blooms you need to be like my grandfather. Without doubt the greatest skill you need is to make a child believe she is special. More than that, to show this in a way that makes her believe she is special whatever happens to her. It is more than saying to her "I love you". It is saying it in ways that allow her to take your love for granted. I don't think Granddad ever said those three words, but I don't doubt that I was loved.

The second skill is to enable your child. Enabling is instilling self-confidence, together with skills such as being able to dress or communicate feelings. More than that it is giving the child the confidence to say "I can". The message can be straight forward "I am confident that you can do it" or more indirect – it is there when you ask her to help you to carry in the shopping. Enabling gives a child confidence and self-esteem. Unquestioned love and powerful enabling work best within clear and firm boundaries, where mutual care and respect are taken for granted.

Contents

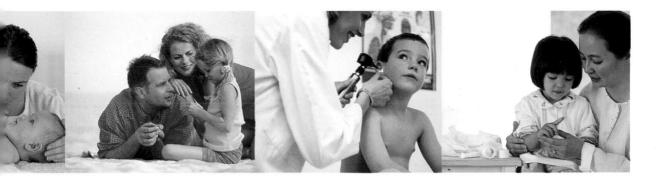

Introduction

Most of us cannot aspire to being a great scientist or a media star. Even with the best teachers we may never win prizes for our embroidery or build the sort of tables that people are prepared to pay a small fortune to own. Most of us are, in fact, quite ordinary, better at some things than others, but average none the less. If we had to list our lifetime achievements they would seem mediocre until we came to look at our children. For most of us, raising children, and raising them well, is our greatest achievement. It is at once the most exhilarating, frustrating, boring, fascinating, terrifying and comforting thing we ever do. No one else loves us with the intensity and acceptance of a two-year-old. Nor does anyone frustrate us quite as much. As he spins into yet another tantrum or refuses eat his dinner we can feel out of control.

Until a child is born it is impossible to understand how absorbed we can become in the minutiae of their lives, or how much we put our heart on the line. Within days of their birth we know that whatever happens to this child from now on will affect the rest of our lives. This is not a relationship that we can set aside and start again. Which is why most of us are so concerned to get it "right". The other reason is, of course, that we are becoming increasingly aware that what happens in childhood can affect the rest of life. The claim "Show me the child at seven and I'll show you the man", is not always true, but it is true enough to make most parents feel that they should try get it right first time.

Being a parent

The good news is that most of us are better and more knowledgeable parents than we think. If we were well parented we will usually find that those skills have been passed on to us. If we were not so fortunate we will often be able to see where our own parents went wrong. While you may have bought this book to teach yourself how, most of you will probably find that you use it to reassure yourselves that you are on the right track. Whatever group you fall into it is wise to remember that there is no such thing as a perfect parent: and that if there were this paragon would be an impossible model for life. We raise children for a world which is far from perfect, peopled by people who are far from perfect. Children need to know we are also fallible. We owe it to them to do our best, but we cannot expect that we will never make mistakes.

Getting it "right" has many facets, and this book is aimed to help you with each one. Sometimes all parents need is knowledge, sometimes all they need is practical skills and workable techniques, mostly what they need is a combination of all three. Where I have suggested ways of doing things I have also tried to explain why some techniques work and others do not.

Using this book

The book is broken down into different sections for ease of reference. In the beginning our major concerns are ensuring our children survive, so the book starts by explaining certain practical skills. As we become more assured in our handling of our small baby we have the leisure to think about how we should parent and how our children are developing. These subjects are dealt with in separate chapters.

The last two chapters of the book deal with problems. The first looks at the problems we all face, giving tried and tested solutions to worrying or irritating behaviours such as tantrums or the child's refusal to eat anything but baked beans. The second deals with the sorts of problems we all hope we will never have to confront – serious and life-threatening emergencies. It would be wise to read this section first, and memorize it. When a real emergency arises there is usually not time to consult a book.

CHAPTER ONE

Childcare

Whether we learn from books, courses, or our own parents or friends, most of us automatically care for our children in the right way. We learn by trial and error, and before you know it, your child will be weaned off breast or bottle, out of his nappies and ready to explore the world around him. If you keep your child's best interests at heart, you will usually get childcare right. A child who is well cared for feels loved and secure so, as he grows, your skill in caring for him will encourage him towards greater independence.

Enjoy your pregnancy

Do not worry about your life as "mother". There will be time to adjust later.

A child is born

Try as we might, few of us can think beyond birth. Who is my baby? Will it be a boy or a girl? What will my child be like? How will my own life be affected? Pregnancy, for many of us, is a time of great expectations.

Until our baby is in our arms, the idea of "parenthood" is made up of the layette, the diagrams in the books and watching the heaving movements of our stomach. Birth frees our dreams and gives them focus. Then, as if we need to make up for nine months without plans, new parents go into overdrive. Is that a smile? Did I see her holding her head up for a moment? How long until she sits? From being frozen out of her future, we race ahead – almost wishing it away. The pressure is on to get to the next milestone. Charts and books (and this book is no exception) fuel that race. In no time she will be rushing into school with her lunch box, our kitchen will be filled with young men, and we are left wondering how on earth it all went by so fast.

So let us start with the first and foremost piece of advice: enjoy your baby. Not for what she will do tomorrow but for what she is today and was yesterday. You have hung your heart out on a line, you are walking without a safety net, the pleasure, the pain, the exhilaration and the sheer boredom of parenthood is like no other. Savour it. Do not expect perfection from yourself or your children. No one can be a perfect parent. Nor should they try. Love them to bits, support and cherish them in spite of their failures and love and cherish yourself in spite of yours.

When in doubt, remember that for most of us parenthood will be one of our major excuses for singing "My Way" at the old folks' karaoke. They are your children forever, but they are only children for such a short time – do not miss it.

A family is not made instantly

Few of us have grown up with small children around us, but if we ourselves have been well parented, many aspects of parenthood will come quite naturally. For those less fortunate, the "right way" will be harder – but not impossible – to find.

Remember that babies are not born into a vacuum. There is always at least one ongoing relationship that must be renegotiated: that of the new mother with her changing self. The very word "mother" has connotations most of us would not choose for ourselves, such as "asexual", "self-sacrificing", "nurturing". The father must renegotiate his own relationship with his changing self, and each parent their relationship to the child as well as each parent with the other. There are other relationships to be renegotiated, too: with other children, family members and friends. This all takes time.

For most women the physical demands of the child take precedent in the first days after birth. She has no time to address her changing relationships, especially if this is her first child. The demands she makes at this stage on the relationship with her co-parent are those of support and shared

THE WAY TO STAY SANE

- Newborn babies sleep much of the time and do not need your or your partner's constant attention.
- Small babies do not miss their parents when they go out for the evening – competent and well chosen baby-sitters can look after your baby.
- The odd bottle of formula is not the end of the world (or of breast-feeding).
- Babies do not need or, indeed, want constant stimulation.
- Babies can manage without being burped at night, and if they are breast-fed they will not need to be burped during the day either.
- Babies do not need their nappies changing at night unless they are soiled. Babies are happy in wet nappies.
- Babies can sometimes (or always) sleep in your bed – as most babies in most parts of the world do. There is nothing special or different about European and American babies (or their parents) that makes this dangerous, nor will it deprive the child of independence, or stop them from eventually learning to sleep alone, in their own beds.
- Babies can have dummies. Comfort objects are positively good for them.
- Your partner can be left in charge.
- Babies can be "topped and tailed" (see p.33) for two days in a row.
- Breasts are a convenient means of delivering food. They do not deliver love or the badge of "true motherhood".
- A natural birth is a fine thing. Having a Caesarean, screaming blue murder throughout labour or not following your birth plan to the letter have absolutely nothing to do with your ability to be a good parent – your feelings of failure, however, can and often do.

SEE ALSO

Establishing a routine **40–41**
Sharing the care **52–53**
First steps to parenting **136–137**
A place in the family **154–155**

Don't try to be supermum
Allow yourself the time to be with your baby, and do nothing else until you are ready. Use your partner's and other people's help in the house and wait – your time will come.

FORGET ABOUT

- **Chores.** You will run yourself ragged if you try to do more than look after your baby in the first weeks. You will be able to do your own thing again, but it will take time to regain your organization and emotional stability. Enjoy what you have. Let your old self rest.
- **Cooking fancy food.** Put aside part of your last month's salary cheque for precooked meals and takeaways.
- **Your figure.** You have the rest of your life to watch your figure. Counting calories is not important.
- **Housework.** If you have the spare cash, pay someone to do it.

critically watched as he tries to lift the child, change her nappy or rock her to sleep. All too often his inexperience is underlined by the mother's relative skills in handling the baby. He may even feel cast out from his child and his partner.

None of this matters in the short term, nor, indeed, does it matter in the long term if everyone remembers that all "characters" within this complicated interplay must take their turn at the back. The changes that a small baby brings into your life cannot all be absorbed in the first days. You will be too tired, too stressed and too engrossed in the new responsibilities of parenthood even to contemplate them.

Good-enough parenting

Good parenting is always a compromise between what you aspire to be and what you can realistically achieve. Reassure yourself that perfect parenting does not exist, nor is it desirable. The child you are raising will have to cope with her own problems and the mistakes of all those she meets. Unless you make some mistakes you would be an impossible act to follow. How could she – with all her imperfections – feel confident if she had perfect parents?

joys, rather than adapting to the changes that have occurred. For the father the pattern is different. He may have been involved with the birth, but now he finds himself on the sidelines. He will be

Lifting and holding baby

The first time you try to lift and hold your tiny baby may well seem a little unnerving, and you will probably worry about supporting him correctly. Yet, although your baby may look fragile, he is already surprisingly robust.

Up you come

Slip one hand under your baby's shoulder. Support his head with your arm, and push the other hand under his bottom.

Close cuddles

Your body supports his tummy, your arms his bottom and neck, as he looks over your shoulder.

As long as you make sure that his head and shoulders are supported, the way you lift and carry your baby – however clumsy it may seem to you or others – will not harm him. Even if his head flops back occasionally it is no cause for panic.

Sitting and watching

The safest resting position for a baby is lying flat on his back. You could place him in a rocking cradle chair or removable car seat which will hold his body fairly flat while, at the same time, enabling him to look around the room and watch you. You can even put a tiny baby safely beside you on your desk or worktop, but always ensure you are within arm's reach, and never leave him unattended. Once he starts rocking the chair, the floor will be much safer. Your baby will move his chair

surprisingly easily, and while you answer the phone or the door, an active baby might topple from the surface.

Lifting your baby

To pick your baby up, slide your left hand under his head and down to his shoulders so that your arm is under his head, and push your right hand under his bottom. Lean into him so your body supports his. As you lift him, move your left hand further towards his bottom, and cradle his head in the crook of your arm. Rest his legs in the crook of your right arm.

Carrying a tiny baby

You can carry your baby cradled in this position, or bring him up to your shoulder. To do this turn him in towards your body, put your left hand under his bottom and

The "hip carry"

Facing your body, he sits astride your hip. His back is supported by your arm.

The "forward carry"

He sits on one hand, his back and chest held by the other.

use your right hand to support his back and head. Slowly pull him up and let his head flop onto your shoulder. You can also carry him in a more prone position, resting his chin and his neck in one hand and his crotch and bottom in the other.

Putting baby back down

Holding your baby close to your body, bend over the cot so that your body continues to support him. Keep one hand under his bottom and the other supporting his head and neck. Slowly move him away from your body and place him on the mattress, then gently remove your hands.

Carrying older babies

Once a baby can support his head, many parents use the "hip carry". Your baby sits astride your hip or waist, supported by the crook of your arm. Meanwhile, you have one hand free to make his bottle.

Another commonly used position is the "forward carry" which allows him to look around. Roll him onto his tummy, then lift, placing one hand under his bottom, the other arm across his chest. Pull him in, to support his back against your chest.

Makeshift carriers

A makeshift carrier will make your baby feel warm and secure, and he can be gently rocked while you carry out your normal activities. He can even attach to the nipple if he is hungry while you vacuum the lounge or prepare supper. Women all over Africa carry babies in pieces of fabric strapped to their bodies, and these babies are rarely heard crying in public.

The style of makeshift carriers varies, as does the baby's position on the body, but the basic principle is much the same. A typical carrier might be made like this: the bottom long edge of a large rectangular piece of cloth is tied around the mother's

hip, while the top long edge is tied across her chest, over one shoulder. The baby is seated in a fold in the fabric, so the bottom edge supports his bottom, and the top edge holds his head and shoulders in place.

Choosing a baby carrier

There are many different types of baby carrier you can make or buy: from a basic piece of fabric to all-weather adjustable pouches with fitted seats and head supports. You will find front pouches easiest for newborn babies, but side pouches are easier on your back because you can support the baby's weight on your hips. Back carriers are easier for toddlers and older babies, but do not use these until the baby can sit independently. Winter babies need more elaborate pouches, with weather proofing. Check that you can take the baby out of the carrier without help. Carriers should have wide seats to support the baby's bottom and thighs, some support for the back and head and wide shoulder straps for your comfort.

Carrying and breathing

Holding your baby close to your chest is warm and comforting for both of you. In addition, this closeness will help him learn to adopt adult breathing patterns.

Newborn babies breathe in slowly and out fast – the same breathing pattern we use when running or doing aerobics. Most of the time, however, we quickly snatch the in-breath and then expel the air slowly in order to be able to speak. Babies cannot vary their breathing patterns before they are about three months old and have gained control over their muscles. Tiny babies are well tuned to your breathing: they synchronize their own movements to your voice and, when held and carried close to your body, they quickly learn how to use your breathing pattern.

SEE ALSO

Bedroom equipment	**34–35**
Have baby, will travel	**42–43**
Seeing the world	**74–75**
Taking control of the body	**82–83**

ALWAYS

● Put your baby down to sleep on his back or on his side. Babies who sleep in these positions are less susceptible to cot death.

● Talk to your baby as you approach to lift him. He may find it frightening to be suddenly lifted into the air by you.

● Ensure that both head and neck of your newborn baby are supported as you lift and carry him.

NEVER NEVER

● Leave your baby lying unattended, especially on his tummy. Even tiny babies can creep in this position.

● Leave clutter on the floor. It is hard to see obstacles on the floor while you are carrying your baby.

● Bundle him up in layers of clothing and/or bedding on a warm day.

● Go out on a cold day unless he is well protected from the elements: wind, rain and cold.

Keeping your baby warm

Newborn babies have relatively poor control over their body temperature – especially on their hands and feet. It is up to us to make sure that they are always sufficiently well protected from wind and weather.

Mummy keeps you warm
Your body is an excellent hot-water bottle – in an emergency, tuck her inside your coat, or hold her close to your body, and wrap both of you in clothing or blankets.

There are a number of reasons why babies need our help to stay warm or cool. Firstly, babies simply do not have a good temperature regulatory mechanism. Secondly, they do not have good blood circulation – so even once they are able to control the temperature of the body, their legs and hands can get cold. Thirdly, babies lose heat at a faster rate than adults. Lastly, babies do not know how to behave in order to regulate their temperature – they cannot jump around to generate heat, or move into the shade to keep cool. Your own comfort is generally a good guide to keeping a small child warm, but it is only a very rough guide to your baby's needs. Babies do not create their own warmth by moving about as children and adults do, and they rarely have much fat to insulate them.

Keeping warm

Before setting out on a cold day, remember that a child needs to be dressed as you would be if you were to sleep out in the park. Even this estimate is conservative. Heat loss is proportional to body surface, heat gain from the metabolism is proportional to body volume: with their tiny volumes and disproportionately high surface area, babies and children always lose heat faster than adults do. Their relatively hairless heads add further to the problem, losing heat even faster. This can be an advantage when it is hot – but it is a distinct disadvantage in the cold.

Coping with the cold

● Remember that a quarter of heat is lost via the head. Do not wait for it to get really cold before putting her hat on.
● Her circulation is poor. Even on days that are cool rather than cold, a small baby needs to have her hands and feet covered when she is outside, and also when she is inside if the room is not heated.
● Change wet clothes (other than nappies) immediately. The water evaporating from wet clothing draws heat from the child's body. Nappies are encased in a waterproof layer so there is no evaporation and they act like a wet suit, keeping a baby warm rather than cold.
● If she is put to sleep in an unheated room, check that she cannot kick off her blankets – or that, if she does so, she is wearing adequate clothing.
● A new baby's room should be around 20–22°C (68–72°F) by day and 15–18°C (60–65°F) by night – overheating is as dangerous as underheating (or more so).
● Even on milder days, protect her from gusting cold winds and rain by popping her inside your raincoat. Put up the rain cover if she is out in her buggy.

• Layers of clothing trap air, so, unless a jacket is padded, two thin layers are warmer than one thick one.

• Even a baby in warm clothing and covered with blankets should not stay out for long when it is freezing.

Choosing cold weather outfits

Once they start to kick vigorously, babies often lose their mittens and booties. Stretch suits with built-in feet and rollover cuffs will prevent this. You can always put an extra layer over the top when it is really cold. Woolly hats which cover the ears are an important component of any winter baby's clothing because they fit snugly around the head and are usually better than hoods – hoods often get in the way of a child's view as they go too low into the face or do not move when she turns her head. On the coldest days provide an extra layer for the head with a hooded jacket, snowsuit or sleeping bag on top of her hat.

Going out in winter

Feed her before going out on a cold day. Keeping warm takes lots of energy, so make sure her stores are renewed.

Always make sure that a baby's legs and feet are covered with a number of layers on very cold days. Circulation to the legs is often poor in the first few months, and in the early weeks babies do not kick and move their legs very much, so that little heat is generated in these areas. Foot muffs keep her cosy in the buggy, but in the carrier she will need a padded snowsuit.

When it is exceptionally cold protect her face by holding her against your warm body and wrapping a blanket loosely over her head and face. Cover her face in a shawl – they have a loose texture so that the airways stay clear. Even better: only take her out if absolutely necessary.

Avoiding frostbite

Babies are very susceptible to frostbite, especially on their fingers and toes. Toes that are cold turn first red, then blue. Those with frostbite are white or yellowish white. If your baby shows symptoms of frostbite get the affected parts next to your body as quickly as possible. Your body is the safest radiator – open your coat, pop her under your jumper and then wrap it back around you both. Get indoors as quickly as possible.

The child should be warmed up very gradually. Immersion in a bath which is just above blood heat (about 38–39°C/ 100–102°F) is safe. A hot bath, hot water bottles, or placing your baby next to a radiator, open fire or stove are not. It may take anything up to 60 minutes for the body to return to normal. Use warm flannels to warm up the ears and other areas which cannot be soaked. Finally, call the doctor, or take the child to the accident and emergency department of the hospital.

Hypothermia emergencies

A baby who seems abnormally cold and inert must be taken to hospital immediately. Do not waste any time. Put the baby next to your skin, wrap yourselves in clothing or several blankets and go right away.

SEE ALSO
Keeping your baby cool   **18–19**
How to dress your baby   **28–29**
Have baby, will travel   **42–43**
Making outdoors safe   **206–207**

Keeping warm
When you take your baby out for a walk in the buggy, make sure she is snug and warm. She is not moving like you are, so she will need extra protection from the cold.

Keeping your baby cool

Much attention is usually being lavished on keeping babies warm, but their lack of control over body temperature also means that they cannot keep themselves cool – which is important in warm countries and hot summers.

Well protected

A sun umbrella and loosely fitting, lightweight clothes help protect your child in strong sunshine, and multicoloured sunblock is fun to look at too!

Summers are getting hotter. We are also taking more holidays in parts of the world where the climate is considerably hotter than in our own country. These lifestyle changes affect babies and little children much more than adults.

Safety rules for sunshine

● In hot weather keep your baby out of the sun during the hottest part of the day, between about noon and 3pm.

● Natural fibres such as cotton and linen are usually cooler to wear than synthetic fibres. In warm weather you can safely let your own temperature be your guide. If it is warm enough for you to sit outside in a T-shirt, then it is warm enough for your baby to do so too.

● Avoid using baby carriers that completely enclose your baby. Never, never leave him in a parked car in hot weather, or lying in direct sun, even for a short while.

● If heat cannot be avoided, remove most of his clothing and give him plenty of cooled-down, boiled water to drink. Protect his head from the sun with a large, light hat and his body with a sunshade or loose-fitting clothing.

● Do not bundle your baby up in layers of clothing and blankets just because he is going to bed. If it is hot, remove some of his blankets. On really hot days let him sleep in just a nappy.

Selecting sunshades

Many baby carriages and buggies come with sunshades that attach to the handles. These are ideal for summer outings. Remember to keep on adjusting the position of the shade so that it keeps the sun off the baby at all times. Babies usually have paler skin than they will have as adults. Even if he has dark skin, however, it is more delicate and will burn easily if exposed to the direct rays of the hot sun. In the carrier, shade can be produced by using a floppy hat or an umbrella. A large sun umbrella is essential for beach and garden – especially if you are staying out in the sun for long periods.

Sun protection creams

Do not rely on the suntan lotions and creams you use for yourself – always protect your baby's skin with a sun block. Cover all exposed areas, especially his face (nose, cheeks and ears) and areas of skin that are not normally exposed to the sun – bare bottoms burn surprisingly quickly! Renew the sun block frequently, especially after splashing around in water.

Sponging down

If your baby is hot and bothered, he may become irritable and start whining, and his face may look flushed. The easiest and quickest way to cool him is by sponging him with tepid water or by putting him into a tepid bath.

The water should be below blood temperature, but not cold. A cold sponge makes the blood capillaries in the skin constrict, which reduces blood flow near the skin surface. This in turn stops your baby sweating which is the best way of cooling the body. A tepid sponge bath, however, provides instant relief and keeps the blood flow going.

Heat-stress emergencies

Heat stress may occur quite suddenly: your baby's skin becomes hot and dry, he seems either lethargic or agitated, he has high fever and may also suffer from diarrhoea. He may even lose consciousness or have a febrile convulsion. Do not delay – act instantly to help your baby.

If you suspect heat stroke

- Soak a sheet or towel in tepid water and wrap your child in it.
- Alternatively, run a tepid bath, place your baby in the bath and sponge him with a tepid cloth.
- Cover his head with a flannel and pour tepid water over this.
- Summon help immediately.

If he is losing consciousness

- Soak a sheet or towel in tepid water, wrap him in the towel and cover his head with a damp cloth.
- Get him to the nearest hospital as fast as you possibly can.
  - Take additional water to pour over him during the journey.

Cool down

Help your baby cope with the heat by gently sponging his face, neck and body with tepid water. You will soon have a happier and more relaxed baby!

SEE ALSO

Keeping your baby warm   **16–17**
How to dress your baby   **28–29**
Sponging a baby clean   **32–33**
Have baby, will travel   **42–43**

HOT IN WINTER

It is easy to forget that there are many situations in cold weather, too, when your baby may overheat. Remove some of his clothing:

- When you get into a heated car, bus, or train, especially on longer journeys.
- When you go into a roofed and heated shopping centre or supermarket, and you plan to spend some time there.
- When you both go indoors – a "quick'" chat with a friend or neighbour may take too long for a baby!

Better health?

Breast milk is said to promote immunity, yet bottle-feeding is just as safe in today's homes.

Breast or bottle?

In the first weeks after birth you will be spending most of your time looking after your baby and adjusting to new joys and worries. Do not allow the choice of breast or bottle to dominate your life and cause you additional stress.

Always remember: a breast is just a breast. How you deliver milk to your baby is a very minor part of parenthood. If you cannot breast-feed your baby, for whatever reason, this should not make you depressed. No-one ever tells you that you should *not* breast-feed, but the advantages of breast-feeding are often overstated. Here we will look at some of the claims in detail.

Breast is best

"Breast milk is designed for rearing human babies, cows' milk for rearing calves", goes the argument. Formula is cows' milk that has been modified to make it more like human milk. It is not perfect, but fairly good – if bottles are made up as directed, formula provides your baby with all the nutrients she needs to grow. It does not change throughout the feed, as breast milk does, nor does it adjust as the child grows, but whether this is necessary is not certain.

Today few women feed babies "as Nature intended". Women in hunter-gathering communities breast-feed for two to three years, and this is probably what happened in Europe, when exclusive breast-feeding was the only available method of contraception (women usually start to ovulate again once they supplement feeds). Nature did not intend us to raise children on modified cows' milk, nor did it intend us to supplement the breast with solid foods in the first year – and this is now common practice.

Breast milk is easier to digest

There is no disputing this: one can smell the difference in the stools of breast-fed and bottle-fed babies! This is caused by the different milk proteins: lactalbumin in breast milk, and caseinogen in formula. In practice bottle-fed babies tend to be more susceptible to colic, wind and being sick. There is also less sodium in breast milk – while this is better for the kidneys, bottle-fed babies are no more likely to suffer from kidney disease. Babies are hardly ever allergic to breast milk, while a small but significant number of babies develop allergies to cows' milk. Breast-fed babies are also less likely to suffer from constipation.

Breast-feeding and immunity

Breast-feeding is claimed to protect against gastroenteritis, cot death and cancer, and to promote better cholesterol metabolism and intelligence. This is difficult to prove or disprove because, in most cases, studies do not compare like with like. Mothers who bottle-feed are more likely to be poor, to live in substandard housing, to be teenagers, smokers, drinkers, drug takers, and to have fewer years of education. On average their children are more likely to suffer from disease, but whether this is a direct result of being fed by the bottle rather than the breast or because of other reasons is unclear.

We cannot even say for certain that the immunity comes directly from the breast milk, although there are strong reasons for supposing it might. Breast milk is derived from the mother's blood, and contains the antibodies she has produced against disease. The baby receives her antibodies against infection every time she feeds. The colostrum, which she receives in the first couple of days of breast-feeding, is rich in antibodies. The milk that follows is less so, but the regular top-up will protect her.

Breast-fed babies may also have more contact with their mother's skin. Her skin is a source of "good bacteria" which could also confer some immunity to the baby.

The immunity breast milk passes on to the baby would far outweigh all the advantages of bottle feeding if we lived in a less sterile environment. However, today bottle-feeding is completely safe as our modern homes are clean of germs. When our immunity is rarely challenged by attack, the advantages of breast over bottle become much less obvious.

Breast-feeding and bonding

It is true that bottle-feeding can be carried out by others, or that by propping the bottle on a cushion you can feed a baby without even picking her up. But that does not mean mothers do not bond as they bottle-feed. Breast-feeding mothers do not always gaze lovingly into their baby's eyes as she suckles. For many of them breast-feeding is a time to catch up on reading or talking to an older child. While it is hard to change a nappy, or spoon-feed, or jiggle a bottle teat into the mouth without having a conversation, it is perfectly possible to slip the nipple in the mouth without doing so. There is no evidence that the breast is the seat of love, and we can safely ignore all claims that it is.

Hormonal love

The role of hormones in breast-feeding and the unconscious connections between our bodies and our minds are harder to determine. Oxytocin, the hormone associated with milk let-down, is also associated with the sexual climax. Women are not automatically "switched on" sexually by ovulation like animals are. They have to learn to enjoy sex, and feelings of love are part of that learning. Before women breast-feed, they have released oxytocin in such loving sexual contexts. So perhaps loving feelings towards the baby when breast-feeding are not so surprising after all. It certainly works the other way around! Most women find that the feelings of love towards a partner, the sight of the baby, or a cuddle from an older child can – in the early weeks of breast-feeding – cause the milk let-down reflex to start.

However, while mothers may develop closer emotional ties to their breast-fed babies, fathers may lose out. They may feel less excluded from this close loving relationship in the early weeks if the baby is given at least an occasional bottle.

SEE ALSO

How to breast-feed **22–23**

How to bottle-feed **24–25**

Weaning from the breast **46–47**

Introducing solids **48–49**

FOR BOTTLE

- Babies may sleep for longer.
- Mothers enjoy greater freedom.
- Bottle-feeding is much easier when the mother needs to return to work in the first few months.
- It is less stressful to bottle-feed the baby in public.
- Bottle-feeding is less problematic for lovemaking, since lubrication and libido return to normal sooner, and leaky breasts are not a problem.
- Fathers can share in feeding and bond with the baby.

How to breast-feed

Breast-feeding is not difficult – if you follow a few simple steps. You lift your baby, stroke his cheek, he turns and latches onto your breast. The milk starts flowing, and you carry on chatting to your older child or watching TV.

Convenience food

Breast milk is always on tap, always the right temperature, ready as quickly as you are, and your baby has access to milk 24 hours a day – wherever you are.

The first few times, breast-feeding is rarely easy. We have too many expectations, and the tenser we get, the harder it becomes. The sooner you start, the easier it will be. In fact, newborn babies come with built-in food stores, and if it takes a couple of days to get feeding established this is not a serious problem. He needs fluid but that fluid does not have to be milk. In the first couple of days the breasts do not even produce milk.

Easy steps to breast-feeding

1 Get into a comfortable position. This is surprisingly difficult. Experiment till you find one that suits you both. Lying on your side may be easiest: you can control the angle of your breast by rocking from side to side, and the position of the baby by moving him up and down the side of your body. Failing this put a cushion on your lap and place the baby on top.

2 Place your baby beside you and stroke his cheek. He will automatically open his mouth as his head turns towards your hand. It is then simply a matter of having the nipple in the right place.

3 Hold your breast between thumb and forefinger (or fore- and middle finger), cupping the rest of it in your hand. Line it up with the baby's head. Push into the breast to direct the nipple into the baby's mouth and expose more of it to him.

4 Bring the nipple towards the baby's cheek and tickle it just above the edge of the mouth. The rooting reflex will cause him to turn and open his mouth. Pop the nipple between his lips and then push it well in so that his lips rest on the areola. His sucking reflex will come into play. Alternatively, tease his lips with the nipple until he opens his mouth, then push the nipple well in, aiming for the back of the throat rather than between the lips. When

latched on, his lips should rest on the alveoli, not at the end of the nipple. If you do not feel the suction he may be sucking his tongue or his lips rather than the breast. Take him off and start again.

5 Once he has latched on, check that his nose is clear. If the milk is flowing too quickly (as it may do at first) express a little before you start by squeezing the areola.

How much to feed

Start by giving 5–10 minutes on each breast. Alternate the starting breast if possible, and more or less equate the use of each breast in the course of the day. But do not worry too much about this.

If you need to stop the feed for whatever reason, pop a finger in his mouth to break the suction. This will help prevent soreness. Each breast contains both fore and hind milk and the baby will usually empty both. As he gets hungrier he will want to feed for longer. Let him. As his hunger is sated, he will suck more slowly and eventually fall asleep.

In the early weeks you may want to put a nursing pad over the unused breast while he feeds because it is likely to leak. You will learn to control this with practice.

When you are starting out, feed him at least six times in 24 hours. Milk is made on demand – if he takes little, you will make little. If you do not have sufficient milk he may stop sucking. It becomes a downward spiral. Using a breast pump to add extra suction, and/or to remove extra milk, can help regulate the supply.

When not to breast-feed

● If you have a serious illness, such as heart or kidney disease, or a serious infection, such as HIV/AIDS or TB.

● If you are seriously underweight.

● If you have to take medication which may be harmful to a growing baby. Most medicines are compatible with nursing, but always check first. Anticancer drugs, lithium and ergots are harmful. Unsafe drugs include aspirin, tranquillizers, antidepressants and antipsychotics, drugs for hypertension and thyroid disease, and sedatives. If there is no safe alternative, and the drugs are necessary for your health and wellbeing, breast-feeding is unwise.

● Breast-feeding mothers may be more susceptible to depression. You may wish to take this into account if you are prone to serious depression and/or have previously suffered from postnatal depression.

SEE ALSO

Breast or bottle?	**20–21**
How to bottle-feed	**24–25**
Establishing a routine	**40–41**
Weaning from the breast	**46–47**

ENGORGEMENT

This is common around day 3–4. Quite suddenly the breasts become swollen, taut, rock hard and extremely uncomfortable. Fortunately it does not last long: but while it does it can be very painful and will almost certainly disrupt feeding. The nipples are flattened by the swelling, making it harder for the baby to latch on. It rarely lasts more than a few days.

● If you are in great pain, sit in the bath and drape your breasts in hot flannels – warm compresses will encourage milk let-down and give relief.

● Express some milk before you start feeding to soften your breasts. This will enable the baby to latch on.

● If your breasts are still engorged at the end of a feed take a mild analgesic (but not aspirin). Use warm compresses to draw off milk and alternate these with cold compresses to bring pain relief.

ADVICE FOR BEGINNERS

● Let the hospital know if you will be feeding on demand. If your baby cannot sleep next to you 24 hours a day, ensure that you can feed on demand during the day, and that he is brought to you at night. Be insistent. Tell the staff that you do not want him to have supplementary bottles of water and glucose which would quickly satiate him.

● Unless he sucks and empties your breasts you will not get your milk supply under control. Ban the bottle until a routine is established, even if you intend to combine breast and bottle.

● If he is correctly latched on, more of the areola should be visible above the breast than below. Do not hold the breast tightly: this can inhibit milk flow.

● Drink plenty of fluids. Alcohol may help you relax, but it is not a good idea to drink regularly. What you drink, he drinks.

● Relax. If you are tense it gets harder. If you are having problems, get help from childbirth classes, your doctor or a friend who has successfully breast-fed.

● In my experience breast-fed babies do not need burping. The suction method means that he does not swallow air while feeding. During the day you may like to put him up onto your shoulder and rub his back – and he will enjoy this – but do not bother with this at night.

How to bottle-feed

Bottle-fed babies are happy and healthy, as are their parents. Bottle-feeding is essential if you need to return to work early, and it provides a unique opportunity for mother and father to share the feeding of their child.

Your breasts will make milk regardless of whether you intend to breast-feed or not, but they will only continue to do so if the milk is removed from the breast. If you bottle-feed from the start, or give up breast-feeding in the first few days, your breasts will feel uncomfortably full for a few days, but this will soon pass.

You will need

● Between 4 and 6 plastic bottles (depending on the method you use to sterilize them).
● The same number of silicone or latex teats; a teat with a small hole for a younger baby, with a larger hole for an older one; the shape is not important – although some babies prefer nipple shapes.
● A means to sterilize the bottles.
● If you wish to warm the milk a bottle warmer is useful.

Making a bottle-feed

Baby formula is available as a dried powder which you add to previously boiled water and shake. Pre-prepared cartons and tins of formula and even ready-to-use bottles of milk are also available. Although convenient, this may be wasteful as it may not come in package sizes that are right for your baby.

1 Always wash your hands before preparing bottles (use sterile wipes at night). Take the bottle out of the sterilizer and rinse in boiled or sterile water if using chemical sterilization.

2 Add the required amount of pure, boiled water to the bottle, then measure the milk powder. Add and shake well.

3 Cool (or warm) to blood temperature and feed. To warm up cold formula, stand the bottle in hot water or use a bottle warmer. The microwave is not safe.

If you are preparing the bottle for later use, cover with the cap and top provided and keep in the fridge.

Sterilizing bottles

Rinse the bottles after use and clean both bottles and teats in water and detergent before sterilizing them. Use a bottle brush to remove the last remaining milk from the bottle and teat, and squeeze soapy water through nipple holes to clear them. After washing, rinse again with warm water.
● **Boil the bottle** if you only give your baby an occasional bottle, or when you are away from home. Immerse bottles and teats in a large pan of water, making sure they remain immersed, bring the pan to the boil and keep boiling for at least ten minutes. Use bottle directly from the pan.

Safe and happy

As long as you can provide a clinically clean environment for preparing feeds, you can enjoy the great advantages and freedom of bottle-feeding.

● **Steaming** is more convenient and quicker. You can buy purpose-built steamers, or ones specially designed for use in the microwave. Follow instructions.

● **Chemical sterilization** uses cold water and sterilizing fluid or tablets. Follow the instructions in making up the solution. Immerse all bottles and other items for the stated times. Do not take them out until ready to use. Replace sterilizing fluids every 24 hours – rinse bottles and teats (using either sterile bottled water or previously boiled water) before using them.

How to bottle-feed

1 Hold your baby close to your body so she snuggles into you. Tilt the bottle so that the teat is full of milk (this prevents her swallowing too much air).

2 Tease the side of her mouth or stroke her cheek so that she turns towards the bottle or your hand and opens her mouth.

3 Pop the bottle into her open mouth, pushing it well back. She should start to suck when the teat is fully in her mouth. Every so often you may need to remove the bottle from her mouth. Teats tend to collapse with continuous sucking, and this can stop the milk flow.

4 Bottle-fed babies swallow air and may need burping during the feed.

Feeding at night

Night feeds are a major drawback when bottle-feeding. The parent must get up and prepare the bottles, sit up to feed the baby and burp her before putting her back to sleep. Plan ahead to reduce waking time.

● Prepare two bottles for each feed, one with previously boiled water, the other with dried formula. Cover and seal.

● When the baby wakes, add the water to the formula, put on a sterile teat (you can store this inverted inside the bottle of water), shake and serve.

● The water can be kept warm near a radiator, in a bottle warmer, or wrapped in a blanket. Do not make bottles in advance – chilled bottles take longer to rewarm.

Returning to work

In the first few weeks: If you are working full-time you may not make sufficient milk at night to satisfy the baby. Using a breast pump during the day – even if you throw the milk away – will keep up the supply.

3–6 months: Introduce a bottle or dummy in the first few weeks, and she will combine breast and bottle. Organize meal times to suit your milk supply: breast-feed before work and in the evening when you come home. Supply may be low at night so you may need to supplement with formula.

6–9 months: Introduce a bottle or a dummy in the first couple of months. She can be weaned onto a cup at about nine months, but she may still need comfort sucking. You may have enough milk for evening feeds without drawing any milk off during the day. If not, give her a little cereal or a cup of milk before going to bed.

9–12 months: Complete weaning before you return to work. Do not combine the two – it is too stressful for the baby.

SEE ALSO

Breast or bottle?	**20–21**
How to breast-feed	**22–23**
Weaning from the breast	**46–47**
Sharing the care	**52–53**

Full of wind

To burp a baby, place a cloth on one shoulder, hold her upright with her head on the cloth, then pat and rub her back gently, or lay her face down across your lap.

NEVER NEVER

● Prop the baby up with a bottle, even if you are busy.

● Reuse formula you have made up for an earlier feed.

● Keep a bottle warm for a long period of time.

● Make up bottles before a journey unless you have a good cool box and they are still cold to the touch when you are using them.

● Feel guilty that you are not breast-feeding.

Changing nappies

The first few nappies may seem easy, but wait till he starts wriggling! With a little practice, though, you will soon learn to handle him so you can change him anywhere – lying across your lap, for example, or in the back of a car.

Initially, you will find it much easier if you assemble everything you need so it is ready to hand, but you will soon get used to changing your baby, however much he wriggles and kicks. You will not have to change him that often – modern nappies keep the skin fairly dry. Even if he is a little wet, he will not find it uncomfortable. Changing is usually unnecessary at night. In the daytime, too, unless he is obviously wet or has filled his nappy, you can usually wait to change him until just before his feeding time.

Nappy changing step-by-step

1 Choose a surface which minimizes your need to bend over. Place the changing mat, or a double thickness towel, on top.

2 Place your baby on the mat and talk to him. Undo his clothing and pull it up so it is well out of the way.

3 Undo his nappy, and use it to clean up if necessary. Fold the dirty nappy over so that the clean outer side supports his bottom while you clean up the front and between his legs. Talk and smile – a happy baby struggles less.

4 Clean all the creases around the genitals (use a fresh wipe to clean faeces from a girl's vaginal area). Make sure that the folds around the top of the legs are clean. Now pull your baby up by his feet so his bottom is clear of the mat. Clean his bottom, especially around the anus and the creases at the top of the legs.

5 Clean a boy from back to front if the back is dirtiest. Always clean a girl's vaginal area before her bottom, and keep soiling or soiled wipes away.

6 Slip the dirty nappy out from under the baby; replace with a clean nappy. Pat his bottom dry if necessary and lower him onto the clean nappy. Talk and smile.

7 You may want to allow a small baby a little nappy-free playtime (especially if he has nappy rash). You can stay with him and talk; or put him on the floor to kick. Never leave him on the table to play.

8 Fold the new nappy around his bottom and fix into place following the packet instructions. If you use a barrier cream wipe your hands afterwards so you do not drop your wriggling child. Put on any clean new waterproofs if using.

9 Put your baby somewhere safe. Drop stools into the toilet. Fold paper nappies over, close tapes and dispose. Put cloth nappies in a nappy bucket to soak.

10 Change any bed linen if necessary. Wash your hands.

A safe place to change
You can change him on a changing table, a chest or a small table. On the bed, use a waterproof sheet – he might wee when out of his nappy.

The contents of a nappy

Newborn: Starts sticky and greenish black. First real stools after about 24 hours, initially quite loose, often with mucus, occasionally with blood; greenish yellow, turning to golden yellow curds; traces of blood are rarely problematic – but always discuss with your doctor. Bottle-fed babies have stools ranging from yellow to brown or even greenish brown.

Black stools: Usually the result of giving iron, or of iron in the formula.

Green and foul-smelling stools: The result of an infection; check with your doctor. If very loose give plenty of liquids (dilute flat soda or cola 50:50 with bottled water). If he develops diarrhoea and vomiting call the doctor or get your baby to hospital.

Runny: Young babies' stools are often quite runny. Watch for changes; if runnier than usual give fluids. For persistent diarrhoea consult your doctor. If he starts to vomit, and the diarrhoea becomes more frequent, call the doctor or get him to hospital.

Bloody: Often caused by constipation and not problematic; do not ignore, however, as it might indicate other problems.

Odd colours, lumps and other changes: Mostly caused by food. What babies do not digest will be in their nappies.

DIFFERENT TYPES OF NAPPIES

Type	You will need	Pros	Cons
Disposables Modern disposables are absorbent and slim, and often contain a gel that draws the wetness away from the skin	About 35 a week	Convenient, simple to put on, unlikely to leak, less work. Baby has a fairly dry bottom	An expensive option – he is likely to use 4,000–5,000 nappies before he is potty trained. Ecologically unsound
Shaped nappies and squares Look like disposables but made from soft padded cloth. Some makes come with a waterproof shell	About 15 nappies of each size plus disposable liners	Quick and easy to put on – side-fastening with Velcro; less bulky than terries; ecologically friendly. The initial outlay is high – but they are slightly cheaper than disposables if the cost is calculated over the two years	Require routine disinfecting, washing and drying; probably not as absorbent as paper nappies. You may end up buying rather a lot of them because the size needs to change as the baby grows
Traditional terry nappies Cloth nappies, fastened with nappy pins, usually worn with disposable liners and plastic pants	24 squares, lidded bucket, bucket for soaking, disinfectant, washing machine, dryer	Cheap and ecologically friendly; one size fits all	Take longer to put on; look bulky; take up more room to carry and store; less absorbent than the best disposables, probably keep bottoms less dry (but liners can help). Worst of all: they need laundering
Nappy services Regular supply of clean nappies; the dirty ones are taken away and washed	The quantities are of no financial consequence	By far the most convenient version; ecologically sound; the cost is slightly lower than that of using disposable nappies	The service is expensive; plus the cons of terries: take long to put on; look bulky; take up more room; less absorbent than disposables

How to dress your baby

Putting clothes on a floppy newborn baby may fill you with anxiety about dropping her or letting her head jerk backwards without support. But you will soon find it easy enough – even when she starts flailing her arms!

You will make dressing your baby easier for yourself if you choose her first clothes wisely.

● Anything that goes over her head should have either a broad "envelope" opening, or buttons or poppers at the neck. Stretch the neck openings before trying to pull them over your baby's head. Do not tug or pull: she will cry and you will almost certainly panic. Just ease them gently past her ears.

● Back fastening makes life difficult.

● Knitted fabrics and those with Lycra allow you to put your hands into the small openings and manoeuvre her hands or feet to the other side. Push up the sleeves so that the whole sleeve can be pushed over her hand and wrist in one movement. Reach through the opening and gently pull her hand through.

● Tight little numbers, and trousers with bibs and straps may look great on – but unless the garment is loaded with Lycra and the legs have poppers from crotch to toe, such clothes are best avoided.

● Nappy changing will be much easier if you choose either a suit with poppers down the legs (or in summer under the crotch), or separate trousers.

● Small buttons are hard to use and zips

Safely dressed

At first you may find it easiest to dress her when she lies on the bed or changing mat. Once you know how to hold her, you can dress her on your lap or in the car.

A FIRST LAYETTE

General equipment

● At least 3 vests. Wrap-around, side-snap or envelope neck styles are easiest to put on. Lycra – at least at the neck – makes it easier to get them over the baby's head. Pull-on styles look smoother and those with snap-button crotches are warmest in cold weather

● At least 3 sleep suits – either night dresses or all-in-one stretch suits. If night dresses have drawstrings, remove these as the baby becomes more active

● Some washable bibs: especially if your baby is inclined to be sick after feeds

For a winter baby

● At least 2 fleecy sleeping suits

● 3–6 stretch suits with sleeves and feet

● 2–3 pairs of booties and mittens

● Warm hats which cover the ears

● 3–5 first size jackets or sweaters

● A sleeping bag or snowsuit for trips out in the carrier or buggy

For a summer baby

● Cooler outfits; either dresses or short-sleeved romper suits

● Hats for sun protection

● 1–2 first size jackets or sweaters

have a habit of catching in other clothing, especially when you are trying to dress a squirming baby. Always pull the garment away from her before doing up the zip.

● Keep changes to a minimum by using bibs, if your baby is often sick, and sponge clothing rather than changing it.

● Talk and coo to your baby as you put on her clothes – dressing is a social occasion.

● If she is frightened when her head is covered, choose front-fastening garments. For an older child play "peek-a-boo" when you pull something over her head.

Putting on a vest

For front-fastening vests: Slip one arm into the vest. Lift the baby, pull the vest across the back, slip in the second arm. Pull the straps across and fasten.

For a wide-necked vest: Lay the baby on the changing mat, pull up the base of the vest to the neckline and pull the opening wide. Now slip this over her head, pulling the front section clear of her face before adjusting the back. (It is easier to deal with problems at the back than risk covering the eyes or snapping the nose.) Take care how you manoeuvre the vest around her ears.

Once around the neck the vest will bunch naturally and you should be able to get the arms through the armholes fairly easily. Bring the arm into the chest and gently manoeuvre the hand up through the gap. Repeat with the second arm. Pull the vest down, then do up any ties or poppers.

Putting on a cardigan or jacket

For a cardigan: Scrunch up one sleeve and stretch open at the wrist. Slip the baby's arm through the wrist opening, then let go of the jacket. Holding the wrist in place, pull the cardigan up the arm. Lift the baby, pull the cardigan across the back, slip in the second arm. Pull across and fasten.

For a jacket: This can be put on in the same way – but the sleeves will be a little more difficult to handle because heavier fabrics cannot be crunched up in the same way. You may find it easier to lower the baby onto the jacket before dealing with the first arm. Alternatively, do the whole thing from the front. Lay the baby on the mat. Open out the jacket and place the jacket on top of the baby with the neck nearest her feet. Slide the arms into the jacket. Lift the arms above the baby's head, then ease the jacket down the back.

Putting on a stretch suit

1 Open up the suit, lift the baby and put the suit underneath her. Do up the poppers around her legs. This holds everything in place while you deal with the task of getting her arms into the sleeves.

2 Scrunch up a sleeve, holding it close to the shoulder with one hand. Slip the child's arm through, holding the cuff wide with your fingers as her hand and wrist enter it. Let go of the wrist and pull the arm forward so the sleeve falls into place. Repeat with the other arm. Fasten the front.

SEE ALSO

Keeping your baby warm   **16–17**
Keeping your baby cool   **18–19**
Changing nappies   **26–27**
Have baby, will travel   **42–43**

There's your hand
Stretchy and woolly baby clothes allow you to push the sleeve right up, thus avoiding the need for panic. Talk to your baby and turn getting dressed into a game you play.

ACCESSORIES

Bonnets
Heat can be lost and gained rapidly through the head. Small babies should never go out into the cold without a warm hat, or into the sun without a bonnet.

Shoes
Until she is old enough to walk, socks or woolly booties will do. In the early weeks her activity is low, and she needs to wear socks inside and out, except on really warm days.

Nightdresses
Much better than today's stretch suits, dresses and nighties provide the tiny baby with fabric she can easily grab. As it touches her palm she will close her hand over it.

Bathing your baby

Cleanliness and good hygiene are essential in the early months when a baby's immune system is still fragile, and while his small size could make any infections or bouts of diarrhoea and vomiting dangerous.

YOU WILL NEED

- Baby soap or bath liquid (use both sparingly, especially on the baby's face)
- No-tears shampoo
- Baby oil – useful for cradle cap (but salad oil can be used instead)
- Ointment for nappy rash
- Cotton wool balls for cleaning the baby's bottom in the first weeks and for "topping and tailing" (see p.33)
- Baby wipes to clean the baby's bottom as well as your hands
- Sterile cotton wool for cleaning around the eyes at all times and around the umbilical area in the first weeks
- Cotton wool buds

Knowing your baby should be bathed two or three times a week is one thing: giving that first bath, however, is quite another! Dealing with a small slippery baby is difficult at the best of times. It is especially so when you are not used to handling him. Most parents will have a chance to practise bathing techniques under the watchful eyes of the nurses in hospital or the midwife at home. If in doubt, remember you can always "top and tail". Until they are mobile, babies do not need a daily bath.

It is also reassuring that, in the first few weeks, small babies enjoy swimming under water and stop breathing when immersed. Even if his head slipped under water for a moment he would not come to any harm.

Clean baby

Dab a little soap or no-tears shampoo on your baby's head using a cotton ball, then gently splash to rinse him clean.

Easy steps to bathing

1 It is safer to wait with the first bath until after your baby's navel and – for boys – the circumcised penis have healed.

2 Find a time that suits you both, preferably during a period of natural wakefulness. Bathing before his evening feed will help settle him for the night, but do not wait until he is hungry or he will protest throughout the bath. If you have older children you may find it easier to bath your baby when they are not around.

3 Choose a warm room: 24–27°C (75–80°F) is ideal. It does not need to be the bathroom; bath him in the kitchen if this is warmer. If you are using air-conditioning or fans, turn them off.

4 Make sure the bath is placed on a firm surface. Kitchen worktops are usually good (the sofa will be too soft).

5 Wash your hands before you start; make sure the baby bath is clean.

6 Assemble everything you need – see the list on the left – and place it within easy reach. Do this before undressing the baby. You will also need a clean nappy, pants and fresh clothes to put on after the bath.

8 First, pour about 2.5 cm (1 in) of cold water into the bath, then add the hot water. There should be no more than 5–7.5cm (2–3in) of water in the bath. The water should feel warm to the touch. Check the temperature by dipping your elbow or wrist into the water. Do not use your fingers as they can withstand much hotter water than a baby's body can.

9 Undress your baby completely, and swaddle him in the bath towel. A small baby's hair and face are easiest to wash before placing him in the bath. Older babies can be washed in the bath.

10 Hold your baby's head over the bath, face up, and gently splash water over his head. Place a tiny drop of shampoo onto a cotton wool ball and gently rub it into your baby's hair. Add a little water, rub gently, then rinse carefully, soaking the flannel or cotton wool and squeezing it out over his head. Pat his hair to dry.

11 Wash his face. Use a sterile cotton wool ball and boiled, cooled (or bottled) water to clean each eye. Work from the nose outwards to the outer eye, using a fresh ball for each eye. Dampen a new cotton wool ball, squeeze it almost dry and wash the rest of his face, outer ears and neck. You do not need any soap for this.

12 Put your baby onto a flat surface, and unwrap the baby towel. Cradle him, supporting his head and shoulders with one hand, his bottom with the other. Slowly place him in the water, talking and cooing softly. Slip your hand from under his bottom, bringing it up to his chest to hold him securely in a reclining position.

13 Apply a little soap on a ball of cotton wool and gently wash him with your upper hand. To rinse, splash him gently or squeeze water from the cotton wool. Work from the cleanest to the dirtiest areas.

14 Now use a little soap to wash his hands (his hands will probably need soaping every day). Rinse his hands. Use your hands to soap his penis.

15 Now lift your baby out of the bath and turn him over, supporting him with one hand on his chest. Talk to him so he will not get upset. Soap and rinse his bottom and back. Rinse finally. Lift him out of the bath, immediately wrapping him in the towel. Pat him dry and dress him.

Selecting a bath

Baby baths come in all sorts of shapes and sizes, from the basic tub to those which offer support, from the solid to those that must be inflated. The latter are useful if you have very little storage space – but they will need to be inflated each time you use them which could be a disadvantage.

Baths with head supports are easier to use but more expensive. Remember when buying a bath that most children only use a baby bath in the first few months. If you have little room for a bath you might consider using the kitchen sink – do this only if the hot tap is not accessible. Always clean the sink well before and after use.

SEE ALSO

Lifting and holding baby **14–15**

Keeping your baby warm **16–17**

Sponging a baby clean **32–33**

Establishing a routine **40–41**

GROOMING

You will also need:
- Nail scissors with rounded ends
- Hair brush and comb if he has enough to brush
- A small bowl to use when giving a sponge bath
- A small basin for use when washing eyes and navel with sterile cotton balls and water
- A few small bottles of drinking water, for a supply of sterile water

Keep him warm

Babies get cold quickly so wrap him in a baby towel as soon as he comes out. The hood keeps his head warm.

UNHAPPY BATHERS

- If your baby does not like bathing, try using a large cut-out sponge to clean him instead. These are available from many department stores and specialist baby shops.
- Consider taking him into the bath with you. (Many parents feel more secure if they are in the bath with the baby.) Undress him first, wrap him in a towel and put him on a changing mat on the floor while you get undressed. Leave his towel and the mat beside the bath. Initially, you will find it easier to hand the baby out to your partner at the end of the bath.
- Use a non-slip mat in the bath and make sure the water is cool enough for your baby. If he still hates bathing don't worry – a sponge bath is quite adequate.

THE NAVEL

The umbilicus is cut and clamped at birth – the stump dries up and usually falls off in a few days. The hospital will show you how to clean around it with surgical spirit swabs and dust it with antiseptic powder.

If you bath the baby before the stump has fallen off, dry all around it thoroughly afterwards.

If the navel starts to weep, or to look red and sore, contact your doctor immediately.

Prevent infection by keeping the area exposed to the air.

Happy bathtime

Have a one-to-one chat with your baby. Smile and play with her while cleaning her body.

Sponging a baby clean

Your baby will not need a complete head-to-toe bath every day – most of the time, a quick all-over sponging, or even just "topping and tailing", will keep her perfectly clean, and save you much hassle.

To give your baby a sponge bath, choose a warm room: 24–27°C (75–80°F) is ideal. Use the kitchen if it is warmer than the bathroom. Turn off any fans or air-conditioning. Make sure the changing mat and bowl are standing on a firm surface – kitchen worktops are a good choice. You could also place it on the floor, but this is harder on your back. Wash your hands. Assemble all you need.

You will need

- A towel – one with a hood is preferable, especially for a winter baby
- Some soap
- Some cotton wool (or soft sponges or flannels)
- No-tears baby shampoo
- Sterile cotton wool balls and boiled, cooled water for cleaning around the eyes, especially if there are any signs of infection
- A clean nappy, pants and clothing to dress her after the sponge bath
- A bowl of water unless you are within easy reach of the sink.

How to sponge your baby clean

1 Remove the baby's clothing except for her nappy, place the towel on the changing mat, lay her on top and wrap her in the towel. (If the room is cold remove her clothing only when you are about to wash and then replace it quickly.)

2 Start with the face. Wash each eye using a clean, damp cotton wool ball dipped in the boiled, cooled water. Work from the nose outwards. Then sponge the face, ears and neck using a second cotton wool swab. Rinse between strokes as needed. Pat dry.

3 Now wash the neck and ears. Soap will not be necessary unless she is very hot and sweaty. Wash any creases. Pat dry.

4 Sponge the upper body next. Wet with a cotton swab or flannel, soap gently

CUTTING THE NAILS

- Cut the nails when they have grown beyond the finger tips. Sit him on your lap and, using small rounded scissors, cut the nails straight across.

- As you cut, hold his hand firmly with your left hand, pressing the pad of his finger away from the nail tip and using your finger to steady his as you cut.

- If you do accidentally cut, he may howl but will soon forget. Some parents find it easier to cut nails while babies sleep.

- Toe nails can be cut in the same way – best while he is lying on his mat.

with a damp soapy hand, then rinse with a second swab or the damp flannel. Pat dry.

5 Extend the arms and repeat, paying particular attention to the hands and the elbow creases. (In hot weather hands and elbow creases will probably need soaping.) Turn her over and wash the back of her neck and her upper body using the same dampen–soap–rinse–dry technique.

6 Wash her feet and her lower legs in the same way as her arms.

7 Remove the nappy and wash the genital area, then turn her over to wash her bottom and upper legs. Always use soap and water unless she has nappy rash.

8 In other body areas the soaping stage is optional. In most cases you can alternate a session of "sponge and dry"

with one where you soap. You may find you need to change the water – especially if the nappy was soiled.

9 To wash the hair wrap her in the towel, hold her head over the edge of the sink or bowl with her face uppermost, and gently splash water over the head, or sponge with a damp cloth. Add a tiny drop of shampoo to a damp cotton wool ball and rub gently into the scalp. Rinse carefully using a wet flannel. Rub gently.

10 Once your baby is clean and dry, dress her quickly so she will not get cold.

"Topping and tailing"

On days when you neither bath nor sponge, you can simply "top and tail".

1 Assemble all the equipment you need: cotton wool; boiled, cooled water in a bowl; facecloths or sponges; a towel; and clean clothing.

2 Undress the baby, leaving her nappy and vest on. Wash her face as you would for the sponge bath, cleaning her eyes carefully and removing any mucus from around the nose, or saliva from around the mouth. Clean the creases of the neck. Pat dry, clean away any ear wax from the *outer* ear using a cotton wool bud. Wipe her hands. Now remove her nappy and clean this area. If it is warm let her kick in her vest. Otherwise dress her.

Cleaning the ears

Never poke anything into a baby's ear. A cotton bud would fit and may seem appropriate for cleaning wax from the ear, but resist the temptation. Your poking is more likely to force wax into the ear than to get it out and, more seriously, you could damage the delicate ear drum. Clean the outer ear with a soft cloth and save the cotton wool bud for the folds of the outer ear only. If you feel wax is building up, consult your doctor or health visitor.

SEE ALSO
Lifting and holding baby 14–15
Changing nappies 26–27
Bathing your baby 30–31
Sharing the care 52–53

CIRCUMCISION

After circumcision, the wound, normally covered in gauze, may bleed and ooze. This is perfectly normal. Double nappies can help cushion the soreness, and stop the baby's thighs pressing against it. Change the gauze when changing the nappy, dabbing a little Vaseline or antiseptic cream onto the wound.

PENIS CARE

At birth the baby's foreskin is still attached. It will detach naturally at about two. Do not force it back – it may tear and scar. It protects the crown from infection and nappy rash. If he has nappy rash, wash carefully and apply a barrier cream. Allow plenty of nappy-free playtime. If soreness persists, contact your doctor. Never try to clean under the foreskin. Wash the uncircumcised penis in exactly the same way as any other part of the body.

INTERCOMS

If your baby's room is out of earshot, you will need an intercom. The most versatile intercoms – but also the more expensive ones – are those that can be plugged into the mains and used in various parts of the house. However, if you are likely to use the intercom only between the child's cot and the lounge, you will not need anything so elaborate – one with a fixed station will suffice.

Baby in a basket

A Moses basket occupies little space and is perfect for moving your sleeping baby from one room to the other with the minimum disruption.

Bedroom equipment

When choosing a cradle or cot, the necessary bed linen and bedroom toys, make sure that they will give your baby the best possible environment – and that you will find the equipment easy and practical to use.

For your baby's first bed you have a wide choice of items, ranging from cradles and Moses baskets to carrycots, nests and buggies. You will also need a number of items for your baby's linen cupboard, and you may wish to think about safety alarms and toys for your baby's room.

Cradles and baskets

To allow your baby to rest comfortably, cradles and baskets are not necessary but they are very practical all the same. They are particularly useful for those with small bedrooms and, with any luck, by the time the baby can climb out of the Moses basket, he will be able to move to a bedroom of his own.

Cradles are portable and can easily be moved up and down stairs as required, or put into the car boot when visiting a friend. Make sure the cradle is sturdy. Rocking mechanisms are liked by the baby,

but I am not sure it is a good idea to get her used to being rocked to sleep: you could be making a rod for your own back.

Carrycots and nests

The carrycot used to be an essential item, but these days it has largely been replaced by portable car seats. A baby nest remains useful as it enables the carer to transfer a sleeping baby from the pram to the cot or sofa without waking him. Always remember, though, how easy it is for a sleeping baby to overheat when you bring him in from the cold. Loosen clothing, keep the room cool and check regularly.

Choosing a cot

● An adjustable base and/or drop sides will save your back and make it easier to get a baby in and out of the cot. Drop-sided cots make life with older babies easier, but check that the drop mechanism can be locked.

● Always check that your cot and mattress meet safety standards, and that the mattress fits properly – a gap of more than 4 cm (1½ in) could trap the baby's head, a smaller gap could trap his fingers. Always remove polythene covers from mattresses.

● The bars should be no more than 6 cm (2½ in) apart.

● Castor wheels are useful, but again check that the cot can be locked in position and will not move.

● On a second-hand cot, check that the wood is not splintered and that any paint on the rails is not flaking.

Mobiles above the cot

Over the last 30 years mobiles have become essential baby toys. Most parents place one over the cot to provide a small baby with something to look at and listen to when they are not at hand.

In my opinion this is not a good idea. Cots are for sleep, not play. A baby needs to be calm if he is to fall asleep, not excitedly kicking as he listens and watches a mobile. They are excellent first toys, but put them in waking – not sleeping – locations. The sooner he learns to tell the difference, the sooner you will sleep through the night.

If you are using a mobile:
● Your baby needs to have a good view: he will be looking from below, and the mobile should be clearly visible from this angle.
● Very tiny babies focus at about 30–35 cm (12–14 in) and do not see outside this range until about 3–4 weeks. Even after they can focus, they are very short-sighted.

Attach the mobile to the cot rather than to the ceiling so he can see it clearly.
● Moving things are easier to see for tiny babies. Place a lightweight mobile in the draught of a fan.
● Long strings are dangerous – they can get caught around your baby's neck. Never hang anything with a long string above or across the cot. Use a pole instead. To tie small items to the rails, use real wool – it is more likely to break if caught around the neck. Make sure that any lengths are too short to become wrapped around the neck.
● Babies love the high-pitched sound of musical boxes, and find them soothing. But do not attach a box to the mobile – one is for resting, the other for waking.
● A voice-activated musical box attached to the mobile may seem a good idea, but you will soon tire of "Golden Slumbers". If you are sharing a bedroom with your baby, make sure you can turn the music off!

SEE ALSO

Changing nappies	**26–27**
Sleepless babies	**36–37**
Have baby, will travel	**42–43**
Sleeping routines	**58–59**

Action toys

Do not attach a mobile where it could over-stimulate your baby.

BABY LINEN

For general use	For the pram	For the cot	For the buggy
● 1–2 wrapping blankets or shawls. Shawls look good but cellular cotton blankets are easier to wash/dry	● 3–4 small sheets	● 3–4 cot blankets (depending on the season), plus 2–3 top sheets and a pretty cover if desired	● Cosy toes, sleeping bag or blanket, depending on season and weather
● 6 muslin or terry nappy squares, or tea towels to protect your shoulder, lap or sofa from your baby's dribbling	● 2–4 cellular blankets (folded, cot–sized), depending on season, plus 3 top sheets and a top quilt or pretty cover if desired (wash in detergent, not in soap powder which may clog the fibres)	● Cot bumpers to stop your baby banging his head on the bars, and to protect winter babies from draughts	
● Small soft cloths, a sponge and/or cotton wool for wiping his face	● 2 waterproof pads to use as mattress covers	● 3–4 fitted cot sheets	
● A waterproof apron and pad for protecting furniture and clothes	● 2 quilted mattress pads, if desired	● 2 waterproof pads and draw sheets if needed (you can reuse unfitted sheets from the pram as draw sheets)	
● 2–3 terry cloth towels	● 2–3 small pillow cases or muslin squares if your baby posits or dribbles		
● Nappy liners – for all-night protection	● A nest or sleeping bag to transfer baby from the carriage to the house without waking him		
● 24 terry nappies or 15 first size shaped nappies or 4 packs of disposables			

Sleepless babies

If you do not get sufficient, uninterrupted sleep, you will soon become exhausted, anxious and restless. Make the best out of your baby's sleeping and ensure that she does not deprive you of vital relaxation time.

Most parents complain of tiredness in the early weeks, even if their babies sleep for 16 or more hours in 24. The problem is not a lack of opportunity for sleep, but the inability to make use of it when it arises. By the time we feel relaxed enough to sleep, our baby is ready to wake up again. We force ourselves awake to feed her and then only slowly relax while she sleeps. Then we repeat the cycle. We never really get an undisturbed stretch of sleep.

The early arrangements for family sleeping are a matter of individual choice. If you are constantly tired, if you have to return to work in the early months, if you have other small children, the obvious priority is that you get a good night's sleep.

Baby in your bed

In the early weeks there is only one way to achieve this and that is to have your baby beside your bed or in the bed with you.

Children around the world grow up to be independent individuals who sleep on their own – whether they share their mothers' bed in the early months or sleep in their own rooms from the start. Independence has more to do with how we treat waking children than with sleeping arrangements. You do not have to continue as you started: once she is sleeping through the night, she will stay in her cot and you can move her to her own room.

Easy night feeds

She needs to be close enough for you to be able to lift and breast-feed her before you are both fully awake, and for you both to be able to go back to sleep as soon as the feed is finished – if not before. It is easy and pleasant to fall asleep while your baby is latched onto your breast. There is no need to insist that your baby stays in your bed after a feed or to ban her from co-sleeping. Just be relaxed about it.

You do not need to actively encourage co-sleeping unless this is your choice. Putting your child down to sleep in her cot during the day and early evening will teach her all the independence she needs. Once she stops taking night feeds she is likely to spend most of the night in her cot if you have started her off this way.

Some babies sleep through the night by the time they are one month old. Most do not. Sharing a bed is perfectly healthy and normal. There is no danger you will suffocate your baby by rolling on to her.

Close to Mum

Having your baby sleep close to your own bed in the first few weeks will relieve you of worries and allow you to look after her without sacrificing a good night's sleep.

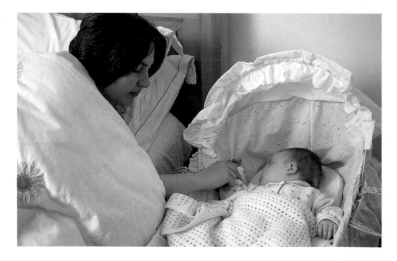

MY BABY WON'T SLEEP

Some people need much less sleep than others. If you and your partner need little sleep it is likely that your baby will follow in your footsteps. Other reasons include:

● **She is used to little sleep.** If both parents work they often keep babies up into the evening. How long you need to sleep is to some extent a matter of habit. If you get your baby into the habit of staying awake most of the evening she will learn to cope with much less sleep.

● **She is being kept awake.** It is hard to sleep unless we are relaxed. If you play boisterous games before bedtime or change her nappy before sleep (or during the night) you are likely to wake her up when you want her to go to sleep.

● **It is noisy.** If you tip-toe around your sleeping baby she will never get used to sleeping through noise, and will wake up as soon as the noise level rises.

● **She has not learned how to fall asleep.** If you always put her down in the same place she will only sleep there. If you always sing her to sleep she will need a song. If she always goes to sleep with a nipple or teat in her mouth she will need to suck to fall asleep.

● **She is over-stimulated.** Is her room awash with light? A dark room is boring and a bored baby will sleep. Distinguish clearly between the lively waking world and the dull world in which she sleeps.

Hours sleep

```
17
16
15
14
13
   0 1   3      6      9     12     15    18
   Age months
```

More or less sleep

The above chart shows the average number of hours babies sleep between birth and 18 months. This will, however, vary widely from one family to another.

Only those who are drugged or drunk would fail to wake up if this happened. Nor would you set up a habit.

You do not have to give up sex – babies are not traumatized by overhearing their parents make love. They are unable to understand the significance of the monotonous sounds they hear. Of course some children wake when their parents start to make love: this is a problem of family life wherever the children sleep. If you find making love in front of the baby a problem move to another room.

Maximizing your sleep

● Do not change the baby's nappies at night unless they are very wet or dirty. If you have to change her, keep light levels low and do not talk to her.

● Do not burp a baby unless she is bottle-fed and shows evidence of discomfort. To burp a baby you need to sit upright and are thus more likely to wake up.

● When all else fails take it in turns with your partner to retreat to the spare room.

● Try to take a catnap in the afternoons or whenever the baby is sleeping.

● Let her learn to go to sleep without your help from the start – she will be less likely to call for you at three in the morning if she can put herself back to sleep alone.

Get a large bed

Even if you are not regularly co-sleeping with your baby, you are bound to have her in bed with you some of time. Yet the average double bed does not easily accommodate a family of four…

Colicky cries

The most likely cause of colic is gas trapped in loops in the bowel. Why it affects some babies and not others, and why in the evening, is unknown.

SOOTHING HIM

● **Swaddling.** Some babies feel secure when tightly wrapped.

● **Rhythmic noise.** Vacuum cleaner, car engine, static or music on the radio.

● **Rhythmic rocking.** Use a swing, carry him in a sling, push him up and down in the buggy. Carrying upright is also good.

● **Fresh air.** Take him around the block in the push chair.

● **Attention.** Babies sometimes just need to be with someone.

● **Sucking.** A dummy.

Crying babies

All babies cry some of the time, and no baby cries all of the time, but some definitely cry more often than others! The trick is to find out what makes him cry and to stop him bawling before you reach the end of your tether.

There are many different cries, from the small, restless whimper to the loud and prolonged scream. They are all distressing, especially if you can do little to stop them. Babies cry for all sorts of reasons. In time you will recognize what some of his cries mean but you are unlikely to be sure of the problem in all cases.

Why babies cry

He is hungry: This is probably the most frequent cause of crying and the solution is obvious. Some babies like to space out feeds, some like little and often. Just because he wants the breast every couple of hours does not mean he is greedy – or that you do not have enough milk. Babies usually settle down to taking food at three- to four-hour intervals, but it can take a number of weeks to get into this routine.

He is thirsty: In hot weather, and if overdressed or in overheated rooms, babies lose a lot of fluid by sweating. Replenish it by offering him boiled, cooled water.

He may want to suck: Some babies just love to suck – and may even cry if the breast delivers milk as they suck! A dummy is the best solution here.

He has just woken up: Babies often cry when they wake up. They stop when picked up, or of their own accord if left.

His birth caused pain: A baby is likely to cry in the first few weeks if he had a difficult birth. There are a number of reasons. First the drugs you received in labour could be affecting him. Second he

may be in pain. If he was a forceps delivery or his head was temporarily misshapen in the birth process, there may have been some compression. This probably produces headaches which may cause problems in the first week or so. If there were more serious complications, pain is also likely. Damage hurts, wherever it occurs. Consult your doctor if you are worried.

He is in pain: Circumcision is painful, and can cause two or three days of unhappiness. Earache is another common cause of pain in the first year.

He is unwell: If he seems listless or restless and/or feverish, consult your doctor. Illness must be taken seriously.

He is uncomfortable: Itchy vests, feeling hot or cold, a tight nappy: there are many possibilities. Check them out.

He is uneasy: Many babies hate sudden change. All babies hate to feel they are losing support.

He is lonely: Babies need company and the older they get the more they are likely to demand it. Some are very demanding, others are happy as long as you are nearby. No small baby likes to spend long hours by himself: nor should he.

He tries to control you: He has learned that crying gets a result.

Pain from colic

Colic is characterized by regular periods of inconsolable crying and screaming. It tends to occur at the same time every day – usually but not always in the early evening.

While the attacks last it is difficult to console the baby. All babies begin to cry more between about 6–12 weeks of age, and all tend to cry more in the early evening. Colic is an exaggeration of this tendency. The onset can begin as early as three weeks, it peaks at about 12 and then declines in most babies. It affects one in five children. No-one is sure why it occurs in some babies and not in others. The good news is that there is no evidence that babies with colic are likely to have more problems later on, nor that they are more likely to grow into "difficult" babies or toddlers.

Your baby is likely to have colic if:

● He burps often, his stomach rumbles or he frequently passes wind (although it is not clear whether this "wind" arises from crying so lustily, or from another cause).
● His crying is accompanied by drawing his legs up as if in pain.
● His tummy is hard and distended.
● Babies who have colic are otherwise healthy – there is no sign of diarrhoea, temperature, or vomiting. If your baby shows such symptoms give boiled, cooled water and consult a doctor. In serious cases get the child to hospital.
● Feeding gives temporary relief – but may make things worse in the long run.
● He cries for hours before falling asleep.

Treating attacks of colic

● If you are breast-feeding, examine your diet to see if certain foods make things worse. Some mothers find that avoiding cabbage and sprouts, or cutting back on cows' milk protein helps. It will not work for all babies, but it may help some.
● A smoky atmosphere can make matters worse – avoid smoking in his presence.
● Simethicone, a component of many medicines that treat "trapped wind", offers relief and is widely prescribed in some areas. It is not absorbed by the body.
● Give him camomile or fennel tea.
● Give him infant colic drops or gripe water before a feed; some babies respond better to gripe water after a feed.
● Place him across your knee and gently massage his back.

Comforting your baby
If he cries a lot, take him in an upright position and walk up and down the room with him. You could also try to talk or sing softly to calm him down.

SEE ALSO
How to bottle-feed   **24–25**
Sharing the care   **52–53**
Is everything all right?   **68–69**
Typical baby problems   **178–179**

IF ALL ELSE FAILS

● Drive him around in the car – but only if you can stay calm.

● Get help. Call a friend, a relative, or a helpline. Talk to other parents and your doctor.

● When you can bear it no more – put him in his cot and close the door. Go to a room where he is out of earshot.

● Say to yourself "I do not have to feel guilty. His tears are not my fault. This will pass." Whether you have a high- or low-need baby is a matter of luck.

● If crying persists beyond three months remember that giving in to his demands will make things worse. A child who controls you with bad temper will be more bad tempered. Try to shape his behaviour by giving him more attention when he is good, and less when he is being bad.

● Check there is no medical problem. Some babies cry because they feel pain or are ill.

Establishing a routine

Until you get used to it, the care of your baby will seem to take up every minute of your waking day – and half your night. It is hard to imagine how anyone could combine caring for a toddler and a small baby – yet they do.

Time for yourself
Do not worry about the housework, getting your figure back or being superwoman – take all the help you can get.

By the time your second child comes along, you will probably find it hard to understand why it seemed so difficult to look after the first one. A large part of the problem is your fear that something will happen to your baby. Even as she sleeps you look to check she is alive. Even as she feeds you worry if she is getting enough food. You know that the vast majority of children survive these days, and that babies are fairly resilient. Yet you find this hard to believe because you know how devastated you would be if anything happened to her.

Feeding routines

In the past, mothers were advised to adhere to strict feeding times. More recently, they were told to always feed on demand. In fact, there is no right or wrong way – babies are flexible. You can mould them, they can mould you, or you can meet halfway. A good routine is one that takes everyone's needs into account. There is little point in waiting for four hours until the next feed to pass if you spend the last hour pacing the floor. There is also no point in giving in to every feeding demand if this causes you to resent that you never have a moment to yourself. Compromise.

If you also have a toddler, your baby will occasionally have to wait. If she can be made to wait while you tend to your toddler's needs, then she can also wait while you finish that phone call. Aim for what seems achievable. Not all babies can go the full four hours between feeds, but that does not mean they need to hang on your breast all day. If she needs a dummy give her one. If she is feeding at two-hourly intervals aim to extend this gradually, adding ten minutes here and there.

Nappy changing routines

It is not necessary to change her before and after each feed. If it is easiest to change her when she is sleepy after a feed, do so then. If you find this wakes her up, do so before feeding her. Keep night-time changes to a minimum. Choose the time to suit you.

Bathing and dressing

"Topping and tailing" is quite adequate most of the time. Until she is crawling around the floor she does not need a daily

A WEEKLY ROUTINE FOR YOURSELF

Every day

- Eat three healthy meals. Drink plenty of fluids.
- Take some aerobic exercise – walking, dancing, jogging, swimming, pushing the buggy up a few steep hills.
- Do some muscular work to build up strength. Do your post-natal exercises. Stretch.
- Find some time for yourself. Read a book, watch TV, ring a friend for a chat.
- Exercise your mind. Try to think about something other than your baby!

Every week

- Go out and socialize. Babies can survive with relatives or sitters. Join a baby-sitting circle. If you cannot afford to pay someone, or if you cannot go out, ask friends around.
- Pamper yourself. Even if it is just putting on some jewellery or doing your nails.
- Get some fresh air. Explore the countryside or a park you have not been to before. Do some gentle gardening. Wrap up well and get out even if it is cold or raining.

bath. If you find bathing difficult, leave it for the days when you have someone – your partner or a friend – on hand to help.

Babies need regular nappy changes but do not need their clothes changed at frequent intervals. She will come to no harm if she wears her nightie all day or yesterday's stretch suit all night. We get dressed in the morning and change at night because the difference between our day and our night is so marked. While she treats day and night as almost one and the same there is little need to keep to this routine. Wash, bathe and change her at times which are easy for you.

Falling asleep routines

When I put my eldest child down to sleep I never used to do so without singing to him, stroking his brow and waiting by his bedside until he fell asleep. He did not sleep through the night until he was two and always expected me to be with him. For two years I felt wrung out.

My daughter arrived almost a month early and I still had a lot of work to finish. So she came to work with me from week one. As I had to work some evenings, I put her into her cot to sleep, said "Night, night, petal" and walked away. From the start she learned to fall asleep without me holding her hand, and although she did not sleep through the night until she was almost a year old, it was never problematic. She could always fall asleep without me.

My youngest son was treated exactly like his sister. Friends used to say "Is that all?", as I took him upstairs in the evening and came directly back down. It was. Babies in my family do not sleep. I did not sleep as a small child and I still get by on about six hours a night. My sisters and their children are mostly the same. If you have a similar family history (and even if you do not), you might want to try my technique.

Waking time routines

A baby who spends extended periods of the day sleeping will be less sleepy at night. You need to encourage her to synchronize with you, to concentrate her waking periods into your waking periods, and her main sleeping period into the night.

Tiny babies tend to fall asleep if they are lying down, and to remain more wakeful if they are sitting up. They fall asleep if there is nothing much to see or hear, and remain wakeful if they have something to watch and do. Your baby will sleep in a cradle chair, but will spend more time looking around before she does so than she would if placed in her crib. She will be more wakeful if you are close by and moving about than if you are in another room.

Try to organize her sleep into three, and later two, major periods. Initially she should have a morning and afternoon nap as well as sleeping at night. Later she can drop one of the naps. Remember that breaking your sleep into two periods means you will need less sleep in total – the hour of sleep you take during the day is worth a couple of hours at night.

SEE ALSO

Breast or bottle?	**20–21**
Changing nappies	**26–27**
Bathing your baby	**30–31**
Sleeping routines	**58–59**

TIMETABLE

- 6am feed, change nappy
- 8am get up, make breakfast
- 9–10am top and tail, dress, feed, do housework; baby-awake time
- 1–2pm feed, make lunch, go for a walk, shop
- 3–5pm baby-awake time
- 6pm feed, hand over to partner, prepare supper
- 8pm change, baby asleep, relax
- 10pm & 2am feed; try to sleep

Mummy or Daddy
Take turns putting her to bed so she will not depend on one of you.

TRAVELLERS

● Airlines often let you pre-board the plane and provide you with a sky cot for the baby to sleep in. Reserve the bulkhead seats which give a little extra room.

● Airlines will warm bottles and baby food for you. Coordinate feeding with take-off and landing: babies are more prone to ear pressure problems, and swallowing helps. Have sterile water in a bottle. If he only takes the breast you will need extra fluids – air travel is very dehydrating. Bottles and food will have been heated in the microwave: check the temperature.

● Many hotels will provide a cot for a baby, but he will be much happier in a familiar travel cot.

● Most hotels and restaurants cater for small children. Many provide high chairs and will heat baby food and bottles for you. If they will not, go somewhere else.

Have baby, will travel

You will not have to stay at home for years to come just because you have had a baby. Make sure you buy the best car seat, pram or buggy to make travelling easy and comfortable rather than one long tale of misery.

In today's mobile society, choosing the right car seat for their baby or toddler is one of the most important decisions that parents have to make. There are now seats and restraints to suit all ages and sizes.

● When buying a seat make sure that it conforms to safety standards.

● Always be wary of second-hand seats unless you know their history.

● Do not try to fit a seat which needs to be professionally fitted unless you know exactly what needs to be done.

● Always make sure the seat is appropriate for your child's weight and size.

Car seats

Stage 1 – birth to 10 months or 10 kg (22 lb): These fit into the front or back seat of a car and face backwards; do not use in the front of a car with passenger air bag. Fitted seat belts make them easy to remove from the car with the child in place.

Stage 2 – 9 months to about 3 years or 9–18 kg (20–40 lb): Larger than stage 1 seats; usually fitted facing forwards in the back of the car. They may be permanently fitted using their own belts or the rear seat belts. Look for comfortable padding.

Stage 3 – 4–11 years or 15–35 kg (33–77 lb): Booster seats bring the child up to where he can be secured in an adult seat belt. Get a shoulder harness fitted to the middle if you carry three children in the back of the car.

Feeding en route

Babies need to be fed at regular intervals. Always stop the car to feed the child. Even when crawling at a snail's pace you should not have the child in the front seat of the car unless he is in a proper baby car seat. In hot weather carry small bottles of sterile

One-handed use
When choosing a buggy, check that it can be folded easily. Remember that you will probably have to do this with one hand while holding your baby with the other.

water (bottled drinking water) in the car and one or two sterilized feeding bottles. Always remember, however, that once the seal on a bottle is broken, it does not remain sterile for long.

In summer, an old-fashioned fan and a damp sponge are also useful for keeping him cool. Never leave a sleeping baby in a stationary car, even if the windows are open. If this cannot be avoided (in a traffic jam, for example) watch him carefully. Small babies are very susceptible to heat stress. If necessary keep his head cool by covering it with a damp cloth.

Choosing a pram

Prams have become an optional item because of our frequent car use. Yet small prams are useful as daytime beds and for rocking fretful babies to sleep. When choosing a pram look for a smooth ride, all-weather protection and ease of manoeuvring. Make sure it can easily be taken up any stairs or steps you have to climb, that it fits into a lift or through doors. A folding pram is easier to carry around, store and transport in the car. A fitted shopping tray or basket may also be useful. Always make sure that the folding mechanism is locked open when the pram is in use and that both wheel brakes are put on when you park the pram – especially if the pram is standing on a slope. Once the baby can sit up, or be propped on pillows, make sure you use a harness.

Combined prams/buggies

Combination prams are a popular choice for many families. They consist of a frame to which you attach a portable cot base in the early months and later a reclining chair. Often they are much heavier than a normal buggy, and if you frequently use public transport you may need a light-weight buggy in addition.

Choosing a buggy

A small baby can only cope with a buggy if the seat can be moved into a fully reclining position. This means that many of the very lightweight buggies are unsuitable for really tiny babies. A winter baby will also need good weather protection, especially in cold climates.

When choosing a buggy, look for stability, good (double) brakes, easy manoeuvrability and a safety certificate. Safety straps are an obvious requirement, and a full harness may be necessary as the child grows. If you use public transport or frequently take the child in and out of the car, weight is an obvious consideration. If you need to shop, a safe place to put a package tray is also important. Big wheels are better if you need to deal with muddy ground, small wheels are preferable if you will need to store the buggy in a small space. Check that the buggy is easy to fold, that the height of the pushing handle is comfortable, and that you can attach both summer and winter weather proofing.

SEE ALSO
Lifting and holding baby   **14–15**
Bedroom equipment   **34–35**
Sitting pretty   **44–45**
Making outdoors safe   **206–207**

Long car journeys
Small children travel remarkably well. They will probably sleep or doze for most of the time.

EATING OUT

● Portable folding seats are useful for eating out with a child. Do not use it on a pedestal table or one with loose leaves, or a loose or glass top. Don't place over a table cloth or place mat.

● Use a chair with a good locking mechanism and secure it properly.

● Always secure a baby in the chair with a harness and never leave him alone. Make sure he cannot push the chair back from the table.

● Take the baby out of the seat before releasing the lock.

In parts of Africa, women traditionally dug small holes to wedge their babies into so that the child could sit and watch them at work. This is a useful technique for the beach, too: Make a hollow in the sand, spread a blanket over it (to stop her eating it) and seat your not-yet-stable baby in its "hole", under an umbrella. You could use a potty in much the same way in the garden or in the house, but take the baby's nappy off before wedging her in position.

Playmats and tent

Many toys, textures and noises give your baby the chance to school all her senses and to learn how to pull, squeeze and grasp.

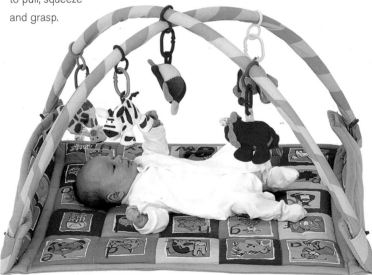

Sitting pretty

Once your baby can sit upright, she will have a better view of the world. It will be more interesting for her and also help keep her awake for longer periods – which gives you a better chance of a good night's sleep!

In order to lengthen her awake times, and concentrate sleeping into specific periods of the day, it is best to prop your baby up in a nearly upright position in the day. She can then watch the world go by, and also observe what you are doing.

Sitting upright also draws you both into conversations. It is easy to walk past the cradle without seeing the baby or being seen by her. It is impossible to walk past the chair and ignore her, especially once her eyes follow you across the room.

Playing on her tummy

Modern advice strongly suggests that babies should not sleep on their tummies because this has been associated with an increased incidence of cot death. This does not mean that lying on her tummy to play is dangerous. Cot death is not common,

even when babies sleep on their tummies, and it never happens while they are awake. Letting your baby play on her tummy is perfectly safe. She will find it easier to reach out for her toys in this position, to look in her mirror and to explore her playmat with her mouth. If she falls asleep just turn her over, or put her into her cot in her normal sleeping position.

Choosing a playmat

Look for a mat with plenty of textures, noises and objects to stroke and grasp. In the early months she will put her mouth onto the different textures – so ensure that the mat is easily washed or wiped clean.

Nappy-free playtime

It is good to get a little air to the bottom, especially if it is usually encased in a tight paper nappy. Most babies kick and wave their arms in excitement once their bottoms are freed. If you are worried about accidents, put a towel on her changing mat and let her lie on this to kick.

Rolling across the room

All babies manage to roll over before their carers expect them to do so. Beds seem to make rolling easy – she certainly won't be the first baby to roll off the edge. Never, never leave a baby unattended on a bed – once they start to roll in a room which has not been child-proofed, it is surprising how far a child can move by combining rolling with creeping on the tummy.

Beware creeping babies

You may think that she is many months from crawling (and she may be) but a baby on her tummy can easily creep forwards. While you answer the door she can move into a danger zone unless the room is child-proofed. Make sure that there is nothing on the floor which she could reach (such as the cat's litter tray), or bump into (such as a sharp corner on a low table), or fall over (such as a step) should she creep.

How to prop a baby on cushions

Babies enjoy sitting with the family. You can prop her up on pillows in a chair or the corner of a sofa. Take two or three pillows and arrange them so they fill the corner of an armchair. The aim is to prop a small baby at an angle of about 45 degrees, but leaving her back in a relatively flat position. The pillows should support both the back and the neck, the bottom should sink slightly into the cushion, and the arms and back of the chair should stop her rolling. Watch her – as she gathers strength she will try to sit and move.

Rocking cradle chairs

Until a baby can control her head (at about 4–6 weeks) and her back (at about 16 weeks), she will need support for both when she sits up. She is too young for an upright chair but can cope with one angled at 45 degrees. Car seats, rocking cradles and lie-back buggies are ideal. Be careful where you place the cradles: an active baby can rock it across a smooth surface.

First chairs

As long as your baby cannot support her back when she is upright, she will need a chair that can be adjusted for her to lean back. If it can be moved to an upright position it will have a longer life. A play or feeding tray makes the chair versatile.

Highchairs

Initially you will feed your baby while holding her on your knee, but as soon as she is ready to start feeding herself she will need a feeding chair.

Highchairs enable us to feed babies while sitting at the table. If you only have one child you may find that a portable chair is all you need, but for a larger family a highchair is much safer. Lively and mobile older brothers and sisters can easily knock a portable chair over.

Look for a chair with a wide, sturdy, non-tip base and good anchor points for a harness. A removable tray is easier to clean, and one with protective lips catches spills. Always use a harness – children try to stand up and climb out; they will also lean over to look for anything they have dropped. A chair with a foot rest and a high back support is more comfortable. If it folds away make sure that it is easy to put up and can be securely locked in position.

SEE ALSO

Introducing solids	48–49
First toys and games	60–61
Sitting and standing	88–89
Making indoors safe	204–205

My own corner
The corner of a settee is a perfect place to prop your baby up. She will be supported on the sides and back by furniture, and her legs stop her from falling forwards.

Rocking safely
You can place the rocking cradle on a table or worktop, but do not leave her unattended even for one minute.

Weaning from the breast

Whether you are returning to work or you just feel that the time has come – at some point you will want to stop breast-feeding your baby. Follow some simple rules and you will easily progress from breast to bottle or cup.

NEVER NEVER

● Introduce solids to a baby under three months. It will not help him sleep through the night, but it will give him a stomach upset.

● Worry that he is still not taking solids at seven months. You can be sure that eventually he will!

● Feel guilty about giving your baby a bottle. Regard the feeding bottle as a liberating tool.

● Feel that you have failed if you need to introduce a bottle. Parenting has very little to do with feeding the baby's body, and everything to do with feeding the child's mind, social development and his long-term emotional stability.

Once feeding is well established you will find your baby spends less time at the breast. It is a two-way affair: he knows how much he needs and how to latch on, suck and swallow efficiently; you "know" how to deliver milk efficiently. Your milk let-down reflex is now conditioned to the sight and sound of the baby, and the hormones that cause the milk to flow are circulating in your blood before you even pick him up. His feeds may be short but if he is happy, healthy and growing he is getting enough.

There will be times when he wants to dawdle – indeed, some babies do this almost all of the time. There will also be times when he needs the comfort of your breast because he is in pain. This is normal. Most babies linger over feeds in the early evening. If he always uses your breast as a comforter consider getting him a dummy.

When to start weaning

Children continue to need milk right through their pre-school years, and this does not have to come from cows! Some people think it is somehow indecent to breast-feed a toddler. By the time the child is three many people will disapprove and suggest you are feeding the child for your own gratification, and that the whole thing is positively indecent. It is none of their business. It is, however, easier to wean your baby from the breast before his first birthday, and if you have to return to work you will probably have no choice anyway.

Weaning from the breast

● Start by distracting him around the time a feed is due. Take him out in the buggy, offer him something to eat and a drink from his cup. Do not drop more than one or two feeds in a period of a few days, or your breasts will become uncomfortable.
● Choose a stress-free time, especially when trying to wean an older child.
● Choose an ordinary time. During the holidays or when you return to work he needs extra comforting – not deprivation.

Partner help

Your baby will refuse the bottle if he can smell your breasts. Your partner can help here. He can also put him to bed if your baby is used to calming feeds before sleeping.

● Introduce a comfort object (such as a dummy, a teddy or a small rag) before you start to wean. Many older babies use the breast mainly as a comforter.

● Keep going. It may not be easy, but when you are feeling desperate remember that all babies manage in the end!

Introducing the bottle

Weaning should be gradual. If you wean from the breast before your baby is about eight months, he may still need to suck. There are two ways of going about this:

● either top up each breast-feed with a little bottled milk, then gradually decrease the breast milk and increase the bottled milk until he no longer needs the breast;

● or replace one breast-feed at a time with a bottle-feed.

If all goes smoothly this should take about ten days. It rarely does. Unless a baby is used to the feel of a teat in his mouth he may simply refuse to take it.

If you return to work before your baby is eight months old, introduce him to a dummy or the occasional bottle of boiled water (or expressed milk).

● Try different teat shapes and texture. Babies can be fussy.

● Try different feeding systems. Those that rely on suction rather than squeezing work in a similar way to the breast.

● If he persistently refuses the bottle, try a sucking cup, a proper cup or even a spoon.

During the transition, make sure your baby gets sufficient milk by mixing a little in with his food. Make all food sloppy.

Using a cup

Many babies walk about with their cups – and spill their drink as they do so! Sucking cups are a little easier to handle than the real thing, but most children can manage with a "proper cup" from about seven or eight months if allowed to practise.

Weaning from the bottle

Babies who suck anything other than plain water through a bottle teat at night are in danger of baby bottle tooth decay. Bottles can also become comfort objects. Replace them with an alternative comfort object before trying to wean him off the bottle.

Weaning older children

● Drop all breast-feeds except the one to which your child is most attached.

● Confine the use of the bottle to certain times. Replace breast and bottle at other times by giving drinks in a cup.

● Find him a comfort object. Tuck a teddy into his arms at night, or give it to him when he is unhappy. Avoid offering the breast or bottle as a comforter.

● Stop offering him the breast or a bottle at bedtime. Be prepared for several evenings of protest. Do not give in.

● Avoid situations and places where he expects to be fed, and distract him when he wants the breast or his bottle.

● With an older child, explain what you are trying to do and why. Bribe him. And praise him for his efforts.

WHAT TO GIVE TO DRINK

● **Breast milk.** This is the best drink for the first year. If you stop feeding him before, you need to give formula.

● **Whole pasteurised milk.** Give with foods from about six months. Do not use skimmed milk – he needs the fats. He is growing fast, and the walls of each cell of his growing body are constructed from fats. Without them he cannot grow.

● **Follow-on milk.** This conveniently fills a marketing niche for the manufacturer but babies do not need it.

● **Plain water and diluted fruit juice.** Both are fine for babies, and there is no need to boil water after six months.

● **Drinks to avoid.** Avoid sweetened drinks, sodas or pops, coffee and tea.

SEE ALSO

How to bottle-feed	**24–25**
Introducing solids	**48–49**
Sharing the care	**52–53**
All about baby teeth	**84–85**

No spills
An unbreakable plastic cup with handles and spout is easiest to handle. Avoid paper, and do not use polystyrene.

ALWAYS

● If you have to leave your baby before he is eight months old, then introduce him to the feel of a teat by giving him a dummy or the occasional bottle of water.

● Introduce foods gradually. Small children do not need a balanced diet of solid food. They only need to get used to the feel of it in the mouth and to get used to swallowing without also sucking.

● Avoid gluten-rich foods in your baby's early months.

Introducing solids

Your baby will have passed another milestone once she has started eating solids. She will become even more closely integrated into your family life and, eventually, it will make your life much easier, too.

Using jars

● Initially your baby will take only one or two spoonfuls of solids. It is easier to open a packet of baby rice than to cook and mash a potato.

● You will be less upset if she spits out food from a jar.

● If you use baby rice as the carrier you can add other, home-cooked or ready-made foods.

● Many jars are based on a single carrier, such as potato. They taste similar and are thus acceptable to a small baby.

Home-cooking

● If you cook for the family, she will learn to eat your foods, and it will be less expensive.

● You know exactly what she is eating, and can introduce new tastes gradually.

● You can use organic ingredients for her food, which is cheaper than buying organic jars.

Do not rush into solids – milk should remain the baby's main food source in the first year. Indeed, solid foods are rarely solid. Most are simply milk with the addition of a little rice, potato, or vegetable.

Do not start with a great variety of foods. Start with one carrier and, once that is accepted, add another. Children have a built-in mechanism which stops them eating strange foods because these could be poisonous. When faced with a new food, they (and adults) taste the smallest possible amount, then wait to see if it makes them sick. If it does not, they taste a little more. This way they gradually accept a new food. By introducing too many foods too quickly you will trigger the "avoid" response over and over again. She is likely to spit out all solids and become very finicky. She is not being awkward. She is just being wise!

Is she ready for solids?

● Is she at least four months old?
● Does she show interest in your food?
● Is she restless after a feed?
● Has her weight levelled off?
● Is she starting to grasp objects?
● If you give her a little mashed potato from your plate does she show interest?

First foods

Initially, your baby's foods need to be smooth, gluten-free, easy to mix with milk and relatively bland.

Solid foods and weight gain

Even if your baby is not gaining weight as she should, do not assume she needs to be weaned before she is four months old. If she is alert and free from illness she is almost certainly getting enough to eat. Babies gain weight gradually over the first year, but they do so in fits and starts. When in doubt always consult your doctor or health visitor. Some children grow more slowly than others, and the tendency can run in families. (The 170-cm [5 ft 7-in] writer of this book spent the first five years of her life in the bottom three per cent growth range – as did her cross-country running, medical student daughter.)

Food hygiene

You do not need to sterilize feeding dishes and spoons, or any of the utensils you use to prepare her food (except plastic sieves). Washing in detergent and rinsing well is quite adequate. You do need to continue to sterilize feeding cups and teats because milk can collect there – an excellent breeding ground for bacteria. Most parents continue to sterilize bottles and cups, although this is not strictly necessary after about 4–6 months. Once she is putting all manner of things into her mouth you have to relax your criteria in any case.

Choosing first foods

The obvious choice of a basic "carrier" food is the potato, the usual choice is probably baby rice. Whichever you choose you need to mix it with plenty of milk so that it is the constituency of cream. Give your baby a small spoonful. If she takes this, offer another spoonful at the same feed the next day. Only when the baby is happy with her carrier solid, should you begin offering other foods.

Puréed vegetables and fruit, often suggested as early weaning foods, should be considered a "second string". Once she has been happily eating rice and milk you could add just a little apple purée to it. Gradually reduce the amount of rice until she will happily eat apple purée without additions. You can add mashed carrots to the rice in the same way – then gradually replace the rice with potato which will give you a second carrier. In time the regular items of a national diet (whether pasta and tomato sauce, or onions, carrots, meat and potatoes) will form the carriers of the diet and the background to more exotic tastes.

Weaning foods for 6–8 months

By six months a baby can have all the foods listed above, including those based on full-cream pasteurized cows', goats' or sheeps' milk. Hard-boil eggs: babies are susceptible to salmonella from soft-boiled eggs. Peanuts are best avoided – they may be a choking hazard, and nut allergies are increasingly common in small children. By eight months children can eat virtually the same diet as their parents. Check that fish is bone-free, take off most of the fat from meat, peel fruit and vegetables and remove pips. Mince or mash, initially to a smooth paste, gradually making the texture more solid and slightly more lumpy as she grows.

Does food have to be bland?

Baby foods are generally very bland. If you offer a tiny baby spicy food she will almost certainly spit it out. But she can be taught to enjoy stronger tastes, if they are

introduced gradually. Start with half a teaspoon in three teaspoons of potato, then gradually increase the proportion of spicy food. Most children learn to enjoy strong-tasting foods if offered this way (although they may continue to avoid hot chilli flavours). All children have some pet hates. Do not expect them to eat everything!

Feeding herself

● Once she is sitting in a chair for feeds give her a spoon to hold. She will not be interested at first. Small utensils are easier for little hands to handle.

● The more she tries to use a spoon the better she gets – but it will be messy!

● Chop up food into tiny pieces which she can pick up and put into her mouth. Peas, cubes of cooked potato or carrot, sliced banana or bite-sized sandwiches are ideal.

● A cup with a trainer spout helps her to drink by herself without spills.

Using implements

Japanese children learn to handle chopsticks by about the time they are three, and Western children can probably advance from spoons to knife and fork by the time they go to school.

SEE ALSO

Sitting pretty	**44–45**
Weaning from the breast	**46–47**
Sharing the care	**52–53**
How babies grow: weight	**70–71**

AVOID

For small babies before six months, avoid these foods:

● Eggs

● Wheat products including bread and wheat-based breakfast cereals

● Dairy products including fromage frais, yoghurt and cheese (but you could make your own from formula)

● Citrus fruits

● Strong spicy vegetables such as onions or peppers

● All kinds of nuts

● Fried foods

● Very salty foods

Potty training

Getting out of nappies is rarely a priority for young children, but with a little encouragement, and once they are ready, most will learn to use a potty quickly and easily, without too many dramas.

If you have an easy-going baby who sleeps all night and feeds at the same time each day, it is not difficult to predict when he is going to fill his nappy. Such babies tend to be regular in all things. Less regular babies may be harder to fathom out but most carers know the signs that precede or accompany the passing of stools. By the time your child is one, you could probably avoid almost all dirty nappies by whipping out the potty at the right moment. If he relies on you to predict his needs, it does not mean, however, that he is potty-trained.

It is more effort, but possible, to avoid most wet nappies: our grandmothers did it, after all! Yet, again, predicting the need for the potty is different from teaching your child to control his bladder and bowels. A child cannot learn control until his brain has developed and learned to control his sphincter and bladder. This happens roughly between 18 and 30 months. Girls tend to be a little ahead of boys.

Accidents will happen

Few children are reliably dry by day and night until they are about two and a half. Some crack it all in one go, others are dry by day for years before being dry at night. Always get him to use the potty before bedtime, but continue using nappies at night and keeping the plastic sheet in place until he is mostly dry when he wakes.

Protect the bathroom carpet with a plastic floor mat. If you have a boy, it is worth investing in a washable surface on the wall surrounding the toilet as he will continue to "miss" for some years, especially when he is in a hurry or deeply engrossed in some game. A half-tiled bathroom with a tiled floor would be ideal!

NEVER NEVER

- Hold him on the potty if he wants to get off.
- Shout, slap, scold, scream, or otherwise punish him.
- Get emotionally involved. If the child learns that refusal is a good way to attract attention he will refuse.
- The message should be simple: using the potty is good! Do not mix messages by telling him pooh is dirty.
- Do not expect too much. He will make mistakes, especially when he is deeply involved in some scheme or with his friends.
- Never compare him with other babies, or try and force the pace to keep up with another child.

SELECTING A POTTY

The main criterion for choosing a potty is that it does not tip when the child sits down, and that it remains stable when he gets up from it. If the potty is for a boy be sure to choose one with a high splash guard at the front.

Many children abandon their potties and start to use the toilet soon after they have gained control of their bladders. Some prefer steps to climb up and perch on the edge of the adult seat, others fare better with a child seat that fits inside the regular adult seat, to make the opening less daunting. Again it is a matter of individual taste which one you and your child prefer. There is a wide range of choices available in departments stores and baby-goods shops, all of them inexpensive.

Inner seat for toilet

Potty with high splashguard

READY...

Before you consider trying potty training ask yourself if your child is ready:

● Is your child mature enough? Can he stand and walk alone?

● Could he get on and off a potty without falling?

● Can he pull his pants up and down easily?

● Does he know the words to use when he wants to use his potty?

Can you detect signs?

● Does he sometimes go for a couple of hours without a wet nappy?

● Does he show that he knows when he wees?

Is this the best time for both of you?

● No illness or problems?

● Can you make light of accidents, laugh at the odd puddle and cope with more washing? Essentially, are you relatively stress-free?

Is the family stress-free?

● No family upheaval such as a new baby, a holiday, house guests, moving home, changes in carers?

● No disruption, change in routine, separations, job loss, illness?

● Is there anything else going on that might disrupt your relationship with your child in any way at this time, no matter how minor it seems to you?

STEADY...

Set an example

● Let him know when you go to the toilet and take him with you.

Let him know that it is possible

● Draw attention to the signs he makes and ask him if he is doing a pooh/wee.

Nappy-free times

● On warm summer days he can run around the garden and enjoy nappy-free playtime for longer spells.

Wee is much more noticeable when it runs down his legs!

Get some trainer pants

● Cloth knickers without plastic outer pants are best because they become cold and uncomfortable when wet, rather like a wet bathing suit.

● Nappies in plastic outer coatings feel warm and comfortable when they are wet, rather like a wet suit:

your child is used to this feeling and will not mind it.

● Like regular nappies, paper trainer pants with their outer plastic coating do not encourage the child to get out nappies, but they are useful because they combine quick release with the avoidance of puddles. Once he can manage trainer pants, regular pants are just a short step away.

Boys and potties

Although most boys want to stand to use the toilet "like Daddy", using a potty in the early months of toilet training is very much easier for you and your child.

GO...

Find the time

● Select a week when you can give him your attention. If he is ready, it should not take any longer.

Watch for the signs

● Sit him on the potty if he seems ready. Let him get off after a couple of minutes whether he goes or not.

Select the moment

● Choose the most likely times for success – after a

meal or drink, before his bath or going to bed, first thing in the morning.

Praise him

● Praise him for sitting as well as for doing.

Show him

● Let him see what he has done. Allow him to help you empty the potty into the toilet. Wipe his bottom and let him flush the toilet. Help him to wash his hands.

If he asks for the potty

Praise him even if he does not actually manage to wee or pooh.

Wait patiently

● If after a week you have clearly made no headway, forget it for the time being. Wait a month or so, and then try again. He may just need a little longer before he is ready.

Sharing the care

In the first months of their lives babies become attached to a few special people – their parents, their brothers and sisters, their grandparents and friends – all of whom can share in looking after your child and making life easier.

Mother and father are not the only ones who can care for their child. In the early months babies do not remember that their carers exist when they cannot see them, and so they do not miss us when we are not there. Nor does a baby under about five months of age realize that there is only one Mum and Dad – they probably think that we are new every time they see us. It is therefore hard to argue that any one person is essential for raising a stable and happy child. What a child needs is love and security. They will not gain this if they have a constant stream of different carers, with nothing secure or permanent. But they can and will gain that security from a small number of different carers each of whom offers love and affection.

Older friends

If there are children of the same or a similar age in your family or amongst your friends, make sure your child learns to spend time with them – you will both benefit from this time.

Getting help

From the start you should get your baby used to being away from you, especially if you will return to work before she starts school. Start with other family members.
● Trust your partner with the baby right from the start.
● Let a grandparent sing to her, bath her and put her to bed. Do not hover – they have more experience than you do!
● Let other people you trust bath her, play with her, or take her for walks in the buggy while you get on with your child-free life.

What fathers can do

Apart from breast-feeding, fathers can carry out every aspect of parenting. If they are less competent than mothers it is usually because they are expected to be so. The fact that few fathers are able to take paternity leave means that, by the time the mother and baby come home from the hospital, the father's baby-handling skills already lag behind. Neither mothering nor fathering comes "naturally" – both parents have to learn. If they interact with love and sensitivity they can become equally skilled.

Grandparent care

Babies develop a secure base for later development through their attachments to their loved ones, first of all to family members: parents, brothers and sisters, as well as aunts, uncles and grandparents. Grandparents have usually done their fair share of child rearing. Most grandparents

SEE ALSO

Establishing a routine	**40–41**
Arranging childcare	**54–55**
Share and share alike	**138–139**
Active co-parenting	**140–141**

TAKE A BREAK

If you are exhausted, feel that parenting is dominating your life and have little time for each other or for sex, perhaps the time has come to take a break.

● Tiny babies soon forget about us. Before about 7–8 months, out of sight is out of mind. This period is a good time to escape for a day or two.

● Make sure the child is looked after by someone they know and you trust. You will not be able to relax otherwise.

● If you are still breast-feeding introduce your baby to a bottle or a cup before you leave her. Take a breast pump with you to draw off milk to maintain your supply.

● Small children will be happier in the familiar surroundings of their own home. For a toddler, a stay with grandparents will be more of a treat, especially if they live near the beach, in a big city, or there is something exciting to do locally.

● Do not travel far: you will feel more secure about leaving your baby if you can rush home in an emergency.

● Do not take a package holiday – especially the first time you leave the child. If you cannot get home it can ruin your stay – even if all is well at home.

Visiting grandparents
If the grandparents cannot see the children regularly, they may try to make up for this with extra presents and by letting them get away with more than the parents would like.

Free childcare

Many mothers can only afford to work if their children are looked after by relatives, for free. If the money is vital to the family, the carer can be put on the spot – they may feel obliged to continue caring for the children even though they wish to stop. Never take such arrangements for granted. Discuss childcare at regular intervals. Caring for a small baby is quite different from caring for an active toddler.

Arrangements with friends

Many friends baby-sit each other's children. Sometimes, a formal baby-sitting circle works best. These operate on a points system: carers earn points by the hour or half hour while they baby-sit for someone in the circle, and spend them when going out. A larger circle makes it easier to find a baby-sitter at short notice.

Professional carers

Many of us return to work, and baby-sitters, nannies and child minders take the place of the extended family. To develop socially your child has to form links and make friends with others. A crèche with other children, a nanny or child minder will automatically provide such contacts.

are an unquestionable asset to a family. They may help financially or look after the children but most of all they love your children. If they do not live nearby, times together may be trying if you disagree on how to care for the children. Hold your tongue – after their visit everything will quickly return to normal.

If they live around the corner things can be more problematic. You should be able to discuss how you wish to raise your children. Tell them how much you appreciate their help and the love they show your children – criticism can seem hurtful. If however they did a fine job of raising you (or your partner) consider whether their "way" is not a better way.

BABY-SITTER

The baby-sitter will need to agree:

● To arrive on time and stay in for the duration of the sit

● To follow house rules on matters such as smoking

● Not to drink or use recreational drugs when in charge of the baby – unless you have allowed this

● Not to pass the baby to another carer except in an emergency

● Not to bring a friend without your permission

● To put your children first; to amuse them and care for them; to check on them and to listen out for them after they have gone to bed. The baby-sitter's own work should not take precedence

● Not to use your phone to call friends far and wide, or to get them to call

● Not to check out your drawers, nose around your house, or read your mail.

Arranging childcare

The most essential ingredients of good childcare are affection and trust. You cannot demand that your carer loves your child to distraction; but you can expect her to treat him with kindness and respect.

Choosing the best childcare for your child may seem like a science, with nannies, child minders, au pairs, crèches and nurseries to choose from.

Choosing a nanny

A full-time nanny, especially a live-in one, provides continuity of care within your home. She can give undivided attention to the child and cover for you at any time. Nannies have undergone professional training so hiring one may be costly. You may also not like the idea of sharing your home or the lack of any external controls.

- The best carer is at ease with children.
- Look for someone who is calm, warm, shares your ideas about child rearing and will fit in with the family. Ask her how she would organize the day and how she would solve potential problems.

Happy together

Make sure that when the carer interacts with the children she gives them her undivided attention. If she is distracted and does not look at them she is unsuitable.

- Always interview, even if a nanny comes from a reputable agency. Qualifications are not always vetted, so check them yourself. Give her the terms and conditions of the job in writing. Make sure she understands them, and stick to your side of the bargain.
- Always check references, especially those from her previous job. Once she is working for you it is wise to make the occasional "spot check". Phone her to check she is

RETURNING TO WORK

- You will need time to settle into childcare. Unless you can work a very flexible day, and/or can take the baby into work with you (or into a workplace nursery) you should not return to work in the first six weeks. If you have to do so, do not exclusively breast-feed the baby. It is almost impossible to achieve this.

- At about 8–10 months babies become aware that we exist even though we are apart from them. They are likely to miss us and cling when we try to leave. Although they settle quickly, turning your back on a screaming child is not the easiest way to start the day.

- The terrible twos are also the delightful twos: for every ten minutes of tantrums there are probably six hours of utter delight. It is hard to leave on a tantrum in the morning – rest assured he will eventually snap out of it. If he does not want to get dressed before he goes to the child minder just put his clothes in a bag and take him in his pyjamas. Once he realizes that his tantrums do not stop you going to work he will accept the situation.

home when she is supposed to be; return home ahead of time. If you feel unsure or uncertain at any time find someone else.

● She should have set hours and not be expected to work beyond these. Expect to pay a reasonable wage. It is an important and skilled job – if you pay too little, you will get a dissatisfied, untrained and unsuitable carer. Costs can be reduced by sharing a nanny with another family.

Employing an au pair

Au pairs join your household from abroad. In exchange for their keep and pocket money they do a little housework and help care for children. They are usually aged between 18 and 27 and may speak very little English. You can expect an au pair to work for a maximum of 25 hours per week, and for no more than 5 hours per day. Usually they stay for a year. Untrained and mostly inexperienced, they are not suitable to take on the sole responsibility for a baby or toddler. Some au pairs are wonderful, others dreadful, a few are dangerous. A major disadvantage is that you usually have little choice in who you take on before they arrive.

The advantage of child minders

Child minders are usually parents themselves. What they lack in formal training they make up for with experience. You can judge their skills by their children. In many cases child minders are registered with the local authorities (always check) which makes them safe care-givers. They look after more than one child, and do so in their own home, so they are also less expensive than other childcarers.

The advantages of a crèche

For most parents cost is one of the main considerations in the choice of childcare arrangements, and a good crèche is rarely a cheap option, especially for a small baby. You will often find yourself paying almost as much for shared care in the crèche as solo care in the home, and once you have two children you may find the crèche is more expensive than employing a nanny. You have the reassurance that many parents are overseeing the care, that the child is rarely left in the charge of a single carer, and that children grow up in a social atmosphere with many friends to play with. Carers are usually trained, and equipment is safe and stimulating.

Choosing a child minder or crèche

● Do you like the carer? Are you made welcome? Do you like her children?
● Do the children seem happy? Will your child have the same carer most days?
● Does the carer break off to deal with the children while she talks to you?
● Does she answer your queries? Does she ask about your child, what he enjoys doing, how you soothe him, about his favourite foods and games?
● What kind of indoor and outdoor play space is available? Is it clean? Is there room to run around?
● What equipment is available? Does it look as if it is put to use?
● Will the hours suit you? Can you stay with your child for a while on his first day?
● How are the children disciplined?
● What is the notice period both ways if arrangements must be changed?

Workplace nurseries

Some companies have established on-site nurseries or provide places with local crèches for employees' children. The advantage is that you can usually visit your child during the day, and you may be able to breast-feed him at lunch time. The disadvantage is that you may have to travel with the child in the rush hour.

SEE ALSO
Weaning from the breast   **46–47**
Sharing the care   **52–53**
What parents worry about **142–143**
The twos and beyond   **182–183**

AGREEMENTS

● State the normal hours to be worked for the agreed wage, how overtime will be calculated and time in lieu taken. Agree a notice period. Pay on time and in full.

● Agree what is included in the job and what is not.

● A live-in nanny needs her own room and use of common space such as the kitchen. You need to agree if you will eat together, whether you sit together in the evening, and if her partner can stay overnight.

● If you are seriously dissatisfied pay her for the notice period and tell her to go immediately.

● Within reason you should know where the children are at most times of the day. You need to have a good idea of what is planned and be able to contact her if necessary.

● Treat the children consistently. Agree rules between you both. Discuss changes (weaning and toilet training).

Naps and early mornings

Your toddler's early-morning visits to your bedroom are one of the great delights of parenthood – unless she arrives at the crack of dawn when you are still enjoying the last precious moments of sleep.

Are you awake, Daddy?
Once your child is mobile and able to get out of her own bed and walk to yours, she will. And before then, she will probably shout for you to come and get her!

There is no way around it – once she is awake, your child will loudly demand your company, and this can be a real pain. It is hard to avoid. You cannot let her wander about by herself, and if you put a gate across her door, she will probably shout and scream until you come and get her.

Afternoon naps

In the beginning babies sleep after every feed. This means that their sleep is divided into six to eight batches. In the first months we struggle to get it organized into three "big sleeps", with only the occasional cat nap at other times. By their second half year most babies have concentrated the main sleep period into the night-time hours and take one, or perhaps two, short sleeps in the day. For many this pattern can continue well into the second year, but at some point one of these daytime sleeps,

and later the other, is dropped. The important point to bear in mind is that studies of adult sleeping patterns suggest that the more we divide sleep the less total sleep we need. A child who has two sleeps a day will sleep for fewer hours in total than one who concentrates her sleep into the night. Increase her night-time sleep by reducing her naps, or cope with her wakeful evenings and mornings by taking a daytime nap yourself. If you can sleep an hour by day it is worth two at night, probably because we sleep our deepest sleep in the first hour.

The child of working parents

If you are working all day you will want to see the children in the evenings. Most mornings you will enjoy their company. When you are stressed at work, however, you need a moment to yourself, even if it is just a lie-in or a child-free evening.

Children's routines are rarely flexible – even when they seem chaotic. She wants to be with you, and you have nurtured that need. The more you push her away, the more she is concerned that something is wrong and the more insistent she will become that she stays with you. The only way around this is to organize a regular bedtime and morning routine – even if this means she occasionally goes to bed before both parents are home or gets up after one parent has left. If her day has a clear structure it is easier to work around it when you need to. Structures give security.

Cutting out naps

If you want to cut out her regular nap time find an activity to keep her awake. Put on a record and have a bop together. Get a chair up to the sink so she can play with water or go to the park. Calmer play should be left until the time she would normally wake up. Once her normal sleeping time has passed her body clock will almost certainly keep her awake until bedtime. Decide when you want her to sleep. Put her to bed a bit earlier and get her up at the same time – or vice versa.

Bedrooms are for sleeping

Children are easily bored, and when they are bored they sleep. It is not just the motion of a car that sends them to sleep – the constant view of the back of the car seat and the lack of anything to do also play a role. If you want her to sleep keep the environment as dull as possible. If you want her to stay awake keep it as lively and stimulating as you can.

In recent years we have tended to decorate children's bedrooms as if they were playrooms. There are pictures around the walls, toys on all the shelves, mobiles, piles of soft toys, night lights, musical boxes, story tapes and more. We put the child in this stimulating environment, not to play, but to sleep. Then we wonder why she does not do so!

When she wakes in the morning she does not come around slowly (as we do in our calm bedroom) but pops out of bed all excited by seeing all the toys around her, and ready to go. The first thing she wants to see when she is in this mood is you. If the windows had a blackout, if the toys were stored away in cupboards, if the mobiles hung elsewhere, if there was, in short, nothing to do but sleep she would turn over and have another forty winks – and so of course could you.

Ways to make her sleep longer

● Make the room dark. Darkness is not a problem if the child is used to it. If she cannot see anything and the house is quiet she will probably go back to sleep.

● Keep the bedroom dull. If she cannot see her toys she is more likely to go back to sleep. If stimulation livens her up she needs company. She is unlikely to lie quietly or play in her room for very long.

● Get a large bed. If you cannot avoid her early-morning visits make sure there is room to escape her restlessness.

● Keep her up. If she only needs nine hours of sleep, decide which nine hours are best for you. Adjust her day accordingly.

● Take her back to her own bed every time she comes into your room. Put her back into bed, turn off the light and close the door. If you do this every night she will get the message. This only works if the child has always slept in the dark. A child who is used to a night light will be too afraid to sleep if the room is completely dark.

● Give her something to do. Take a toy she has not played with for a while such as a puzzle, or set out a game with a group of toys, such as a tea set and a couple of teddies, for her to play with first thing. This can either be left in her bedroom (it is best placed where it will attract her attention as she sets out to your room), or in your bedroom. Even if this wakes you up, lying in bed listening to her happy play is very relaxing.

Out of sight

Toys in stackable plastic boxes are hidden from view in the bedroom. Easy to carry to another room, you can swap them when interest in one lot of toys wanes.

SEE ALSO

Sleepless babies	**36–37**
Sharing the care	**52–53**
Sleeping routines	**58–59**
First toys and games	**60–61**

STORAGE

For toys

● A toy box on wheels is easy to move around.

● Short kitchen wall units make a good low work surface. As the child grows you can move them higher up the wall.

● Under-bed drawers are big and get messy. Place storage boxes inside.

● Cupboards with fitted shelves and/or mesh drawers. Keep toys out of sight.

For clothes

● Children need to be able to reach their clothes. Lower the rails in the wardrobe and add a small drawer unit.

Sleeping routines

Many parents complain about sleepless nights, but the definition of what constitutes a problem depends very much on your expectations. The simple rule is that if his sleep pattern is causing you problems it needs attention.

Fast asleep at last
Once your baby is old enough to have one big sleep, you can help him learn to sleep through the night without help.

DELAYING

All children use delaying tactics. If you say, "Just a minute", and mean five, they will take all five and ask for more. If you ask three times before you get cross, they will let you ask three times. Say what you mean and mean what you say.

● **Warn.** "I want you to start packing up now. Bath time in five minutes."

● **Insist.** "I'm running your bath now, you have one minute to pack up, and then I expect you upstairs."

● **Act.** "Up you come right now. No more delays."

● **Ignore.** "But Mum! One minute! Please!"

● **If necessary.** Carry him up.

Most babies do not sleep through the night until they are about six months old, so we cannot call the frequent waking of younger babies problematic, even if it causes parents problems. Sleeping problems fall into three categories:

● Baby who won't go to sleep.
● Baby frequently wakes in the night.
● Baby wakes early.

Whichever category your child falls into, the chances are that you will suffer more from his sleeplessness than he does. He may be a bit irritable if he has not had enough sleep, but he will just take a few extra naps during the day to make up for it – something his parents can rarely do.

Growing is painful

Children tend to grow at night, and can do so at phenomenal rates. He may grow 1.5 cm (1/2 in) in a single night. No wonder he cries! In these growth periods all babies go through relatively irritable and sleepless patches. We tend to call them teething – and their teeth do grow at such times – but it is much more than that. His bones lengthen, his muscles extend and, because his brain also grows, he is unsettled by his rapidly changing abilities. At birth only a third of the brain is in place. He is a helpless individual who cannot control his body, does not understand what he sees or hears, has little ability to think or remember and no language.

By two he is mobile, bright, can communicate his own thoughts and feelings and remember what he did yesterday. He is more like his adult self at two than he is like the baby he was at birth. Imagine how it must feel to change so rapidly. These unsettled periods are usually followed by a time of relative calm. Crisis points occur between about six and 12 weeks (when some babies develop colic and all cry more); somewhere around seven to eight months when many babies are thought to be teething and all begin to show fear of strangers; around nine to ten months and at around two years.

Preparing for bed

Children need to wind down before bed. The problem is that many of them are at their silliest in the last hour.

Silly time: If the sensible bits of his brain seem to have switched off (quite normal) you can wait for the tantrums and the sulks, or squeeze out the silliness with a wild game. Chase him round the garden, orput him in the buggy and go for a jog.

Clear up time: Select a disc, put it on and see if the room can be cleared of toys before it is finished. If you make a game of this necessity, and it forms part of the daily routine, he will grow up expecting to put things away *and* think it is all fun.

Start the wind down: It is time to calm down – a warm bath, a warm drink and a cuddle, in that order.

Say goodnight – to everyone and everything: children should not be made to kiss strangers if they don't want to do so.

Take him to bed: Pop him in, pull up the covers, kiss him, turn off the light and go. **Play a story tape:** Once he can control the bedside light and the tape recorder by himself he may like to listen to a tape, or read a book, before settling to sleep. It is an excellent habit for an older child.

Learning to fall asleep

Children need to learn to "go to sleep" by themselves. If he needs you to put him to sleep he will always call out for your help. By not allowing sleep routines to develop which involve your presence you encourage him to find ways of falling asleep when he is alone. However elaborate the family calming-down routine, cut it short at the bedroom door. A kiss and a quick "goodnight" are all that is necessary.

We all wake in the night, but we simply turn over and sleep. If there are changes in our lives, or we are worried, we can have sleepless nights. We do not wake up more often, we just do not fall asleep as easily. A child who does not know how to go to sleep without the help of a carer will demand that his carer comes to his aid.

What if he protests or cries?

If he knows the regime he will not protest. If he thinks by crying he can get you back to sit with him and stroke his hair why would he fail to cry? If a child who normally settles quickly cries he should be heeded. If he always goes unwillingly he is best ignored. Check once and leave.

If he carries on protesting, you have a choice. You can tough it out now, or live by his demands. His protests will fade, he will probably – reluctantly – accept the situation a few days later, and be firmly settled into the regime by the end of next week. Until then use earplugs, play some music, close all the doors, be firm and say "No, no and no" – as often as necessary!

DOES HE DREAM?

When we first fall asleep our bodies are restless and our minds "relaxed". After an hour or so the body becomes inactive, while the brain explodes into action, the eyes rove. We dream. After 15 minutes or so we return to the resting inactive brain state. This cycle repeats about six times through the night with about 10% of the night taken up with dreams. Children dream more the younger they are; premature babies dream most of all. What do small babies dream about? We can never know. Maybe just flashes of sounds and sights. Adults sometimes have nightmares in non-dreaming sleep; pre-schoolers have them more often. After a nightmare or night terror he wakes afraid or in tears.

SEE ALSO
Sleepless babies **36–37**
Naps and early mornings **56–57**
Typical baby problems **178–179**
Typical toddler problems **180–181**

Good-night story
Read a story or sing a song with your child – but do so downstairs, in the living room. This way she will not come to expect you to sit with her when she goes to sleep.

First toys and games

Today's children are showered with toys from the day they are born. But which toys and games are the best to choose for a child's development in the early months, and how many or few should she ideally have?

There is a fine balance to be struck between over- and under-stimulation. Both can be detrimental to the child's development. The optimum balance lies somewhere in the middle – where parents create an environment which raises the child's interest, captures it and draws it into productive activity.

Too little or too much?

If a baby is left without stimulation she will sleep, but after a while she will wake and cry. If you do not respond she will whimper for a little longer, then fall asleep again. If this is her daily routine the baby will gradually expect less and less, ask for nothing and, of course, get nothing. If, on the other hand, she is used to constant attention and suddenly faces neglect, she will initially protest loudly, then withdraw into depression and eventually give up interest in the world.

At the other extreme, the continuously over-stimulated child is faced with a barrage of toys and activities. She looks at one but, before she can begin to explore it, another toy catches her eye, then another one. She flits from one thing to another without ever doing more than skim the surface. She is excited, but unsatisfied, stimulated but not lured into creativity.

Between the two extremes there lies a happy medium, where the child can rest as well as work, think as well as play, listen as well as talk, walk as well as run, settle quietly as well as squeal with delight.

Quiet spaces for sleeping

There is such a wide choice of cradle toys available, it may seem bizarre to question whether or not we should provide them. If cots were the major daytime place for babies, making them interesting would be an obvious priority. But cots are rarely used as playpens – most babies sleep and nap in them. Once they wake they cry, we rush to the bedroom, scoop them up and take them away from their cot and its toys.

So why bother? If we want a child to sleep, is turning on the mobile the best thing to do? If we start by teaching her that she needs a mobile to turn before she feels sleepy, we may find ourselves having to switch it on every time she wakes in the night. By all means buy a mobile, but fix it to her chair, her pram or her playpen – not to the place where she sleeps.

A year of two halves

In the first six months, babies look, reach out and touch, hold and bang, or take things to their mouths. If they can hold it, they will bang it, if they can get it to their mouth, they will chew on it. They do not use toys in a unique way.

By the second six months the child is beginning to treat each object in a unique fashion. We might compare this to the beginnings of language. It is as if she is saying: "I know what that is, I know what that does". And, in fact, this is what she is doing, because at this age she is beginning to use signs as if they were words.

TEN TOP TOYS

For 0–6 months

Mobiles
Most mobiles are fixed to the side of the cot, a few fix onto the sides of chairs. A tiny baby sees best at a distance of 30–35 cm (12–14 in), sees moving objects better than stationary ones, and dark objects better than light ones if they are presented against a white ceiling.

Musical boxes
Babies love the high-pitched notes of musical boxes. Beware those that turn on automatically when the baby cries!

Rattles
First rattles should be light and well balanced. Dumbbell shapes are good. Later she can cope with other shapes.

Wrist rattles
Wrist rattles cannot be dropped – and leave the hands free for her to watch.

A mirror
Place it where she can see herself moving, and where it will reflect light in interesting patterns.

Pram beads
Traditional but still good. They give the child something to watch and later swipe at when lying in her pram.

Toys to swipe
A teddy on a string, a pompom, anything small and interesting.

Toys to grab
Rattles, rings, her nightdress or the bits and pieces on her play mat

Toys to hold and chew
Interesting textures, bobbles and places to explore with her lips and tongue.

Toys to feel
A play mat, a soft toy with "feel appeal".

For 7–12 months

A jack in the box
A "surprise" toy where someone or something hides and is found.

An activity centre
A classic with lots to investigate, to stimulate a variety of hand skills – poking, prodding, twisting, turning.

A soft toy
To cuddle, to throw, and later to take the dull bits in games.

A posting box
A hide-and-find toy which also encourages careful placing.

Soft bricks
Large, soft bricks are easier for unskilled hands to hold and stack than the real thing.

A car
To "brmmm brmmm" back and forth.

Books
To look at, to listen to new words, to point at what she sees and hear the names, to play at eating the sandwich or smacking the naughty dog.

Saucepans and a tea set
To play with in the bath, to fill and empty, and to start to imitate.

A ball
To roll and let go.

A play mat
A play mat or a soft toy with a variety of textures to grab, stroke, pinch, pull and grasp.

For 1–2 years

A toy vacuum cleaner
A brush or mop to follow you around the house and imitate you when you are cleaning.

A toy kitchen
With sets of plastic crockery and cutlery, for early imitative cooking, serving and eating.

A trike
A tricycle or a sit-and-ride, a pull-along and a push-along to make the most of her mobility.

A simple tray puzzle
To encourage her to turn her hand and to line up shapes.

A simple construction kit
A simple kit of building blocks which does not require accurate placing is a good first choice.

A crayon
Wax crayons, or a stout brush and a pot of paint, plus plenty of paper (wallpaper is ideal) for young artists.

A car
A car or similar vehicle into which the child can fit peg people.

Stackable toys
Large bricks or stack of rings to fit over a pole.

A shape sorter
A sorting box with about four different shapes.

Books
Books with pictures of familiar objects that the child can try to name

CHAPTER TWO

Child growth and development

At birth, a child's muscles and bones are weak, making it difficult for her to move, and she cannot yet control her movements, recall events, think, or reason. Most children develop in a similar way, but reach milestones in their development at different times. All children, however, will control their arms before their legs, and communicate by action before they speak. And it is watching our child's progress to walking, speaking and understanding that makes parenting so special.

At birth the average baby is about 52 cm (20 in) long and weighs between 3 and 4 kg (7–9 lb). His head is relatively large for his body and his limbs are rather puny and short. In fact his head makes up a quarter of his total body height. He is still curled in the foetal position and will remain so in the first weeks.

Small but mine

You may be surprised when you first see him – is this really what I carried for nine months? He seems so tiny, and so strangely adult. Yet you will soon adopt him as your precious child.

Your newborn baby

He is a little miracle – and so incredibly tiny. It comes as quite a shock: the size of his mother's bump seemed to promise something much larger. In the first weeks he will carry on growing at almost the same rate as in the womb.

As a rough rule of thumb, your baby's growth rate will halve as time passes. He grows as much in the first month as he will in the following two, as much again in the first three months as he will in the following six, as much in his first year as he will in the following two, and so on. What this means in practice is that we very rarely see anyone quite as miraculously tiny as he is just after birth.

First impressions

Babies often begin to breathe before the body is completely born. Most breathe within about 2–3 minutes, some need to have their airways cleared, and a few need the stimulation of a slap to get going. Crying is not always the first sign of life – some babies just splutter into independent life. The condition of your baby is now assessed according to the APGAR scale.

The initials stand for Appearance, Pulse, Grimace, Activity and Respiration. Each is assessed on a three-point scale (0, 1, 2), giving a maximum total of 10. Babies with less than six points may need resuscitation, those with less than four may need life-saving. A score of seven or more after five minutes is good. Not all babies with lower scores have problems later, but some do.

First looks

Immediately after birth most babies are wide-eyed and serious. He will probably be rather red, with puffy eyes. Beauty, they say, is in the eye of the beholder – which is just as well: a vaginally delivered baby is not always a pretty sight.

The head, which is rather large in all newborn babies, may well be misshapen, lopsided, or pointed. This is especially likely in babies that were delivered face first. The baby's eyes may be bloodshot, the nose will be flat, and he will seem rather chinless. The body is small with pale skin (even in black babies), with visible blood vessels. There could be some bruising – especially if forceps were used in his delivery. The upper part of the body may be covered with a downy fuzz, and here and elsewhere there may also be a waxy covering to the skin. All these minor "imperfections" will, however, quickly disappear, as will the swollen breasts (which may be present in boys and girls) and the vaginal discharge (which may be bloody in some girls).

The most beautiful baby

He is of course beautiful. And you come to him like a new lover. Reaching out tentatively at first, you move your hands across his body, smiling, talking to him, crooning endearments. In between you will beam at your partner and other first visitors. Like all momentous occasions language fails. Words are far too banal to express your deep emotions.

The hospital may encourage you to put your baby to the breast, and if he is alert, and you have had few drugs during the birth, he may well latch on to the nipple straight away and start to suck.

Initially his breathing is soft and shallow. Often it will seem as if he is not breathing at all. When he sleeps he may become so pale and still that you could believe him dead. And you will check many times to make sure! Circulation and breathing quickly mature but it will be some time before he can control his body temperature well – and before you can rest peacefully that this pale baby is viable and healthy.

HOW BABIES CHANGE

Skin
Babies' skin gets darker with age. Mixed-race babies are usually much fairer at birth than they will be by the time they reach their first birthday.

Eyes
Caucasian babies usually have blue eyes at birth, but many darken later and take on other colours. Darker-skinned children are born with brown eyes.

Hair colour
The first hair is often a very different colour and texture from later hair. It gradually falls out over the first months. It can take up to two years for the hair to regrow and thicken. The time it takes to grow bears little relationship to its eventual thickness.

Nose
Noses are quite prominent at birth, giving new babies an oddly adult look. As the cheek muscles develop (which they do thanks to baby's regular sucking), the nose starts to look less dominant. This gives him a typically sweet baby face.

SEE ALSO
A child is born   12–13
Your baby's first reflexes   66–67
Is everything all right?   68–69
In his genes!   114–115

My precious baby
Birth is such a momentous event for both of you, you may be stunned into silence. Soon you will start to explore him, his feel and smell, and you will inevitably fall in love!

Your baby's first reflexes

You have delivered your little miracle, and there she lies, all bundled up. You may think that all she can do at this stage is sleep and, after a little practice, feed – yet numerous automatic responses are already active in her tiny body.

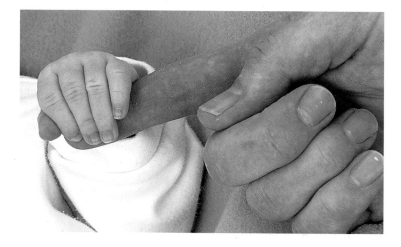

Hold my hand

The grasping reflex is one of the first that we come to notice and appreciate – she clings so tightly and seemingly lovingly on to our hands! In fact, the grasping power of her hands and feet is so strong that she could be hung out on a washing line!

Much of what a newborn baby can do are in-built reflexes – things that all babies around the world do in exactly the same way. New babies have no choice about reflexes: if the right stimulus occurs they respond in a pre-programmed way. And their response will be exactly the same way as that of all other babies. Some of these reflexes will stay with her throughout life, others will disappear as she grows older.

A newborn baby's reflexes

The following reflexes are present in most babies. The hospital or midwife will test for some of them, but you will probably notice some of them yourself.

The blinking reflex: A flash of light or a puff of air on her face causes her to blink.

The rooting reflex: If you touch her face she will turn towards the touch, opening her mouth as she turns, searching for something to suck.

The sucking reflex: Once something enters the mouth she lowers her tongue to create a vacuum and then begins to suck.

The swallowing reflex: If something enters her mouth she swallows. Although the reflex is present at birth, she has to learn how to coordinate it with her breathing. She will often splutter and cough until she has done so.

This coordination problem arises because she also has a reflex to breathe when her oxygen level is low. She needs to learn how to breathe before she makes these reflex gulps for air, and how to let her breath out slowly when she needs to.

The Babinski reflex: Gentle stroking along the foot causes the toes to fan out and the big toe to flex.

The Babkin reflex: Pressure applied to both palms of the hands while the baby is lying on her back will cause the eyes to close and the head to return to the centre.

The grasp or palmer reflex: Babies automatically close their fingers over anything that presses the palm of their hand. If you touch the sole of her foot she spreads her toes and then, if the pressure remains, she will curl them. This is one of the reflexes the doctor will check – he will offer his fingers to the baby and lift her up. The grip is lost from the toes at about three months and from the fingers at about seven months.

The stepping reflex: If you hold her upright and let her feet touch a firm surface she will walk with a high step. As

Like a duck

Amazing as it may seem, your little baby may be a better swimmer than you! The diving reflex enables her to hold her breath for a short while and swim under water.

her legs become plump she will stop walking (though many light babies often continue). These movements keep her joints supple. Kicking both legs serves the same purpose and is, in fact, the same reflex response.

The crawling reflex: If you place a baby on her stomach she will crawl so that her knees come up under her body. She may even creep along.

The Moro or startle reflex: A startled baby spreads her arms, legs and fingers, and arches her back. Then she curls, clenching fingers and toes, bringing her arms across her body and bringing up her knees into a protective foetal position.

The diving reflex: If water suddenly splashes onto her face, her heart rate decreases and the blood moves away from the surface of her skin. If she goes under water she stops breathing.

The patella reflex: This reflex is familiar to us because it is still present in adults. It is the one the doctor often checks: a tap on the patella tendon just below the knee causes the knee to jerk upwards.

The rage reflex: If both hands are placed on the side of an alert baby's head so that movement is restrained, and the infant's mouth is then momentarily blocked, the baby cries and struggles.

Some other things she may, but will not always, be able to do:

● Turn roughly towards your voice – especially if the sound comes into her left ear. She may even reach out with an arm.
● Move in time to the rhythm of your speech (but this will be so gently you would need a video tape to see it).

Some things she may be able to do in the next two to three weeks:

● Copy your facial expressions. For example, she may poke out her tongue if you poke out yours. You will need to face her and be within about 25 cm (10 in) of her face for this to work.
● Move her lips as if she were talking back if you pause when talking to her. You will need to face her and be close in to her.
● Recognize your smell.

- Extra fingers and toes. Common; often just tiny flaps of skin; easily removed.
- Minor bends and twists in arms and legs. Will straighten once he is active.
- Clicking hips. Caused by the mother's hormones. Mostly rights itself; double nappies or a a cast may help.
- Umbilical hernias. A loop of intestine pokes through a weak muscle and rests under the skin; surgery usually not needed but possible.
- Scrotal hernias. A bulge above the scrotum; cuts blood supply to it; needs to be corrected.

Incubator baby

Even if your baby is placed in an incubator for observation he will usually be all right.

Is everything all right?

Rest assured that if doctors suspect there is anything wrong with your baby, they will be making checks. However, you have spent more time looking at him than anyone else, and you will spot worrying changes first.

If the birth has been difficult, or your baby is in some distress, he may be placed in an incubator. If he has been born prematurely he will be taken to the special care unit. In both cases there is usually no need to worry – most babies are perfectly fit and well. If you do have a worry, speak to the medical team. It is perfectly natural to worry – to look and check, and almost invariably there is something that looks a bit strange. Naturally there will be! The baby has just been pushed, with difficulty, through a narrow birth canal. It is the rare baby that gets through without the odd blemish or worrying sign. Within a few days, most of these will have disappeared.

The head and face

The shape: The head is squeezed by the force of labour and birth. Because the bones of the head are not yet fused, it can be pushed into quite odd shapes, especially if the baby is born face first. Do not worry. The bones are pushed and squeezed to get the head through the birth canal. This is why they move and put the head into strange shapes. The movement protects the brain from damage. The bones will gradually return to their rightful places over the next week or so. When they have done so, he will look perfectly normal.

During a difficult labour the head can also become swollen and bruised. Again this is quite normal, even if it looks rather alarming. The swellings on the back of the head (which are caused by the head pushing against the undilated cervix) disappear in the first few days, as do the swellings or grooves caused by forceps if these are used in delivery.

The eyes: Most newborns have puffy eyes, and many are bloodshot. Most babies look as if they have a squint (this needs checking if it persists beyond about 10 weeks). Watery eyes are also common. They are caused by a blocked tear duct. Any discharge from the eye needs the doctor's attention.

The mouth: Spots that rub off the tongue are milk curds, those that remain could be thrush. Babies' tongues are quite small and do not stick out far – which makes them look as if they are tied by a membrane. Most are not. If you are worried get a professional opinion.

The ears: Ears are often pushed out of shape by birth. Most will soon return to their normal position and shape.

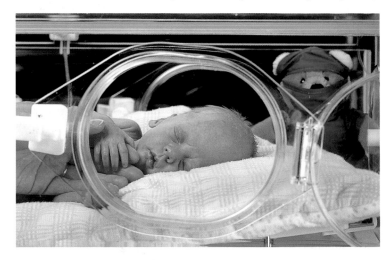

The fontanels: The soft, pulsating spot on top of the head is the surface of the brain. Do not be afraid to touch it. If it looks taut or starts to bulge (which may be caused by a swelling of the brain following brain damage or infection), or if it seems to have fallen away from the skull (because the brain has shrunk due to dehydration) – do not delay and get the child to hospital immediately. Both are very serious.

The skin

Waxy: Before birth the skin is covered in vernix, a waxy yellowish coating. Some of it may be still be present at birth, especially in an early baby. It will wash off, but since it protects the skin from infection it is best to leave it in place until it rubs off.

Flaky skin: Common, especially on the hands and feet, it is usually caused by the baby being overdue, and will disappear.

Jaundice: Mild jaundice (yellowing of the skin) is common; it mostly disappears in the first few days. It can make the baby sleepy and you may have to wake him for feeds. If it gets worse or persists give boiled water and call the doctor immediately.

Very pale: Pale faces, red bodies and blue limbs are common because circulation and temperature control are still immature.

Hairy: Lanugo is the downy hair which covered the baby's body in the womb. Most babies still have some of this at birth – especially on the shoulders and ears. It will go. Wrinkled skin will also disappear.

Spots: *Urticaria neonatorum* looks like nettle rash. It is of no consequence and rarely lasts more than a couple of days. *Milia*, tiny white spots caused by blocked sweat glands, are common in young babies. They will disappear within a few weeks. *White pearl spots* are caused by the mother's hormones (they pass to the baby via the placenta), and will clear as the hormones disappear from the baby's bloodstream.

Birthmarks

While few babies have major problems, many have minor abnormalities. About half of all babies have a birthmark. There are three main types, which are mostly caused by abnormalities of the small blood vessels. The two most common birthmarks usually disappear by the time the child starts school, but the third type is permanent.

Stork marks: Small pinkish marks between the eyebrows and at the nape of the neck; turn darker as the baby cries; fade over the first couple of years. Almost 50 per cent of babies have these marks.

Strawberry naeves: A bright red, slightly raised area; may not appear until the baby is a few weeks old. They are more obvious and more distressing than stork marks because they tend to enlarge over the first months. After this they begin to fade to a pinkish colour. Most have disappeared by the time the child is six – sometimes they leave a slight puckering of the skin. They can be removed surgically.

Port wine stains: Present at birth; often on the face; permanent; caused by a malformation of a larger blood vessel. The dilated capillaries give a purplish red colour to the affected area. Some can be treated with lasers or plastic surgery, most can be covered by cosmetics. Very rarely they are associated with other more serious vascular malformations in the brain.

Mongolian blue spots: Large bluish patches on the back and buttocks; look like bruising; mainly in Afro-Caribbean and Asian babies; fade in the first five years.

Moles: Small, brownish pigmented spots; occasionally present at birth but mostly appear in the second year. They can occur on all areas of the body. Malignant change is rare in children, but any mole that changes colour and size, starts to itch or bleed should be seen by a doctor.

MORE WORRIES

• **Undescended testicles.** One (or both) may fail to descend. More typical of premature than full-term boys. If left untreated, an undescended testicle may cause infertility. There is also an increased risk of malignancy.

• **The following problems** may occur due to the mother's hormones being passed to the baby via the placenta. Once they have cleared the baby's blood, the problems will disappear.

• **Very large genitals at birth.** Women secrete male and female sex hormones, so the growth occurs in boys and girls.

• **Bleeding from the vagina.** It looks like – and is – a small and slight period.

• **Swollen breasts.** Both boys and girls may have these. Some babies, again both sexes, have some milk in the breasts at birth.

PLUMP KIDS

- Long-term habits are picked up from the family, so keep the family active. Plump people are often less active.
- Avoid rewarding with sweets, but do not ban them. Moderation is less likely to encourage binge eating.
- Discourage food between meals.
- Do not eat in front of the TV. We eat less when we concentrate on it.
- Do not ban fats and sugars – they are vital for growth – but regulate intake. A balanced diet, eaten sitting at a table with other people and in moderate amounts, is the best way to control weight.

How babies grow: weight

There are many reasons why your baby may be smaller or larger than other babies. Understanding the causes will help you follow your child's progress and steer her in the right direction towards long-term health.

At birth most babies weigh about 2.75–4 kg (6–9 lb). Rapid growth will make your baby put on weight surprisingly quickly: she will double her birth weight by 4–5 months, and will have tripled it by her first birthday.

Charting your baby's weight

The charts below show the percentile weights for boys and girls between birth and 12 months. You can compare your child's weight with that of other babies by checking her age along the bottom of the chart and her weight on the side. Using the lines on the chart to guide you, place a dot on the chart that represents both the age and the weight of your child. If you do this every month, you can produce your child's personal growth curve. Children grow in fits and starts, so this is unlikely to be as smooth as the printed lines. If your child's

weight falls below the 10th percentile line, more than 90% of all babies of her age are heavier than her. Most (82%) of all babies fall between the 9th and 91st percentiles.

Do fat babies become fat children?

About one in every five fat babies becomes a fat adult, which means that about four in every five do not. The common belief was that our fat cells were mainly laid down in infancy. This meant that, if extra fat cells were laid down, they would persist into adulthood where they could easily be filled with fat again, causing adult obesity. If, on the other hand, an individual had not laid down extra fat cells as a baby, this would not happen and they would be less likely to become overweight.

Unfortunately, this is no more than a nice idea. Recent research suggests that fat cells can be laid down at all ages and stages

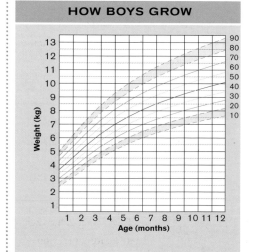

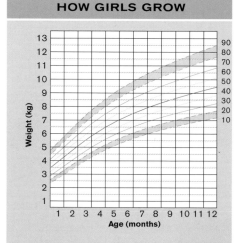

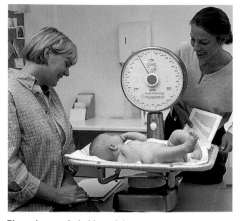

Plump legs and chubby wrists

Your baby will grow at a phenomenal rate, up to 12mm (½ in) in 24 hours! Her growth will be monitored at the child health clinic: electronic scales give the most accurate readings.

of development. They can also reappear after they have been surgically removed by liposuction. It is their distribution that changes with age.

How plump a person is, and how they distribute that fat, tends to run in the family. There is a very strong genetic component to obesity. A child with two overweight parents is very likely (80%) to follow in their footsteps – to start plump and to remain overweight. A child with one plump parent halves that risk. It is possible, but not easy, to kick the family trend. It is worth attempting to do so – the longer a child remains plump, the more likely she is to be overweight as an adult.

Parenting an overweight child

Plump children may be the butt of jokes, they are the last children selected in games and often have fewer friends. This can make them feel bad about themselves. Teasing and low esteem in turn may lead to comfort eating. Not joining in with games leads to inactivity. There is thus a vicious circle of overeating, inactivity, increased weight and unpopularity.

Breaking this circle can be extremely difficult. The child needs to know that she is loved, not for what but who they are: your beloved child. They need to feel good about themselves, and to recognize their own strengths and abilities and, above all, their own value. If they are constantly reminded that they are fat (and thus feel ugly), this is hard to achieve. Constant dieting, banning ice cream, never ever being allowed sweets, all say: "We would like you better if you were thin". It is also likely to lead to an obsession with the desired goods, which may then be eaten hurriedly and excessively, in secret.

Fat children should, of course, not be fed chips and syrup pudding every night. They need a well-balanced diet, plenty of exercise and activity, and no overeating or snacks between meals. Most of all they need their self-esteem building up. It will take plenty of knocks. Don't let any of them come from you. Never, ever call her fat names – even in jest! It hurts.

Active play

Active play with friends is good for your child, socially and physically, and swimming is the best exercise for those who are overweight.

How babies grow: height

Babies are not just miniature versions of adults: they are a very different shape. As they get older, different parts of their bodies will grow at different rates, gradually changing all their body proportions until they look like us.

At birth, your child's head measures a quarter of his whole length, and his forehead is a much larger part of his face than it will be. Eventually, his body and limbs will grow at a faster rate than his head, but in the first phases of growth this is not the case. At birth, his brain is only one-third its adult size. By the time he is two years old, it will be almost fully grown. This means that his head has to grow a lot in the first couple of years.

Growing and changing

At birth your baby will stretch from about your elbow to your fingertip. By the time he is one-year-old, he will already be as tall as the kitchen table. At the same time, much else is happening. His muscles are strengthening and losing their watery texture. His bones, which bend easily at birth, become harder and less flexible. His heart strengthens and becomes more efficient, and his blood pressure decreases. He is now able to digest food, and at the same time his immune system improves. He also learns to control his breathing in the same way as adults.

Charting your child's height

The charts opposite give the average heights for boys and girls between birth and 12 months. You can compare your child's height with that of other children.

1 Check your baby's age along the bottom of the chart and his height on the left side. Using the lines on the chart to guide you, draw a horizontal line across from his height, and a vertical line up from his age.

2 Place a dot on the chart where the height and age lines intersect. You can now check if your baby is taller (above the 50th percentile line) or shorter (below the 50th percentile line) than average. Half of all children are taller than the 50th percentile, and half shorter.

On a percentile chart, if your child's height falls above the 91st percentile, only 9 percent of children of the same age are taller; if it falls below the 9th percentile, 91 percent of children of the same age are taller than your child.

The tendency to be tall or small seems to run in families – tall parents, especially if both are tall, tend to have tall babies, and short parents tend to have short babies.

Look how tall I am!
Children – and their parents – will proudly measure progress on the height chart. Yet, the rate of growth is considerably slower now than before the birth of the child.

PHENOMENAL GROWTH RATE

When the fertilized egg cell passes down the Fallopian tube and nestles into the wall of the uterus, it weighs 0.00000057 g (0.00000002 oz). By the time the baby is born, nine months later, he will be between 3 and 4 kg (6–9 lb). If the rate of growth in the initial three months of life was to continue until the age of 21, this man would weigh considerably more than the Sun and all the planets of our solar system combined.

HOW BOYS GROW

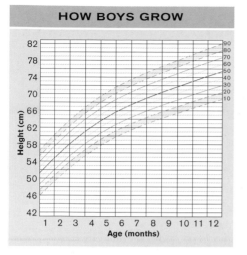

HOW GIRLS GROW

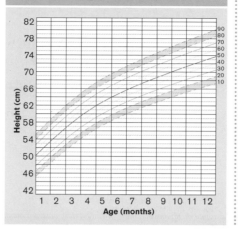

SEE ALSO

How babies grow: weight　**70–71**

How the senses develop　**78–79**

Taking control of the body　**82–83**

Becoming mobile　　　　**92–93**

Relative height

These charts allow you to map your child's height and to compare it with that of other children of the same age. Follow the instructions opposite.

HOW BABIES CHANGE AS THEY GROW UP

Digestion

Sickly babies

Babies are often sick and rarely digest everything we give them (which can be seen in the nappies).

Milk drinkers

Their digestive systems remain immature during the first two years. This suggests that babies are "designed" to survive mainly on milk until they are about two, rather than on the solids we now feed them.

Friendly bugs

Digestion is helped by friendly bacteria which begin to take up residence in the baby's gut within the first few weeks. Your baby "catches" these bugs from you, so contact with your skin is important for him.

"Mummy, I'm hot"

Older children are able to sweat – the most basic way in which the body keeps itself cool.

Temperature

Sweating it out

Sweating lowers the temperature of the skin. In hot weather the blood moves into the small capillaries below the skin surface (which is why we go red). We sweat, and evaporation of the water from the skin cools the blood in the capillaries. In cold weather, the opposite happens.

Activity levels

We feel warm when our muscles are working, so we shiver and jump up and down to keep warm. Heat loss is proportional to the amount of exposed body surface. We reduce the exposed surface area by curling up into a ball when it is cold; we increase the area by stretching out in hot weather.

Babies lack control

Babies are not very good at controlling their body temperatures, and parents therefore need to keep a careful eye on them during very hot or cold weather.

Breathing

Taking a breath

The most obvious difference between a baby's breathing and an adult's breathing is that a baby breathes by using his stomach muscles, an adult by using his ribs and diaphragm. The other difference is more subtle. Older babies, children and adults have two breathing mechanisms.

Automatic breathing

The basic mechanism works by monitoring the gases in the lung (oxygen and carbon dioxide). When oxygen is low we automatically take a breath. This is what stops us holding our breath until we die. In the first weeks this is the baby's only mechanism.

Voluntary breathing

Somewhere between six and twelve weeks a second, voluntary breathing mechanism develops. This enables us to take a deep breath before blowing up a balloon or to control our breathing as we speak. It is this voluntary mechanism which tunes our breathing to our movements and our breathing to our speech. We use it most of the time.

Seeing the world

Our ability to see and make sense of the world around us is truly remarkable. Babies start with very poor "viewing equipment" – yet their brains develop remarkably quickly and help them make sense of what they see.

Happy to see you

When we talk to our child we tend to move close in, or hold her close and move her up or down because of her fixed focus. And she will encourage us to do so!

The eye can only "work" if the brain interprets the image and, like the brain, a baby's eyes are still very immature. While we see in colour, and have 20/20 vision, a newborn baby sees in shades of grey and only has 20/800 vision. (She can just make out an object 6 m/20 ft away which we could see 245 m/800 ft away.)

Your newborn baby's problem is not one of getting things into focus (although she has that problem too), it is a matter of having the right equipment. The centre part of the eye, which we use in daylight to see colour and detail, is not fully developed – in fact, most of it is missing. The baby has to rely on the outer parts of the eye, which are specialized for dim light and movement. To get an idea of what she sees, draw the curtains and light a candle. The way the room looks to you now is probably rather like it looks to her. She sees outlines but not detail, big things but not small, greys but not much colour, and only when the cat moves does it suddenly become visible. When we talk to her, we move to make ourselves more visible. She reinforces us in this: if we give her what she wants she responds; if we don't she does not. We soon learn.

A baby's visual equipment improves very quickly. By the time she is six months, her eyes will be as good as yours, but she will still not perceive the world quite as you do.

MILESTONES IN SEEING

Birth	4 weeks	6–12 weeks	12–20 weeks	20–28 weeks	28–52 weeks
Pupils adjust to light; she blinks, can detect movement and is sensitive to changes in brightness. She can focus in front of her face. Her eyes follow her turning head. She wants to watch, but her visual acuity is very poor.	Babies are now very interested in faces. She can recognize her mother's face. She can also cry real tears.	A baby can see out of the "corner of her eye". Her eyes work together and move to focus. She is interested in edges, corners and curves. On a projector, she could operate the focus (by sucking a nipple) to focus slides.	By now a baby knows when things are familiar – she looks at her hands, watching them move, and will focus on her reflection in the mirror, although she will not yet recognize herself for at least another 15 months.	A four-month-old child prefers to look at complex things. She can see 800 times better than she could in the first weeks. She can now pay attention to very small objects, and her sight is within the adult range.	During this period, a child's vision improves so much that she can see almost as clearly as an adult, although she still remains a little short-sighted. By now she can follow rapidly moving objects.

Visual constancy

We see the world as static and stable, but babies have to learn about seeing, and they do so in the first months of life.

Size constancy: When we park the car and walk away from it, it does not shrink, although when we look back at it, it appears smaller. Babies learn about size constancy between about 22 and 28 weeks.

Shape constancy: On the retina a closed door is a rectangle. As it opens, the edge nearest to the eye becomes bigger and the edge further away becomes smaller – it becomes a trapezoid. We know this, but when we look at the open door, we just see a door. By 12 weeks babies learn that shapes do not change even if they move.

Position constancy: Stationary objects stay where they are, but if we move, their position relative to us can change. This is another constancy babies learn in the first year – and, not surprisingly, it is one they learn as they become more mobile. Some signs that this is starting to happen are present at just over six months but most children are not all together clear about this until about 10–15 months.

Depth of vision

We see the world as having length and breadth and depth. The retina of the eye only records two-dimensional images, but our brain reconstructs the third dimension, which tells us how things are placed at different distances from us, by combining the pictures from both eyes. We also use some other cues – such as the fact that regular patterns seem to get smaller (such as parallel railway tracks), and that things nearer to us may partly hide things that are behind. It is a complicated set of rules for a baby to learn and, not surprisingly, they seem to take quite some time to do so.

Babies learn about depth between about 12 and 30 weeks. This has been tested in research. When a baby is placed on one side of a big drop that is covered by clear perspex, and her mother calls her from the far side, most babies under seven months will happily crawl across. After that they refuse. Even younger babies seem to "know" about depth: their heart rate increases.

SEE ALSO
Your baby's first reflexes **66–67**
Is everything all right? **68–69**
How the senses develop **78–79**
Not like others **132–133**

Mirror, mirror

When your baby is about 4–5 months old, she will pat her own image in the mirror. She won't know it's her, but she will adjust her position to get a better look.

MILESTONES IN VISUAL PERCEPTION		
0–20 weeks	**20–26 weeks**	**26–32 weeks**
A baby does not know that things (or people) continue to exist when she cannot see them. She does not look for an object she drops. She does not miss you when you leave her, nor does she realize that there is only one of you. If she sits at a dressing table and you adjust the mirrors to give multiple reflections of you both she will be very happy. By 20 weeks things are beginning to change. She may now be upset by seeing many reflections of her mother, and she may even look for something she drops – but most babies will not do so until much later.	When you have hidden a toy, a baby will expect to find something in that place, but she is not sure what. You can hide a teddy behind a screen and then move the screen to reveal a ball, and she will not look surprised. She knows something should be there, but cannot remember what. She will watch you choo-chooing her train behind the chair and will expect to see it come choo-chooing out the other side. She knows that when something moves in a certain direction, it keeps moving even when out of sight, but she cannot remember what that something was.	By now most babies look for objects they drop, and they will also look for an object that is partially hidden.

For years parents have said that they could tell by their cry whether a baby was hungry, afraid, or just bored. Psychologists dismissed this, but carefully controlled studies have proved the parents are right. Babies *do* mean different things by the way they cry, and parents *can* tell the difference.

When mothers listen to their babies, they tend to repeat what they hear, and babies respond by repeating this back. This continues, but only as long as the mothers do, otherwise the baby stops!

During these conversations, babies copy their carer's facial expressions. As we move our mouths when we speak, mouth movements are the most common copy-cat activity.

Listening to the world

In the first twelve weeks of their lives, babies are much more responsive to sounds than to sight. The auditory canal, initially still filled with fluid, soon clears, and a baby's hearing is then as good as that of his parents.

Your newborn baby's hearing is fairly acute immediately after birth, even while it is still partly muffled by fluid. Tests suggest that babies have surprisingly good auditory skills – newborn babies can, for example, tell the difference between sounds of different durations, sounds of different loudness and those of different pitches.

From the first day, babies are almost as sensitive to sounds as their parents – that is, they can hear very quiet sounds. This ability stands in stark contrast to their poor visual sensitivity at this age. Babies are born with the ability to hear both high- and low-pitched sounds, but they much prefer those of a higher pitch. They hear sounds most adults can no longer hear, such as the high-pitched whistle of the TV.

Newborn babies prefer human voices to all other sounds. They have a preference for vowel sounds (a, e, i, o, u, ar, ay, ee, oh, oo, ey) – which are, of course, the sounds we normally make for them. Who has not said something along the lines of "coochee, coochee, coo" to a baby! Babies also move in time with the human voice, and look interested when someone starts to speak.

Young babies are able to locate sounds, especially voices, in space – but only those which are made almost directly in front of them. From a very early age they link hearing with seeing and will look to see what is making a particular noise, or who is speaking at that moment. However, unless you are right in front of him, he may not be able to find you. By eight weeks he will look in approximately the right area, and by 16 weeks he will often find exactly the right place.

The foundations of language

Babies have a particular affinity for language sounds. If you give a baby a dummy to suck, he will suck happily while he listens to a new sound. Sucking is a sign of interest – for as long as he is interested

			MILESTONES IN HEARING		
Birth	**4–5 weeks**	**8–12 weeks**	**12–16 weeks**	**16–24 weeks**
He startles at a noise, turns roughly towards a voice and moves very slightly in time to speech. He is quieted by low pitch and rhythmic sounds.	He can distinguish the sound "p" from the sound "b". He prefers to listen to complex sounds, and likes to be told stories even though he cannot understand them.	He will turn his head to the right or left in response to a voice from that direction – but he will not necessarily be able to find the speaker.	He can roughly locate where a sound is coming from, and will look in that direction to check.	He will look up to find a sound made above his head. He can distinguish complex sounds ("baba" vs. "baga"; "ba" in "kobabo"). He can tell tunes apart – and knows individual voices.

he sucks. If you make the sound "bah", he starts sucking, but if you make it too often he will become bored and stop sucking.

You can alter the "bah" sound by saying it with a different intonation, or making it last a bit longer – yet he will not start sucking again. If, however, you change the "bah" to a "pah", he immediately starts sucking again. He is already responding the same way we adults do: ignoring the intonation and speed of language but being acutely aware of the little sounds that make up words.

What you can do to help him

It is natural to call his name and wait until he looks for you, and then to call again. Natural – and exactly right. His biggest problem in the first few months is learning how to precisely locate sounds in space.

We play with a rattle in the same way. Shake, wait, then shake again. Such games are excellent practice. Beyond this, all you really need to do is talk and give him plenty of opportunity to join in and make his replies. Babies get bored and switch off if they miss their turn. Looking at the things you talk about will later help him to pair up words and objects. Most of us do this quite naturally, so we do not have to make a special effort. From about six months, babies start to look in the same direction as we look when we speak, which will help them to learn the names of the things we talk about.

Expecting sounds

By about three months your baby will expect certain sounds to accompany certain familiar activities. His toy duck makes a funny squeak, and if you change this to a "woof" sound he would probably cry. If you stand on one side of the room and a recording of your voice is heard from the other side, a four-month-old will cry.

By six months, he can match voices with faces, and he will remember sounds. By seven months, he uses hand and body signs as if they were words. His problem is not one of understanding sounds and recognizing words but of knowing how to make them himself. This is the age at which deaf babies – and indeed hearing babies – can begin to learn sign language. He will probably already have a sign he always uses when he wants to be picked up, and another which means "no".

24–32 weeks	32–52 weeks
He will respond to hearing his name when he is called.	He responds to simple commands such as "how big", "show me", "no", as well as to the names of familiar objects such as "dummy" and the names of people in his family.

SEE ALSO

Smiles and babbles   **86–87**
Learning to speak   **96–97**
Perfecting language   **100–101**
Talking to children   **150–151**

PROBLEMS

About 85 per cent of deaf babies are born to hearing parents. All babies ignore sounds occasionally. If, however, a child consistently fails to respond to sound, or fails to respond to certain sounds, or to sounds in one ear, he needs to be tested. There are some tests you can do yourself:

● Call from different areas of the room. Does he respond? He may locate you by sight, but did he actually hear you?

● What happens if you use a bell or something with a much lower pitch?

● Even if he does respond, remain vigilant. If he does not react as he should, make sure you request a hearing assessment.

Shake, rattle and roll

Shake a rattle on the left, then on the right, above and below her head. Does she respond? Tests at home cannot replace a professional assessment but they can reassure.

Tiny tears

Some babies will start to cry real tears at the end of the first month, most will do so by 6 months.

Peas, please!

Most babies will pay attention to a small object such as a pea by the end of the fourth month, and reach for it after about six months.

How the senses develop

It is fascinating to chart your baby's progress, from the world of blurred sounds and images to the sharply focused adult world. Here are the milestones in a child's perceptual development in the first few months.

A t first, babies do not look at objects in a systematic way – they concentrate on one bit and then move on to another. If you show something to your baby, she will look at the edges and corners, and ignore the middle. When she looks at your face, she will gaze at your eyes and your hairline, and she will be especially interested if you have dark hair or wear glasses.

By two months a baby becomes more concerned with the relationship between the parts of an object. She will look from your eyes to your hairline and back; from the eyes to the mouth and back, as if she were building up a picture. This change in the way babies look at the world has led some people to suggest that, at first, babies do not have a "picture" – they see only the parts and not the whole.

By the age of two months she has a definite preference for faces, and likes eyes to be open. She prefers you to face her, and she shows interest when you meet her eyes with both of yours. By five months she can differentiate between faces she has seen before and faces she has never seen. Her perception of what is "pretty" is the same as her parents', and she will generally prefer pretty faces.

Early colour sense

At the age of five months, your baby will like bright primary colours and sparkly, glittery things. Soon she will start to prefer red to blue.

What do babies like to hear?

Babies love the human voice above all other sounds, and they like higher-pitched female voices and those of children better than lower-pitched male voices. We react to these preferences, and everyone – including children – raises the pitch of their voices when they talk to babies.

When a baby is awake and alert, she prefers gentle sounds. She learns what each sound means, and becomes more alert when she hears familiar sounds such as footsteps approaching, the tap running for her bath, the slow hum of a fan, or the vacuum cleaner. She finds slow, rhythmic sounds calming, especially if she is sleepy. You can use such sounds to change her breathing and heart beat from the alert pattern to one that is more typical of sleep.

HOW THE PERCEPTION OF BABIES PROGRESSES

Month	Virtually all babies will	Most babies will	Some babies will
1	Startle at a loud noise. Show interest in voices. Focus on a face, at first only for a moment. Look towards a voice at the midline. Respond to the sound of a bell.	Follow an object which moves in an arc above the face until it reaches the middle. Respond to a high-pitched sound.	Follow an object which moves in an arc above the face, past the midline. Turn eyes to light. Be very interested in faces.
2	Follow an object which moves in an arc above the face until it reaches the midline. Respond to a high-pitched sound. Show interest in faces.	Follow an object which moves in an arc above the face, past the midline. Visibly recognize their mother.	Work both eyes together. Focus on edges and corners. Turn the head towards a sound at ear level.
3	Move the head to follow an object which starts a little to the left or right of the midline and moves in an arc above the face, past the midline and to the other side.	Move the head to follow an object which moves through the full 180° arc, from left to right or vice versa.	Work both eyes together. Focus on a near object, edges and corners. Turn the head towards a sound on the left or right. Recognize their mother by sight.
4	Move the head to follow an object which moves through the full 180° arc, from left to right or vice versa. Recognize their mother.	Pay attention to a small object.	Turn in the direction of a voice coming from an arc 45° to the left or right, particularly if it is that of her carer. Respond to familiar objects and people. Watch her own hands while she is on her back.
5	Pay attention to a small object. Turn in the direction of a voice coming from an arc 45° to the left or right, particularly if it is that of her carer.	Watch her own hands while she is sitting or lying. Focus on her mirror image. Watch her hands reaching for an object.	Turn to face the speaker. Look to see where a voice comes from.
6	Watch her hands while she is sitting or lying. Watch her hands moving towards an object.	Look for a dropped object. Turn to face the speaker.	Turn towards a voice except if it is behind her. Prefer to look at real objects rather than looking at pictures. Guide her hand by using vision. Look for a sound above or below the head. Begin to respond to her name. Pat mirror when she sees image.

How babies learn

Now you see it
A small child will expect to find something in the box, but it does not have to be the Jack.

Babies do not think or remember the same things as us. In the early months, a child's attention span is very short. He hears a sound and, while it lasts, it holds his attention, but as soon as it stops, he will forget that it ever occurred.

Small babies do not look like miniature adults, and they certainly think differently. They have no sense of continuity in time – if a toy drops out of view, it also drops out of a baby's mind. For a baby to understand that two things are linked both need to happen very close to each other in time.

There are three things a child learns in the early months: he learns to ignore something that is always there; he learns to predict that something will happen; and he learns to make something happen.

Early learning
Learning to ignore: Switching off our attention to what is always present enables us to notice what is new, or has changed. In practice this means that a baby does not need total silence to sleep – he can adapt to noise – but also that he will ignore toys that are always in exactly the same place.
Learning to predict: When you hear the signature tune of your favourite soap, you expect the programme to start. A baby in his cot learns to predict that a face will appear when he hears and smells you approaching. He will expect to be fed when you hold him in a certain way. In the first year, babies learn to anticipate bathtime, feeding, Mummy coming home from work and the actions of some toys.
Learning to make things happen: Tiny babies cannot make much happen, but they are born with the mechanism that enables them to try. They can cry, which

will make us rush to them, they can smile, which will make us interact with them, and they can feed. They can also sleep and urinate but they cannot control when they do this. First, your baby will start to respond to you, then he will begin to knock things with his arms or legs.

Learning that he can learn
The most important thing for a small baby is not what he learns, but learning that he can make things happen. Until he knows he can influence his world he is not motivated to act with intent. Although babies may learn how to do things by 6–8 weeks, their body control is so poor that learning is very limited until 12 weeks. Small babies learn almost all they learn by practising over and over again.

Watch with mother
Probably the first progress you will see is that he responds to you – he smiles when you are there and he imitates your facial expressions.

Paying attention

- **Adults** have an attention span of six or seven which allows us to memorize a six- or seven-figure telephone number, but not a 16-figure credit card number. We can remember things from the past and relate past and present. This suffices in most situations, without the use of special strategies or memory aids.
- **Children of seven** only have a span of five, so school-age children need props and memory aids to help them remember.
- **Toddlers** have a span of three. It is almost impossible for them to relate what they see or think about (the same thing) to complex ideas they have stored away.
- **Tiny babies** have an attention span of one. They cannot think of anything other than the one thing they see now.

Early memory and thought

Tiny babies do not remember events. They only recognize that they have seen something before. By ten months they will remember that something happened in a particular context or place, but they cannot think about it when lying in their cots waiting for sleep. When a baby realizes

Bedtime stories

By about ten months your child will be able to remember what happened in a context or place, that this is where you read her a story yesterday, for example.

that you can exist even when you are out of sight, he will start to cling to you as you try to leave. When he knows there is only one "you", he will be upset to see multiple reflections in the dressing table mirror.

His memory span increases quickly: he looks up from his game, smiles at you and then carries on playing; sometimes he looks for things he drops. He is just beginning to remember the events of a moment before.

SEE ALSO

How the senses develop   **78–79**
Learning to speak   **96–97**
Attention and memory   **104–105**
Learning to think   **106–107**

MEMORY AIDS

- Toys that always do the same thing will help a baby remember the game: if the teddy always gives him a kiss he'll come to expect it.
- Songs with typical actions help him learn to predict what will come next. Sit in the same chair when you sing it and use the same actions every time.
- Do things in the same place to help his recall – sing or shout under a bridge, read a book on the sofa, look for a cat in the garden.

MILESTONES IN THINKING				
1–4 months	**5–8 months**	**8–12 months**	**12–18 months**	**18–24 months**
Produces "effects" with his own body. Looks where objects were last. A baby does not look for an object he drops, nor will he cry if you leave him in someone else's care.	Plays with his toys. Picks up, mouths, bags and chews them. Knocks objects. Watches an object go behind a screen; is surprised if it is not there when the screen is moved – but is not surprised to see a new toy. Watches if he drops an object; will look for a half-hidden object.	Purpose in mind: crawls to get a toy. Imitates others. Uncovers a hidden object; moves one toy to reach a hidden one. Plays at dropping objects. Looks for an object where it usually is – not where he has watched you put it; by 12 months looks for it where he last saw it.	Trial and error learning: a child can now consider several solutions to a problem but must try each one in turn. Imitates. Lifts cover to search for a hidden object and will search under other covers if he does not find it.	Can think, find solutions and novel combinations. Not everything is trial and error. Thoughts are still of images and actions. Does not yet think in an abstract way, nor use language to work things through. Can imitate after a delay: will wash up his toy pots after watching you.

Taking control of the body

A small baby is soft, her muscles are weak and watery. They move but she has no voluntary control over them. When she gets excited, her legs and arms fly – but she cannot yet touch a spot on your nose with her hand.

Development is not a race nor is it an intelligence test. "Average" means in the middle – half of all babies are above average, and half are below. Most children (some 60–70 percent) are close to the middle. It is the ones at the very bottom (and sometimes those at the very top) who cause concern – not those who walk late, but those who walk last; not those who talk late, but those who talk last.

Premature babies

A child who was born prematurely takes a long time to catch up. When charting her development, use her due date as the base line, not her birth date. If she seems a bit slow to make her milestones according to her birth date, everything will probably be perfectly normal if you use her due date instead. Remember that the trauma of her early months may well have held her back. Very premature babies rarely reach their milestones "on time" until they are about three. If in doubt, always ask your doctor for a developmental check.

Babies who are damaged at birth will be very slow at first. Their rate of progress will give a much better indication of future development than their age. Remember also that specific disabilities may well have far-reaching ramifications in the early months and years. A blind baby, for example, will normally be slower to move and slower to talk than a sighted child. There is so much less to tempt her into moving – and so much more to frighten her – and it is harder for her to learn the names of objects she cannot see.

WHAT CAN GO WRONG IN DEVELOPMENT

Genetic faults	Chemical faults	Cell migration	Infections	Growth
Sometimes faults occur which mean that the brain develops incorrectly, that parts are missing, or are "wired up" incorrectly. Faults can produce relatively minor problems (such as dyslexia) or more serious ones (such as mental handicap).	Sometimes there is a chemical imbalance in the body (often a faulty enzyme) which causes the build-up of poisons in the cells of the body (including the brain). Over time, they will damage the brain cells (Tay Sach's disease is an example of this).	Brain cells migrate from the centre to where they are needed. This can go wrong, so they end up in the wrong place. Not only are they of no use here, but they also displace cells that would be useful. It's best to avoid drinking alcohol during pregnancy, as this may affect the migration of cells.	Infections (of which rubella is the best known) can disrupt brain development, causing blindness and/or deafness.	Sometimes the baby does not grow normally. This can be the result of the mother's illness or poor nutrition. It may also be caused if the placenta does not supply the baby with sufficient nutrients, and this affects brain growth.

Hardening bones

At birth, most bones, apart from some in wrist and ankle, are present. Composed mainly of cartilage, they are still soft and pliable. Calcium and other minerals are deposited in the bones during childhood, which hardens and strengthens them. This process starts before birth and continues till adolescence. It begins earlier in girls than boys, and in children of African origin than in children of European origin.

Strengthening muscles

All the muscles are present at birth but they are still immature. They mature in the same order as the nerves that control them: from the head via the neck to the shoulders, down the back to the hips, from the shoulder down the arm and from the hip down the leg. The arms are controlled before the legs, and the legs before the feet.

The developing brain

The brain is only partly developed at birth; much of it is missing and much more is poorly connected. There is a very obvious reason for this: if women had to deliver a baby with a full-sized brain and a full-sized head, they would need hips as wide as a table, and with these they could not walk.

The brain develops from the spinal cord up, and from the centre out. At birth, the bottom part of the brain (which controls involuntary processes such as breathing, sleeping, digesting, urinating and blood flow) is in place. So are the areas which control the senses and the reflexes. It is the upper areas, in control of voluntary action, memory and thought, that are largely missing.

A newborn baby is entirely dependent on others, and will remain so for a considerable period of time. As she needs to take control of her body and exercise her mind, other areas of her brain will develop. Voluntary control begins at the mouth and moves out to the rest of the face and down the body. The areas which control the shoulders mature before those which control the hands, and these in turn mature before those which control the fingers.

SEE ALSO

How babies learn	80–81
Sitting and standing	88–89
Crawling and walking	90–91
Reaching and grasping	94–95

Ready to walk?

Your baby cannot walk until her bones have hardened, her muscles strengthened, and her brain can decide which muscles to move and control balance.

Oxygen	Prematurity
Brain cells need oxygen, and any disturbance to the supply can cause permanent cell damage. Cerebral palsy is often caused by a loss of oxygen during the birthing process. Hydrocephalus can damage babies by producing too much pressure in the brain.	Because premature babies do not always breathe properly or consistently, their brains can be starved of oxygen. Very premature babies may also have problems with blood circulation and bleeding within the brain. Both can produce cerebral palsy.

All about baby teeth

Your baby's first tooth will be another milestone in his development. Some babies do not have any teeth until after their first birthday, but most will cut their first tooth between about five and seven months.

Toothy grins
Once your baby's front teeth have erupted, there may well follow a long gap before the next ones emerge. Then, however, they will all come quickly, until the set is complete.

ALWAYS

Plan ahead
The teeth are formed in pregnancy – a baby depends on you to provide a good diet. Tell the doctor you may be pregnant if he prescribes drugs. Avoid tetracyclines in particular.

Clean teeth
As soon as the teeth appear they can develop plaque, which causes tooth decay. Instil good cleaning habits as soon as you can. Let him use his own toothbrush, then give his teeth a good "wipe dry" afterwards. He will not notice that you are doing most of the cleaning!

An adult set numbers 32 teeth, but there are only 20 baby, or "milk", teeth. It is the back three top and bottom teeth that are missing in the first set. Early or late teething tends to run in families. If you or your partner cut your teeth late, you should not be surprised if your child does too. Once the first tooth has broken through the gums, the other front teeth tend to follow in rapid succession. The teeth are clearly visible beneath the gums before they erupt. At first they form little white patches in the gums, and just before they erupt these turn to pale bumps.

How teeth erupt

Very few babies (about 1 in 5,000) are born with a tooth, but typically a baby cuts his first tooth between five and seven months. Usually, this is the lower right or the lower left incisor, which is followed by the upper incisors, the upper side teeth and then the lower side teeth. In fact, these last three sets can come in so fast and furiously that the order may be slightly different. Often babies get two or three teeth in a matter of days or weeks. After the front teeth have erupted, there is sometimes quite a wait until the next phase begins. It starts with the first upper molars and is followed by the first lower molars. Another pause may then occur before the final two phases. The four middle molars erupt (upper before lower), and finally the four back molars (lower before upper). By this time he will be about two and a half.

Taking care of the teeth

● Make sure your baby has plenty of calcium – milk, cheese and yoghurt are good sources once he reaches six months. Formula or breast milk will be his major source of calcium before then.
● Make sure he gets plenty of vitamin D – hard-boiled egg yolk, oily fish and dairy products are good sources. Only use vitamin supplements designed for babies and never give more than the stated dose.
● An apple is better than apple juice. An orange is better than orange juice.
● Diluted juice is better than squash.
● Water is the best drink if he is thirsty. It is also a useful emergency tooth cleaner.
● Watch out for hidden sugars. Honey is a sugar – and a sticky one at that. Sucrose and glucose are also sugars. The teeth do not discriminate between different sorts.

• Limit sweets, cola and ice cream to special occasions and always clean the teeth afterwards. Wiping with a soft rag is easiest for a small child.

• Give chocolate, cake, or biscuits in preference to toffee, marshmallow, honey, or sweet drinks. Sticky sweets will stick to the teeth, while chocolate cake and biscuits tend to fall off the teeth.

• Do not add sugar to drinks or cereals. Sometimes ready-sweetened cereals are a better buy – they may contain less sugar than your child would add to the unsweetened variety.

• Never dip dummies in sweet substances such as honey or sugar.

• Public eating is better than private bingeing. If you forbid all sweet things, he may well eat them when you cannot police the tooth cleaning which should follow.

• It does not matter how children clean their teeth (or how you clean a baby's teeth) as long as you do. A soft cloth with a little toothpaste is the easiest for a baby. As he grows up he may want to use his own toothbrush. If he is less than competent, simply wipe over the teeth with a cloth afterwards. The last thing you want to do is to discourage him from brushing.

• Go steady on the fluoride – although small amounts protect his teeth, too much can discolour them. He does not need fluoride toothpaste, fluorinated water *and* fluoride tablets. Just one of these products will be plenty.

• Do not let him go to sleep sucking a bottle of milk or juice. If he does, remove the bottle from his mouth. Never ever put him to bed with a bottle of sweet juice or milk. Sweet sticky fluids can sit in pools around the teeth – and the bacteria in the plaque will have the whole night to work away and multiply. The resulting acid can begin to pit the enamel of the teeth before all of them have erupted.

Using the mouth to explore

We say, "he is teething", as he puts all his toys into his mouth to gum. But is he? Probably not. Babies use their mouths to explore the world around them because they have learned to control their tongue and lips before they can control their hands and fingers. They can hold objects when they are about 4–7-months-old but they cannot yet manipulate them properly with their hands.

Even after this time children often enjoy putting things in their mouths, especially once they have been weaned from the breast or bottle. If babies had a choice, they would suck for comfort, and would probably take most of their meals from the breast for at least another year. Since we are in control they often miss out!

Tasty toys

Tongue and gums help your child explore the taste, texture and shape of a new toy – much better than his hands are able to at this stage.

SEE ALSO
Crying babies   38–39
Introducing solids   48–49
Reaching and grasping   94–95
Nursing a sick child   208–209

TOM THUMB

Don't worry too much about thumb sucking. Dentists are now agreed that it is most unlikely that thumb sucking causes buck teeth. Bottles of sweet substances are more problematic for the health of your baby's teeth.

NEVER, NEVER

Never say, "It's just teething." Illness in small babies can become serious very quickly, so never ignore a fever.

Teething – or rather crying because of pain – can make the baby red in the face. It does not give him a fever. Nor does it cause convulsions, diarrhoea, or sickness. Babies become overheated quickly, which may be dangerous. Loss of fluid can cause a loss of blood pressure; this may stop the heart working.

Always take him to see the doctor if he is feverish, suffers convulsions, sickness, or diarrhoea.

Happy smiles

Some babies are born happier than others, but all will learn to use smiles and laughter – or tears – to get their way.

Multilingual babies

By about 30 weeks, the babble of babies starts to sound like the adult speech they hear around them. French-listening babies will begin to sound different from English- or Chinese-listening babies.

Smiling and babbling

From an early age, babies need to communicate, but initially they have just two ways of doing so: they can cry or they can smile and coo. They do both – some babies tip the scales towards the tears, others towards the smiles.

Babies start to smile soon after birth – and, even at this stage, girls smile more than boys. The first smiles are usually little half-smiles during sleep, which we call "windy smiles". In fact, they occur when the baby moves from a light to a deeper sleep, or the other way, not because of wind. Within a week or so these are followed by elicited smiles, which also occur in sleep, when the baby hears a sound (a high-pitched voice or a bell). Soon after, between three and seven or eight weeks, we see the first real waking smiles. "Late" babies smile early, premature babies late.

At first, babies smile when we raise our voices and bob up and down. Later they prefer a stationary face, and later still a face they know. Blind babies start the same way, but they stop smiling when the cue is a stationary face. Initially, babies' smiles just surround the mouth, later they light up the the whole face. The mouth opens wide and they invite us to play – just like puppies or cats. They want to interact with us, copy us, look for us, "talk back". If you laugh, a baby will repeat what made you laugh. Do not underestimate the importance of this – it is the cornerstone of her security.

Smiles to laughter and coos

We smile for different reasons and have two different smiles: a faint, closed-mouth and an open-mouth smile. The smiles have different roots. The closed-mouth smile evolved from the "keep your distance" face we see in dogs. The open-mouth smile from the "come and play" face we see in many young animals. This face is common in babies and a delight to parents. We respond by coming in close, tickling the baby's tummy, chasing her – and so she steps it up, squeals with delight, laughs out loud. She will not lose this skill.

In the first days, babies mainly cry, but by the end of the first month, most have discovered other noises. By the second month they will use their own cooing noises to talk to anyone who wants to talk.

CHILD GROWTH AND DEVELOPMENT

Month	Virtually all children can	Most children can	Some children can
1		Vocalize in ways other than crying.	Smile at you. Take turns in a "conversation" by responding. Begin to coo. Use different cries for different basic needs.
2	Smile at you. Vocalize other than crying.	Make cooing noises. Use different cries for different basic needs.	Take turns in a "conversation". Make throaty sounds.
3	Take turns in a "conversation". Make cooing noises.	Make throaty sounds. Talk to family members.	Use h, b, p sounds. Laugh and squeal in delight.
4	Laugh. Make throaty sounds. Talk to family members.	Squeal in delight.	Change their babbles in pitch and volume, and with mood. Talk to objects and faces. Use h, n, k, f, b, p sounds. Blow a raspberry.
5	Squeal in delight.	Change their babbles in pitch and volume, and with mood. Talk to objects and faces. Use h, n, k, f, b, p sounds. Blow a raspberry.	Make vowel sounds, say most consonants. Try to imitate sounds.
6	Use h, n, k, f, b, p sounds.	Begin to combine consonants and vowels. Begin to vary pitch and rate of speech.	Combine consonants and vowels. Vary pitch and rate of speech. Talk to toys and mirror image. Babble, putting together vowels and consonants in continuous streams of sound.
7	Change their babbles in pitch and volume, and with mood. Talk to objects and faces. Blow a raspberry.	Babble, putting together vowels and consonants in continuous streams of sound.	Repeat sounds such as "dada" and "mama". Join in and "talk" with adult intonation when others are talking.
8	Babble. Repeat syllables such as "dada" and "mama".	Repeat sounds such as "dada" and "mama". Join in and "talk" with adult intonation when others are talking.	Shout for attention. Show emotion through speech. Respond to "no" and "bye-bye". May label an object with a sound ("wowow" for a dog).

Sitting and standing

You will be eagerly watching your baby, especially if he is your first, for signs of progress. He will always seem to be about to do something. Can he sit yet? Is he about to crawl? Here we look at his first motor milestones.

Never mind that he only just firmly sits on his bottom, you will spot him leaning forwards and about to get on all fours! Never mind that he only just crawls, today he let go for a moment when he was holding onto his chair. Tomorrow he could be walking.

It is so easy for us to wish his babyhood away. You are not alone in this. We all do it. It was not until I had my third child that I learned to fully appreciate him for what he was that day.

Part of the problem is that we are always unsure. Whatever reassurances we are given, fear lurks at the back of our minds

that something could go wrong. Totting up his milestones reassures us that all is well. We worried about him before he was born, and it is only natural to worry even more now we know and love him so well. All parents are aware of how easily their hearts could be broken, and how desperately they want life to be good to their child.

Not a sign of intelligence

When considering a child's milestones it is important to remember that physical development and mental development are not closely correlated. A child who walks at eight months is no more destined for a

This is good fun
The more he can see, the more excited he becomes. Everything around him seems interesting, and this is how he will learn.

MILESTONES TO HEAD CONTROL			
1–4 weeks	**8–10 weeks**	**16–20 weeks**	**24–28 weeks**
If you use your baby's arms to pull him up from a lying to a sitting position, his head lags behind his body completely.	If you use your baby's arms to pull him up from a lying to a sitting position his head still lags – but not completely.	If he is held, he will be able to turn his head in all the directions. If he is pulled up to a sitting position, his head lags only slightly behind.	He is now able to lift his head spontaneously, tucking his chin to his chest as he comes up.

MILESTONES TO SITTING				
1–4 weeks	**5–7 weeks**	**8–15 weeks**	**16–20 weeks**	**21–24 weeks**
His back is uniformly rounded when he is supported in a sitting position. He has no head control as yet.	If you support him in a sitting position, his back is rounded, but he will already hold his head up intermittently.	When sitting, his back is still rounded, but he can raise his head and flex his knees. He sits for 10–15 min with cushions as support.	His back is now straighter and he holds his head without a wobble. He can sit for 30 min if propped up by cushions.	He sits with a little support and can pull himself up to sit. He is now well balanced if he is strapped into a chair.

MILESTONES TO BECOMING UPRIGHT			
1–15 weeks	**16–24 weeks**	**36–44 weeks**	**48–52 weeks**
Your baby is still quite passive and will not "join in" if you pull him up to a standing position and hold him by his hands.	He begins to push up by raising his buttocks, but he cannot yet hold this position without your help.	If you hold him up, he will lower his legs to find a surface and push down on it. He will stand in a more erect position if he is supported under his arms.	He stands erect when holding on, and when he is one-year-old, most babies can stand for a moment or two. About half of all babies will stand well and some will walk.

SEE ALSO

Taking control of the body **82–83**

Crawling and walking   **90–91**

Becoming mobile   **92–93**

Making indoors safe   **204–205**

On my own two feet

Soon, sitting still will feel too limiting, and your child will start to pull and push herself up to a standing position – another milestone in her motor development!

Nobel Prize than one who walks at 18 months. Even language development is largely uncorrelated with later intellectual ability. By all accounts Einstein did not talk until he was two.

In the genes

Most of our physical development is pre-programmed – there is very little we can do to speed it up (although we can slow it down by failing to stimulate the baby). Identical twins tend to walk within days of each other, and within families most children will walk at approximately the same age. If you come from a family with a "slow" programme, all his milestones are likely to be a bit late. Similarly, if you come from a family with a "fast" programme, all the milestones are likely to be early. This includes hand skills as well as walking and crawling.

Girls tend to be faster than boys, and Caucasian babies later than those of African origin. There are a couple of exceptions to this: not all babies crawl, and an efficient crawler may walk a little later than a child who never crawled. Since he can move about very efficiently, he does not feel the need to learn to walk. Some children get around by bottom shuffling, and since they are both mobile and able to carry toys around with them, they have even less motivation to walk. Consequently, they are often late finding their feet.

Sitting pretty

Sitting gives a baby a better view of the world, and gives the world a better view of him. We rarely walk past a baby who sits propped on his chair without saying "hello". If he sits strapped in the shopping trolley, everyone in the checkout queue will return his smile. A baby lying on his back gets a good view of the sky and the ceiling – but these are rarely very interesting. Once upright there is all the world for him to see and to get excited by. Bored babies switch off and go to sleep and, eventually, they start to lag behind in their development.

25–28 weeks	**29–32 weeks**
By now he sits steadily, if only briefly. He can push himself into a sitting position without help.	He sits alone, he can lean forward, move about and bounce while sitting without toppling over.

Crawling and walking

Mobility changes everything. We can no longer put the baby down to play while we get on with other things. Before we know it, she has darted out of the carefully baby-proofed room and into the – as yet unsafe – kitchen.

Rocking baby

At about 20 to 26 weeks, when lying on her tummy, your baby will begin to push her legs under her body, raise herself on all fours and rock a little back and forth.

The books come out of the bookcase, the cat's dishes are explored (and the food tasted) – in short we cannot take our eyes off a mobile baby for one moment, and this makes her much brighter! When they first become mobile, all babies take a great leap forward in their development.

They become more interested in the world, more social and generally more capable. A baby "IQ" test at this stage would put the mobile babies way ahead. All babies make this jump when they become mobile. By two, when virtually all babies are mobile, there is no great difference between babies.

Children make this leap because they are excited by their mobility, and excited children are quick to learn. They also

MOTOR MILESTONES: CRAWLING AND WALKING

1–14 weeks	15–20 weeks	20–26 weeks	27–33 weeks	34–38 weeks	38–52 weeks
Crawling On her tummy, a baby makes crawling movements, moving her arm and leg on the same side of the body. She cannot turn from front to back.	**Crawling** On her stomach, a baby pushes up using her arms, and flexes her knees. She rolls onto her back. If carried, she begins to hold her posture. If you move her out of balance, she will use her arms to regain balance.	**Crawling** A baby turns her head to the side and towards the back, raising her shoulders and curving her spine; she eventually succeeds in rolling from her back to her tummy. When on her tummy she pulls herself along with her arms.	**Crawling** A baby pivots from side to side on her stomach and creeps forward. She may start to crawl forward unsteadily, on her hands and knees.	**Crawling** A baby combines rolling with creeping and pivoting to move across the room, even if she does not crawl. If she does crawl, it will become more efficient.	**Crawling** A baby rolls into a sitting position, and then crawls. She sits back when she arrives. She turns before attempting steps, but she will crawl up stairs.
Walking If supported under the arms her posture is limp, but when her feet touch a sloping surface, she steps using high knees. Lying down, she "kick-steps" when crying or excited.	**Walking** If you hold her under her arms, she will start to support most of her weight as she stands on your lap.	**Walking** Held under her arms, she supports most of her weight and may step or push down on her feet.	**Walking** Her postural adjustment improves. When standing on your lap, her feet move. She may begin to cruise around the furniture.	**Walking** When held and cruising around, she will adjust her balance with each step. At first she clings with both hands, but then she uses one to hold on and the other to explore.	**Walking** Stepping gets better. She can let go for a moment, and reach for a toy when holding on. She pulls herself up to standing, and can stand alone. She walks holding your hand. She can lift one foot when standing.

interact much more with their carers. We watch them with eagle eyes – however well we try to baby-proof, there is always something we have forgotten – and as we watch, we talk and interact much more. After a few weeks we feel more secure that they are not going to hurt themselves, and we relax. At the same time the initial excitement of mobility wanes, and the child continues her former steady progress.

Watch out for early crawling

You may think that your child is many months from crawling (and she may be), but a baby on her tummy is capable of creeping. While you leave her to answer the door, she can move into a danger zone, unless the room is child-proofed. When you put a baby on her tummy – even a young baby – make sure that there is nothing on the floor which she could reach or bump into, such as a sharp corner on a low table, or fall over, such as a step.

How to encourage crawling

● Babies do not crawl until they are ready, but unless she is put on her tummy to play, she may never try. Some parents do not place a baby on her tummy because of the dangers of cot death. While it would be unwise to let a baby sleep in this position, it is perfectly safe for her to play.
● A nice soft surface helps. If her knees hurt, she is unlikely to get up on them.
● Crawling babies love to be chased and to play hide and seek behind the furniture.

How to encourage walking

● Barefoot walking encourages strong feet, ankles and leg muscles.
● Sofas and small tables are great because she can support herself as she walks along their length. Once she can rest against a surface, or hold on with one hand, place toys along the sofa to encourage her.

● Extend her range and make her explore more of the room. Once she is stepping, you can push pieces of furniture together to make a longer run for her.

Progress after the first year

52–58 weeks: She walks holding your hand. She soon starts to walk alone, but loses her balance if she stops suddenly.
18 months: She goes up and down stairs without help. She leads with one foot and follows with the other.
24 months: She runs, walks backwards and picks things up without overbalancing.
30 months: She balances on one tip toe and jumps with both feet.
3 years: She hops and runs with flat-footed action. She cannot change direction when running. She shuffles if asked to skip.
4 years: She carries on going up and down stairs by stepping and then bringing both feet together on one step until she is about 52 months; then she will start to step alternately. She runs in a controlled way and can start, stop and turn suddenly, but may not be able to change speed without stopping first. At 4 she can hop about eight hops, and go up and down the climbing frame. She can alternate feet for about eight steps when walking on a wall. All these skills will improve in the next year. She skips in a flat-footed step, if at all. She can do a hurdle jump.
5 years: She skips with both feet alternating. She gallops starting with either foot, runs, dodges and changes speed and direction. She hops ten or more hops. Most children can climb a rope ladder. She jumps smoothly, using an arm thrust to take off and a crouch to land.

SEE ALSO

Taking control of the body **82–83**
Sitting and standing **88–89**
Becoming mobile **92–93**
Making indoors safe **204–205**

Hide and seek
Children love crawling into tunnels and reappearing on the other side. You can buy folding tunnels or you can create your own with boxes from the supermarket.

Becoming mobile

Children will not all venture from lying to sitting to creeping and crawling and, eventually, standing at the same time, and some may miss out entire stages. But the following chart will give you a good idea of your child's progress.

MOTOR SKILLS MONTH BY MONTH			
Month	Virtually all children can	Most children can	Some children can
1	Lift head briefly when lying on stomach.	Lift head to 45° when lying on stomach.	Lift head 90° when lying on stomach; move a little on stomach.
2	Begin to uncurl when lying on stomach or back; lift head and hold briefly when on stomach.	Lift head 45° and hold briefly when on stomach; move a little by squirming when on stomach.	Hold head steady when upright; raise head when lying on back; roll over from front to back.
3	Lift head to 45°; lie flat on back or stomach, arms up towards head; move forward a little by squirming with arms and legs.	Lift head to 90°; raise their head while on back; roll over from back to front.	Hold head steady when upright; raise head when on stomach, supported by arms; move forward a little on stomach.
4	Lift head 90° when lying on stomach; raise head when lying on back; move forward on stomach (head raised 45°).	Hold head steady when upright; raise head supported by arms when lying on stomach; roll over one way.	Keep head level with body when pulled to sitting; bear some weight with legs; roll over from back to front.
5	Hold head steady when upright; raise head supported by arms when lying on stomach; roll over from front to back.	Bear some weight on legs; on stomach squirm forward a short way, shoulders raised; keep head level with body if pulled to sitting.	Sit without support; on stomach, push up with outstretched arms or legs; roll over both ways; creep across room in swimming motion.
6	Keep head level with body when pulled to sitting; creep forward on stomach using knee and thigh.	Bear some weight on legs; sit without support; push up with outstretched arms or legs.	Stand when held or holding on; push up to sitting; get into crawling position and rock.
7	Sit without support; roll over with great ease in both directions.	Creep forward on stomach by bringing knee and thigh forward; get into crawling position to rock.	Stand when held or holding on; crawl on hands and knees; push up to sitting from stomach.
8	Bear some weight on legs; push up with outstretched arms; creep across room with swimming motion.	Stand when held or holding on; push up to sitting from stomach; crawl on hands and knees; get into crawling position and rock.	Walk holding onto furniture; crawl (if they are going to); pull up to a standing position from sitting, holding on to furniture.

s your child becomes more and more mobile, he will delight in all the new areas of the home he can now explore. Sitting upright will give him a better view of his surroundings. Better hand skills allow him to handle and examine the things he can pick up. And his ability to walk, finally, will open up a whole new world to him –

there are other rooms in the house to explore, there is the garden, and the entire outside world. No wonder his intellect also takes a great leap forward at this time.

Enjoy this time of exploration with him – but be also aware of the problems that his new-found mobility brings: access to things and places that may be dangerous.

SEE ALSO

Taking control of the body **82–83**
Sitting and standing **88–89**
Crawling and walking **90–91**
Making indoors safe **204–205**

MOTOR SKILLS MONTH BY MONTH

Month	Virtually all children can	Most children can	Some children can
9	Get into crawling position and rock; push themselves up with outstretched legs.	Stand when held or holding on; get into a sitting position from stomach and pull up to a standing position from sitting.	Begin to take steps when standing and holding on to furniture (cruising).
10	Stand when holding on; pull up to standing from sitting; crawl on hands and knees.	Get into a sitting position from stomach; begin to walk when holding on to furniture (cruising).	Stand alone for a moment; stoop to pick up toy when holding on; take steps with minimal support.
11	Get into a sitting position from stomach.	Walk, holding on to furniture; stand alone for a moment.	Walk alone using wide-legged waddle; stand alone.
12	Cruise around furniture; pick up a toy when holding on.	Stand alone for a moment; pick up a toy when holding on.	Take steps between furniture, and one or two beside furniture.
13	Take steps with minimal support; stand for a moment.	Occasionally take independent steps beside furniture.	Walk at different speeds; change direction easily.
14	Stand alone.	Walk at different speeds; turn.	Pick up toy; walk and carry toys.
15	Walk alone.	Pick up toy; walk and carry toys.	Run in straight line; stop to turn.
18	Pick up toy; walk and carry toys.	Run in straight line; stop to turn.	Go up steps, lead with same foot.
21	Run in straight line; stop to turn.	Go up steps, lead with same foot.	Run and change direction.
24	Go up steps; lead with same foot.	Run and change direction.	Jump on the spot; tiptoe.
30	Run and change direction; walk up and down stairs alone.	Walk on tiptoe.	Balance on one foot for one second.
36	Walk on tiptoe.	Balance on one foot for one second; jump across.	Balance on one foot for two seconds.

HAND MOVES

● **Swiping.** Your baby is lured into swiping by the movement of her toys, so she will need toys that move when she hits them. Soft toys tied loosely to the cot rails are ideal. Fix a rod across her cot and dangle toys from it, directly above her chest.

● **Grabbing.** Toys need to sit still for a baby to grab them.

● **Stroking and patting.** Your baby needs toys with a variety of textures that "feel nice to the touch".

● **Pincer movements.** Your baby still puts most things in her mouth so let her practise her pincer movements on food such as peas or banana slices.

Reaching and grasping

In the beginning a baby's hands are tightly closed and her vision is too poor to see detail. Even if she saw her hands she would be unlikely to realize that they belonged to her, and that she could use them at will.

By her first birthday, your child will grasp, poke, prod, stroke, pat and pass toys from one hand to the other. She will pick up a pea, drop her cup, feed herself a biscuit and bang her plate with a spoon. She can take a toy you offer, draw squiggles and even turn the pages of her card book.

Before then she has a lot to learn. A new baby cannot move her hands at will. When something touches the palm of her hand her fingers close in reflex. Initially, her hands remain closed most of the time. As the reflex weakens her hands will open, but she will still not be able to control her fingers. Until she is about eight or nine months old, she will grab using a weak reflex grip called the "mitten" grip.

Seeing her hands

Your baby will uncurl from the tight foetal position in the first weeks of life and, soon afterwards, she will start to wave her arms and kick whenever she is excited. She loves such movement, and seeing her waving arms will excite her, but she probably does not know the hands belong to her. Gradually, she realizes that when she sees hands moving she can also feel herself move. By 16 weeks she will like to lie on her back and look intently at her hands. If you attach a bell to her jacket or mittens, she will find her hands more easily.

Taking control

At first a baby can only control her mouth and tongue. As other parts of her brain mature, she will learn to control her muscles at will and make use of them. Brain control and muscle development start at the neck, move to the shoulders and then to the upper back and out along the arms. At first she will swipe from the shoulders, then from the wrists and finally move her fingers separately and to order.

Give me!

Once your baby can sit upright, after about six months, she will reach out for and grab hold of any toy that is placed near her.

Yum, yum!

Initially, all toys first go into a baby's mouth. She uses lips and tongue to explore while her hands are not skilled enough.

Coming to grips

The mitten grip is made with a flat hand, the fingers coming down in a preset order (3-2-1-4) and the thumb touching the first finger. It works well for holding things, but is no good for manipulating objects. The mitten grip will eventually be replaced by the "pincer" and "palmer" grips.

For the pincer grip, your baby uses forefinger and thumb like a crab's claw to pick up small objects. In two stages, she first uses her fingers like tweezers, then she curls her fingers to use the tips.

For the palmer grip, she cups her hand around an object, curling the palm and using the thumb in opposition to the fingers. Because each finger can now be moved separately, she can adjust what she holds. She can also hold with one hand while she explores with the other.

Reaching

Reaching is a complex skill. Adults always prepare before they reach: they judge whether they need to use one hand or two, the angle of the hand as it makes contact and how open each hand should be. We do all these things automatically but like all motor skills they must be learned.

In the first weeks, babies are surprisingly good at reaching – but this initial reach is a reflex. They do not visually guide their hands, they shoot them out to grab for anything that captures their attention even a noise. This reflex soon disappears, and babies then have to begin the slow process of bringing their hands under visual control. At the same time, their hands are maturing and they become able to control their fingers so that they can pick up, hold and put down what they see.

A baby starts by swiping from the shoulder. One day, while kicking in her cot, she hits a toy. It moves, she gets excited and waves her arm more vigorously.

By chance she hits again. From such beginnings, she learns how to swing more accurately. As the reflex grip slackens, she uses her open hand to hit, and from this grabbing develops.

Helping her to grab

A rod or dumbbell is the easiest shape to grab. Hold it so that your baby can see it. As she reaches, she will look between the object and her hand, and since her hand is familiar and interesting she will often forget about the toy and watch her hand instead. Shaking a rattle will remind her. Gradually, her hand will distract her less. In fact, at first she will get her hand close to the toy, then grab with her eyes closed.

Letting go

Small babies do not intentionally let go. They see a new toy and, as they open their hands to grab it, they drop the first toy. At 8–10 months she intentionally lets go of one toy before she grabs another. Initially, she just unclasps her hand and lets the toy roll out. Then she unclasps her fingers and tips her hand. Eventually, she turns her hand over before she tips, and she will practise it over and over again!

SEE ALSO
First toys and games   **60–61**
Your baby's first reflexes   **66–67**
Clever hands   **98–99**
Making indoors safe   **204–205**

Bang, bang!
Once your baby is older than six months and can control her hands, she will have moved from indiscriminate "banging" to an exploration of her toys – and nice noises!

DON'T

● Give your baby too many toys. Reaching and grabbing are very important skills, but so is exploring. Babies automatically reach for anything that attracts their attention and it is counterproductive to shower them with toys. Instead of exploring one toy, they will just reach and grab for others.

● Strings should never be so long that they could wrap themselves around your child's neck.

● Don't let a baby play with anything small enough to swallow.

● Don't give a baby anything she could ram into her throat or eye as she tries to reach her mouth with her hand.

Learning to speak

A child's first "words" are not words at all but signs which he makes to let us know what he wants and what he knows. Most children then quickly progress from signs to babbles, and from babbles to words and sentences.

All toys are ducks
Initially, your child may use a word like "duck" to signify all his toys. It is only when you correct him that he will learn to apply different labels to his other toys.

He may use a few signs as "party pieces" such as lifting his hands in the air when you ask him "How tall are you?" or, less obviously, putting an empty cup to his mouth to say, "I know what this is for". You will recognize a host of other little signs which he uses again and again. My son used to imitate the actions of the "wheels of the bus" whenever he saw one, his sister always put her nose to pictures of flowers, as she did to the real thing.

The very first word

The average child will say his first word at around 10–11 months, usually a simple repetition of a single sound – typical examples are "Dada", "Mama", "bobo" (for bottle), "psspss" (for cat), "wowow" (for dog) or "numnum" (for food). Often these sounds are accompanied by a sign, such as pointing a hand at an object to mean "look at this".

Not all babies manage to produce words this early, and a significant minority may not say anything at all for the next three or four months. Almost all understand more than they can say – and for some the gap is larger than it is for others.

Words and more words

By the time they are 16 years old, most young people have a vocabulary of 40,000 words, and double that number if we count proper names and idioms. This means they have to learn a phenomenal 100 words a week throughout childhood. The only workable strategy for the child is to "grab" a word, hope it is right and wait to be corrected if it is not: "Yes, it is a lorry", or "No, not a lorry – a tractor".

In practice this "grab-and-use" strategy means that he starts by over-extending the use of the word, then fines down its meaning. So at first all men are "Daddy",

LANGUAGE MILESTONES

About 30 weeks	About 34 weeks	About 10 mths	About 11 mths	About 1 year
He may use a simple sign such as raising his arms to indicate "pick me up", or closing his mouth tightly and shaking his head to mean "no".	He shouts for attention, and shows emotions by making noises such as whining or squealing. He responds to "no", and "bye-bye". He may make a sound like "psspss" when he sees a cat.	He may say "Dada" and have one other meaningful word or sound. His babble sounds like language. He understands a number of words. He may lift his foot if asked "Where is Joseph's foot?"	He may say "Mama" and have two or more meaningful sounds such as "hi" or "no". He babbles as if he knows it means something. Some children embed "real" words in a stream of babble.	He says about three words and has a number of meaningful sounds. He points, jabbers, understands more than he can say. One word may cover a whole class of objects: animals are all "psspss".

later he learns the word "man" for the rest and uses Daddy for one special person.

Most children's first words refer to the things they can see and point to, and of the first 50 words about 40 will be nouns and seven verbs. Some children speak first about relationships, feelings and needs. They use "me", "you" and words they run together: "go-away", "love-you", "do-it".

Putting two words together

When children are between about 21 and 26 months, they start putting words together to form simple two-word sentences. A small child's two-word sentences are far from random. Each sentence will normally have one pivot word and one noun. Typical examples of pivots are "there", "where", "that", "give", "bye-bye", "gone", "want". These are combined with nouns and noun-like words to say "Daddy gone", "Teddy gone", "Bye-bye bus", "Bye-bye Mummy".

Helping your child

● Repeat and expand his sentences: "It's a dog", "It's a nice dog". This makes it clear to him that you have understood what he said, and it helps him form new sentences.
● Interpret and repeat what he means. If he says, "Joseph sock", say, "Yes, that is

Joseph's sock", or "Where is Joseph's sock?"
● Use short simple sentences and complete them. Use simple basic grammar and straight-forward word order.
● Use emphasis. "*Here* is *Teddy*".
● Look at the things you talk about – he will follow your gaze and match the sound he hears to the object he watches.
● Talk about what you see and hear. Point to the picture in a book and say the word.
● Talk about what he is doing, and ask him to fetch things for you. Talk as you feed, change and bath him. His first sentences are often about such routine, familiar activities. Make the time to sit down for a "chat" at some point every day.
● Talk about possessions. Early sentences are often about "my" things.
● Keep your language simple enough for him to follow. Use just a couple of new words a day so he can progress, but do not expect too much all at once.

When to worry

● Early detection of deafness is important. If you are worried, ask for a hearing test. All children should have their hearing tested in the first year, and between 12 and 18 months, especially if they have had ear infections.
● Late onset of speech is not necessarily related to hearing problems – it is often found in families with a history of dyslexia. If your child successfully communicates with actions and noises, and obviously understands what you say, his hearing may be quite normal.
● Always consult an expert if he does not understand one word by 14 months; if he does not say anything by 18–21 months; if he starts to talk before then but makes no progress; if what he says is still unclear at three years.

SEE ALSO

Listening to the world	**76–77**
Smiling and babbling	**86–87**
Perfecting language	**100–101**
Talking to children	**150–151**

Quiet! Don't talk!

Gestures speak louder than words. Your child will soon link the finger on the lips with the fact that she has to be quiet, perhaps in conjunction with a "sh" sound.

About 21 mths	About 22 mths
He has a vocabulary of about 50 words and starts putting these words together in two-word sentences.	He will typically select one or two pivotal words and combine these with a variety of nouns. Typical sentences would be "Daddy gone", "Teddy gone", "Bye-bye Daddy", "Bye-bye car".

Clever hands

Your child will soon progress from her early hand and palm reflexes to reaching, grasping and holding. And regular playing practice will teach her to advance to more complex activities involving a high degree of control.

Moving from one toy to another, as well as – eventually – exchanging toys such as a football with you or another child, will help your child develop a good coordination between both hands.

Placing

This is a complex skill. Your child must turn her hand over while still gripping the toy, twist the hand into the right orientation, line the object up for placing, then very gently let go. If she gets any of these wrong, she will place the toy incorrectly. At birth she has very few bones in her wrist, and these do not start to grow until after she has gained control of her fingers. Until her wrist has fully developed, she cannot twist her hand or place anything with any great accuracy.

Rolling

As soon as she can bring her hands together to play "pat-a-cake" she will be able to "catch" a large ball you roll to her. Sit opposite her, with your legs apart, and roll the ball directly into her open legs and arms. Her legs will stop it rolling out of reach. Although she can "catch" like this she will find it harder to roll the ball back until she has learned to let go.

Throwing

Most children begin to throw between 12 and 18 months. A soft foam ball or a bean bag are the easiest (and safest) toys for this. A child's ability to throw will gradually improve, but even when she starts school she will not yet throw very accurately.

Catching

It is even harder to catch a ball than to throw it. Teach her to catch a beach ball. Stand very close and almost place the ball in her hands. Gradually, move further and further away and use a smaller ball. By about 3–4 years, most children can catch and throw a large ball over a short distance.

Kicking

Start with a large stationary ball and move on to a ball which you roll directly at your child's feet. Kicking is more difficult because she has to be able to balance on one foot. She may be able to balance long enough to kick a ball by 18 months, but she will not be able to make a running kick until she is about four, and can change pace and direction as she runs. She will not be able to dribble the ball for at least a year or two after that.

Skilled play

For a simple ball game, a surprising number of hand skills are required: turning and twisting of the wrist, throwing and letting go, catching, grasping and holding.

HAND CONTROL MONTH BY MONTH

Month	Virtually all children can	Most children can	Some children can
2	Open hands at will; grasp a finger placed in palm.	Swipe at an object with entire arm; clasp (and drop) a rattle.	Raise one arm or both together; watch hands; suck fingers.
3	Bring both hands together; when shown a reachable object, bring hands together to clasp.	Raise one arm or both together; bring hand to mouth; turn body towards object.	Hold hands open; reach for an object with one hand, without accurate clasping.
4	Glance from hand to object; raise one arm independently; bring hand to mouth.	Reach for an object with one hand, without accurate clasping; raise both arms together.	Watch and play with hands; use mitten grasp: thumb opposes fingers and palm.
5	Bring both hands together; hold rattle; reach out to hold object; turn body towards object.	Reach for and clasp object from above; watch/play with hands; transfer toy; use mitten grip.	Hold on to their bottle; reach for object – the aim is now fairly good; loosen grip to let go.
6	Use mitten grip; reach for and clasp object from above; transfer toy from one hand to the other.	Hold onto their bottle; reach out accurately for an object.	Pick up object and take it to the mouth; pass from one hand to other; let object roll out of hand.
7	Pick up an object and take it to the mouth; hold onto their bottle; reach accurately.	Reach for a toy; pick up a small object with fist; pass from one hand to other.	Stroke with open hand; try to get toy which is out of reach; drop toys intentionally by tipping out.
8	Pick up small object with fist. Pass from one hand to the other.	Try to get toy which is out of reach; drop toys by tipping out.	Use thumb when holding large object; bang objects together.
9	Try to get a toy which is out of reach; drop toys intentionally by letting them roll out of hand.	Use pincer grip to pick up pea; use thumb to hold a large object; bang two objects together.	Play pat-a-cake; drop by turning hand, then opening it; let go intentionally.
12	Pick up pea with fingers; let go intentionally, turn hand and drop; bang two objects together.	Play pat-a-cake; place objects; poke with finger; turn over the pages in a card book.	Remove covers from containers; put one object into container; rotate and stack toys.
15	Use tips of fingers to pick up pea.	Scribble and point.	Build a tower of 2 bricks.
18	Scribble and point.	Build a tower of 2 bricks.	Kick a ball forward.
21	Build a tower of 2 cubes.	Throw ball overhand.	Build a tower of 4 cubes.
24	Build a tower of 4 cubes; kick ball forward; throw ball overhead.	Build a tower of 6 cubes; throw ball overhand.	Complete a simple puzzle; catch a beach ball.

Perfecting language

Within a few years, your child will pick up the rules of grammar and intonation of his mother tongue. He will advance from "telegraphic style" to complex sentences – although there may be a few mistakes along the way.

BILINGUAL

Bilingual children pick up words in both languages. This means that, at first, their progress in each language is a little slower than that of monolingual children, but most bilingual children catch up long before they start school. The effort of learning two languages in the early years seems to have a positive effect: research has shown that bilingual children often do better at school.

The language of small children misses all the little words and word endings. They say "go school" rather than "go to school", and "two bus" rather than "two buses". Your child hears all the words you say, and knows what he should say, but he cannot organize a complex sentence.

He expects you to interpret what he says rather than repeating back what he did say: he says "Mummy shoe" and means "Where is Mummy's shoe?", but his memory span is small and he cannot organize more than one or two words at a time.

Memory span

Most adults have a memory span of about seven items. This limited span affects how we organize a sentence. We can only follow a long sentence if it is made up of a number of short and distinct phases. A small child's memory span is only two to three words long, so he has problems even with much shorter sentences. He copes by picking out the parts we emphasize, so that his sentences sound like a telegram.

At birth, a baby is aware of what he sees – he looks away and all thought of what went before has gone. His span is just an instant long. Through the first year, it slowly increases, and by eight months, he can look away from what he is doing and then go back to it, because he remembers what he had been doing.

By his first birthday his span is large enough for him to combine actions and words, such as pointing and saying "bus". He makes this easier for himself by first pointing and then saying the word rather than organizing the two together – as he would have to do if he said "Look bus!"

By the end of his second year he can follow what you say, and will know how things should be said, even if he cannot yet say them. As his span improves further, his sentences get longer. He begins to add in the little words and the word endings he has, up to now, missed out.

Goody-two-shoes

One day, your toddler will start to say "two shoes" rather than "two shoe". He has learned the rule for making a plural and will now practise it all the

Learning and using rules

Toddlers learn many words. They listen to how we put them together, and from this they extract the rules of language. When he can form the plural, he will also say things he has never heard such as "Two sheeps" and "Two foots". It is these mistakes which tell us that he has learned the basic rule for making a plural. You can test this by making up a word like "wump" and asking him what two would be called – he will say "Two wumps". As he listens to you and learns the rules, he will also begin to add in little words such as "in", "on", "the", "a".

Forming complex sentences

By three children begin to use complex sentences, but at first they do this by simply tacking on additional clauses: "See the teddy that I got". Only later will they start to interrupt the main clause of the sentence to insert a new clause "The girl with the pink dress runs fast". Although children have mastered almost all the rules of language by the age of five, there are still some complex constructions they cannot use, such as "She did do it, didn't she? He wouldn't do it, would he?"

The first rules a child learns

- Present progressive -*ing*: He is sitting.
- Prepositions: *in* the chair; *on* the table.
- Plural -*s*: Two cats.
- Past tense: He asked. He went home.
- Possessive '*s*: Meg's car is here.
- Copula (contracted, uncontractable) *be*: That's a horse. Is that a dog?
- Articles *a, the*: a pig, the bus.
- 3rd person singular: He runs fast. Does the dog bark?
- Auxiliary *be*: They're running very slowly. Is he running?

My teddy bear says

Children learn from listening to adults but also from each other, and by practising "teddy speak".

SEE ALSO

Listening to the world	**76–77**
Learning to speak	**96–97**
Attention and memory	**104–105**
Talking to children	**150–151**

HOW CHILDREN LEARN ABOUT SENTENCE STRUCTURE

	Stage 1	Stage 2	Stage 3	Stage 4
Basic grammar	Children never use the rules of grammar.	Children learn some of the irregular cases, such as "went" rather than "goed", and "feet" rather than "foots".	Children learn the rules and apply them across the board.	Children learn when to apply rules and when not. They will not always get it right (even early rules like plurals) until they are 7–8 years old.
Asking questions	Children aged 12–30 months use intonation for questions. They say a sentence and raise the tone at the end of the sentence to form a question. "I have dis?", "Have some?"	By 36 months children start using the "wh" questions – when, what, who, etc. Often the earliest such questions run two words together: "Whatsat?", "Whatisdis?"	Children begin to get the order right in positive questions, but not in negative ones. They can say: "What will you do now?", but not "Why can't you sit down?"	Children can form positive and negative questions accurately.
Negative sentences	Children form negative sentences by adding "no" at the beginning, such as "No do it". They feel instinctively that important words such as negatives should be at the beginning or the end of a sentence, not in the middle.	Children put the negative element in the right position within the sentence, but they do not always use the right word: "I said not that", "I not hurt Jamie."	Children get both the position and the word right in most situations: "I didn't say that", and "I didn't hurt Jamie."	Children get both the position and the word right in all situations: "I didn't say that", and "I didn't hurt Jamie."

Drawing and painting

Children do not draw what they see – they draw what they think should be there. Their drawings are not attempts at photographic representations of the world; they are symbols, just like letters and written words.

If you show a young child a cup with a flowery pattern, and ask her to draw it, she will draw what she considers to be the essentials of all cups – the cup shape and the handle – and then add the essence of this particular cup, a flower pattern. Neither the "universal cup" nor the "universal flower pattern" will necessarily be like the cup in front of her. Her cup may have a different shape, her flowers may have straight stems and look like daisies, while the flowers on the cup she is looking at have curly stems and look like honeysuckle or roses. Not until she reaches about eight or nine years does she attempt to recreate on paper exactly what she sees in front of her.

Young artists

It is fascinating to watch the child's progress from uncontrolled round-and-round scribbles to lifting the crayon off the paper more frequently, then to drawing defined shapes and realistic images.

MILESTONES IN DRAWING	
18 months– 2 years	Patterns may look like scribbles but the lines are not aimless. The picture is well balanced: something on the left is usually balanced by something on the right. Drawings are not meant to represent anything. At this age she draws continuous lines, which go round and round and curl over the page.
2–2½ years	She will still not aim to draw anything specific, but if you ask her what she has drawn she tells you. The next day she may say it is something different. She will take her crayon off the paper more often, and sometimes draw a circle, break and draw another. It looks less like dense scribble.
2½–3 years	Children begin to see their drawings as representing something (probably because we expect them to do so and often ask them). She may tell you what she intends to draw before she starts – but may not stick to the plan. If she thinks it looks more like something else she will change her mind.
3–3½ years	She draws lines, dots, squares, big and small circles and crosses. She begins to enclose things within her circles. Lines radiate from a "sun" circle. She will suddenly realize she has drawn a person, and she will want to repeat it. Things are not always in the right place, but she is happy with this.
3½–5 years	Positioning becomes important: eyes in the face; no body, but the legs are there. She uses circles for head, eyes, nose and mouth. By four she adds detail: people with arms, buttons on coats. If something is important to her she draws it: if she grazed her knee, her people will suddenly have knees.
5–8 years	Her drawings remain symbolic. The most interesting part is always bigger. If she draws a dog from the side, it with be seen with all four legs in a line underneath and its face looking out of the picture. She may also draw things she cannot see, such as a baby inside a pregnant woman.

Drawing people

Children do not draw stick men, they draw potato men: they have large heads, they may or may not have stick limbs, but they will usually have faces.

• In the earliest drawings the face will have eyes (sometimes more than two) and possibly a nose and mouth, although these are not always present.

• Later, hair may be added to one area of the head and arms and legs attached to another. These remain optional and may vary in number. The important point is not where they are, or how big they are, but that they are there. If she thinks about them she adds them, if she doesn't she may forget.

• Gradually, the number of "must have" elements increases. She starts to add arms or a body, then both. After the arms she adds fingers, then she draws in clothes.

• Size always represents interest in her early drawings. When fingers become important they take up most of the page. If asked to draw her family she is usually at least as big as her parents – if not bigger.

• She places elements randomly at first. Arms come out at waist level, faces always

look out of the page, feet turn to the side.

• One other thing you may notice about her people: they are usually positioned on the right-hand side of her pictures.

Chimneys askew

Small children look at the part of the drawing they are working on as they draw. You can see this when they draw things that should be vertical or horizontal. Under about six, they line each object up with the nearest straight line, so, if they are putting a chimney on a sloping roof, they will position it at right angles to the roof.

Little scribbles and writing

Soon she will start to "write". You can encourage her in her efforts, but do not force things. As long as she is having fun she is learning to control her pencil.

• Refer to big scribbles as drawing and little ones as writing. If she asks you what letters look like show her, but wait for her to ask. Let her write her own shopping list.

• If she draws a letter by chance point it out to her: "What a lovely O". If she draws several letters spell them out: "This says ummoo – I wonder what that means!"

SEE ALSO

Clever hands	**98–99**
Learning to think	**106–107**
Ready for school	**108–109**
From toddler to child	**186–187**

POSITIONING

Small children have problems positioning items relative to each other.

• A house rarely nestles in the hill. Most five- and six-year olds will perch a house on top of a round or pointed hill or draw it sideways on the slope. Older children may prop it up with foundations.

• The seat of a stool is seen from the top, the legs from the side. The man floats above so as not to hide the stool.

• An elephant gets a typical face. The child does not know that the trunk is the nose, and so she will place it wherever she has left some space! She does the same with a giraffe's neck – it is attached anywhere it fits.

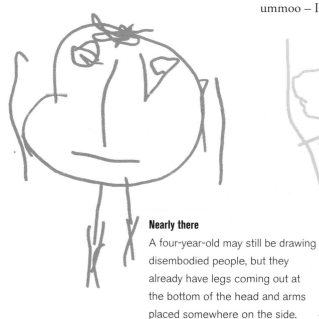

Nearly there

A four-year-old may still be drawing disembodied people, but they already have legs coming out at the bottom of the head and arms placed somewhere on the side.

"My" house

You can be sure that "her" house will have a central door, two or four windows, a steep roof and a (smoking) chimney – even if her real house looks nothing like that!

REMEMBERING

● Even premature babies recognize that something was seen a few moments ago, but cannot remember over longer periods.

● By five months, a baby can recognize a pattern he has seen two weeks before.

● Babies cannot remember the past until they are about seven months old. They then remember sensory events and movements (much as we remember how to ride a bike).

● By two he will remember completed past events, but he cannot reconstruct their sequence. He remembers that Grandma came yesterday and they went to the shops – but he cannot remember which happened first.

Past imperfect
Your child will know that it was her birthday, that she had a toy rabbit as a present from her brother – but she will not know which came first.

Attention and memory

We know that children do not think like adults, or solve problems as we do. That is what makes their explanations of the world so endearing to us. Children do not just know less than we do – they think differently from us.

Compared with adults, children are not just unsystematic, disorganized and easily distracted, they see themselves as the centre of things, and they grab at the first solution to a problem or situation that comes to mind.

Space for thinking

Preschool children do not think like adults because their brains are different from ours. Children know many things, but do not organize their thoughts logically because they do not have the "working space" they

need to be able to do this. It is a bit like preparing a meal without having a work surface. You can cut the ingredients into the stew, but the chances are that something will be forgotten. If you have a work surface, you can prepare all the ingredients first, and check that you have everything ready before you start to cook. Thinking, like cooking, needs a work surface, or to use the term psychologists have coined, a "scratch pad".

To solve a problem, we need to think through a number of possible solutions, compare ideas and see which one works best. How well we can do this depends on the size and organization of our scratch pads. If it is tiny (as it is in babies) it is impossible to think about complex ideas or explanations. It is also impossible to compare different solutions – what a baby thinks now is what he thinks. Once the scratch pad has become larger we can "turn things over" in our mind, and decide on the best solution. Adults are not "captured" by their current ideas in the same way as children are because their scratch pads hold both current and past experiences.

How children differ

● Children are dominated by what they see at the moment. If the eye can fool them, then it will. They cannot push their current experience into the background.

● Children lack the experience and knowledge to solve complex problems, but they may be surprisingly knowledgeable in a specialist field they have been exposed to.

Learning to concentrate

Attention involves focusing on certain aspects of our environment and ignoring others. As children grow up they become better able to resist distraction. We know that infants are interested in curved lines, faces, three-dimensional objects, sounds and smells. These are likely to attract them, but their attention is never captured for very long, and they are easily distracted when something else comes into view.

Strategies for memorizing

As children grow up, they use a wide range of strategies to help them remember. One of the simplest is rehearsing. Children under three can rehearse – but will only do so if they are told that it is a good idea, and then may only do it for the task at hand. By ten, almost all children spontaneously rehearse anything they need to remember.

Other strategies are breaking items down into components or grouping them into larger classes. Again, they only do this spontaneously from about ten. A telephone number like 883514 is easier to remember when broken down into three groups: 88–35–14. When asked to remember what they saw in a picture, ten-year-olds will group similar items together (such as food or people). They remember the items, by first recalling everything in one class before recalling everything in another.

Changes over time

Recognition: At all ages, recognizing that you have seen something before is better than recalling that you have seen it. If asked to sort the things they have seen before from those that are new to them, two-year-olds get it right 80 per cent of the time, four-year-olds 90 per cent of the time, and adults rarely make a mistake.
Recall: If the same children are asked to recall what they had seen, four-year-olds

only remember 20 per cent of the items, those under four even less. All children remember actions and activities (the game) better than things (the toy).

Autobiography: Remembering specific events that happened to you seems to start at about three or four years of age. This slowly improves until about eight years.
Sequence of events: By four or five years of age children can remember a sequence (such as the order of clothes on a washing line), but they have trouble putting events in chronological order. Children remember the first event in a sequence very clearly, but have problems with those that follow.
Using memory strategies: When asked to remember where something is hidden, two-year-olds watch you hide it, then look away and forget. Three-year-olds watch and then keep on looking at the hiding place until you ask them where the toy is. By five years, children have learned that telling someone else where they have put something helps them remember. By seven, children use a variety of memory strategies, such as rehearsing and questioning.

SEE ALSO
Learning to think	**106–107**
Ready for school	**108–109**
Caring about others	**110–111**
Becoming independent	**164–165**

DISTRACTIONS

- When reaching for toys, babies get distracted by their own hand, so they close their eyes.
- Children under six prefer visuals. They prefer TV to music and books.
- Bright colours and loud noises attract children most.
- Preschoolers learn best when there is no music or noise.
- They learn best when focusing on one thing only. Keep other toys hidden.

CHANGES IN ATTENTION WITH AGE	
At three	**At six**
In a picture, a child registers colours, sizes and shapes, then integrates these into a "whole".	He sees the whole picture from the start.
He scans the world impulsively.	He searches for what he wants
He simply enjoys looking.	He looks systematically, and tries to make sense of what he sees.
Looking for his shoes, he checks in a couple of places, then settles down to do something else.	He will look where the shoes are "supposed to be" first, and then check in other possible places.
Asked to find the "odd one out" in a series of pictures, he will glance from picture to picture, hoping to spot the difference.	Asked to find the "odd one out" in a series of pictures, he will compare two at a time, then two more, until he finds it.

Learning to think

Thinking involves more than just a recall of past events – creative solutions may be required. An understanding of cause and effect as well as the ability to abstract and symbolize are formed at an early age.

PAST PRESENT

To remember, babies need cues. They need the familiarity of their surroundings – room, faces, toys and routines – to experience the feeling of having been there before.

This is also why babies under one hate going on holiday: everything is new and different, and there is too much to take on board in one go. If you holiday with a small baby, take along as many familiar things (blankets, teddy, toys) as possible, and repeat familiar routines if you can.

One of the most frequent ways in which we need to "think" is problem solving, and this, too, is different in small children. In order to solve a problem we first gather all the useful facts – that is, we assess the current situation and think back to any relevant information we might have stored from another, similar occasion. We then compare the old and the new, and we check if this helps us to understand. We apply strategies, we make best guesses, we come up with interim solutions and then we test these out. All this occurs in the work space of the mind.

Developing symbolic thought

Between birth and two, children come to understand the world by acting on it. Their understanding is not couched in terms of words or symbols, but in terms of their sensual experience and their activities. As adults, once we have learned to swim or ride a bike, we are in a similar situation: we cannot easily describe how we do it, nor explain to another person how they should do it, we do it more or less "automatically"; but we can tell other people how we saw a monkey in the zoo climb up a tree.

During the early preschool years: A child's early sensing and moving way of understanding her world is gradually joined by symbolic thought – that is, thoughts based on language and symbols. Symbolic thought allows the child to make comparisons, to think about things that have happened before and to use language

Pretend play
From about two your child will understand events and actions beyond herself – "Tea for dolly".

to describe them. Now she can also tell someone else what she has done and that she saw the monkeys at the zoo.

In the later preschool years: With an increasing capacity for symbolic thought, children begin to separate objects from events, thoughts from actions. So, for example, they recognize that the high chair is not part of the eating process itself. Between two and four, the child learns to use a familiar action pattern on things outside herself. Not everything revolves only around her: she can imagine relationships between her toys – Teddy is the driver, the rabbit is the passenger.

Logical thought

Between four and seven, a child will come to understand relationships (such as mother and child) and contingencies. She will, for example, know that the heaviest bucket is the one with the most sand in it.

But none of this means she thinks in a logical way. Her tendency to focus attention on one aspect of any situation stops this. If you show her two tall glasses of water, and ask her if they have the same amount in them, she will say "Yes". Now, if you pour the water out of the tall glass into a short fat glass, she thinks it has less water in it. In the same way she thinks there are more buttons in a long line of six buttons than in a short line of six. Children at this age are still fooled by their eyes. It looks higher, it looks longer – so there is more. Because she concentrates on one aspect (height), she ignores the other (width).

Cause and effect

● Preschoolers assume that one thing causes another if two things are closely associated in space or time, even if they have no obvious connection, or if the connection is reversed. For example, she might say that the sun stays in the sky because it is yellow, or that she fell off her bike because she broke her arm.

● Preschoolers generalize from one situation to all. If, for example, one black dog knocked her over in the park, she will assume that all black dogs will knock her over. If she bumps into the table leg, she will assume they are all going to hurt her.

● Preschoolers cannot make the correct inferences about a sequence of events. If, for example, you tell her that the ball hit the hammer, the hammer fell off the shelf, onto the cup and the cup broke, she will not be able to conclude that the hammer broke the cup. If, however, you give her two possible choices, she can pick out the one that is the most likely answer. So, for example, if you ask: "Was it the hammer or the ball that broke the cup?", she will probably opt for the "hammer".

Changes between 4 and 7

Theory of mind: At three, she does not put herself in another person's shoes or realize that her thoughts and feelings are separate from other peoples'. She is always at the centre. If asked if she has a sister, she will say "Yes" – but if asked whether her sister has a sister, she will say "No". As she approaches four, she will begin to realize that her thoughts and feelings are separate from other peoples.

Understanding permanence: A child under four will know that she is a girl, but she may still think she will grow up to be a Daddy. A child over four knows she will always be the same gender.

Quantity theory: Most preschoolers can count, and they also know that two is more than one. But at this age, they do not yet know that seven is also more than six.

SEE ALSO
Learning to speak   96–97
Attention and memory   104–105
Ready for school   108–109
Caring about others   110–111

TELLING YOU

There is so much to learn from seeing and observing that it takes a few years before a child has sorted out some of the basics. It is only after about two years that language will play a significant part in her life and that she begins to understand some concepts.

She will start to give reasons, to compare and to understand rules. From about four she will ask many questions and understand the answers. It is only now that she can learn by being told.

Which is more?

Before the age of seven, a child will still think that the flattened ball of play dough is more than the round one – because it looks "larger". Her eyes deceive her.

Ready for school

Your child has learned an awful lot over the first few years of his life. He has grown enormously in weight and height, he knows how to move and speak, he can express his feelings and relate to others – but is he ready for school?

There are a number of basic skills that are required of each child before he is ready to leave the safety and emotional security of the home and go out to school with others for the first time.

Sitting still

It may seem obvious that children need to be able to sit still at school, but it is a serious problem for many small children. If your child cannot sit still for more than a minute or two, you would be wise to delay school. A disruptive, restless child can get a reputation that will stay with him through the school years.

To help your child learn how to sit still, start the day with some wild activities – running around to loud music or jumping off the stairs, for example. Now turn off the music and ask him to do something that involves sitting at the table. Eating breakfast, for example, or reading a story, playing with toy bricks, drawing a picture, standing at the sink to play with water – these are all good quiet tasks. Follow this with another wild session, then another quiet one. Do not expect your child to be able to keep still for very long. Start with a few minutes and build this up. Praise what he does. Ignore the fidgeting.

Paying attention

Children need to know that they have to listen when people speak to them. They need to be able to pay attention to what is being said, and then do what is asked of them. All of this is difficult for many children, especially for young boys. To help your child, set the table for meals and sit opposite him so that he looks at you, and you at him, as you talk. Turn off the music, radio, TV and all other distractions. Excitement makes children flit from one activity to the next. Put most of the toys away in the cupboard. In short, provide the sort of environment that allows him to concentrate and give sustained attention.

Fun and imagination
Playing with toy bricks, farmyards and other scenes "forces" your child into a quiet period. It also allows him to develop his creative imagination by transporting him into a different world.

Getting on swimmingly
One of the best ways to help your child learn to cope with the company of others is a visit to the swimming pool – fun and sociable.

Concentration and perseverance
Your child will find it much easier to concentrate on the task in hand if he is used to playing in a space that is not scattered with toys. Distraction is the enemy of concentration, so keep his stimulation (other than the task in hand) to a minimum. Reward him if he succeeds in sticking with and completing a task.

In a crowd, without Mum
Practice is the only way to learn survival in a crowd. All children gain from the experience of going to a preschool play group or a baby gym. The swimming pool is another good noisy environment where he will learn to be surrounded by other children. Experience will teach him to be without his carer. He has to be confident that he can cope on his own – and that you will return when you say you will.

Making friends
Not all children know how to make friends when they start school, but those who do will be much happier. Few children make long-term friends at this age. They just need to know how to join in and how to give and take. The only way of learning this is repeated practice in other social contexts, such as the kindergarten.

An ability to express himself
A child who is still having problems with language is at a great disadvantage in the early school years. He will find it difficult to communicate with both the teacher and the other children.

Self-confidence
A confident child can take things in his stride. If he believes he can do it, then he probably will. If he believes he cannot, then he almost certainly will not. You can help build his confidence by telling him how special he is and how well you know he will cope. If he behaves badly, criticize his behaviour, not the child.

Writing and reading
It does not matter whether he can write his name or whether he can read, but he should be able to control a pencil. He should also know that print is what one reads, and that reading can give pleasure.

Knowing learning is fun
A child who has played alone and has been free to explore and discover his world will start school with much enthusiasm. One who always follows others will wait for the teacher to prompt him, rather than striving to find out on his own.

Pencil control
Drawing with pens and pencils of all sizes will teach your child how to hold her writing utensils and how to achieve the desired results – even if she cannot yet write.

SEE ALSO
Perfecting language 100–101
Attention and memory 104–105
Learning to think 106–107
Caring about others 110–111

HELPFUL PLAY

● **I spy.** Listening for sounds and connecting these with objects.

● **Watching insects.** Observation and discovery.

● **Jigsaw puzzles.** Shape recognition; completing tasks.

● **Colouring in.** Pencil control and colour sense.

● **Spot the difference.** Attention to detail; comparing.

● **Nonsense rhymes.** Sound recognition and fun.

● **Write a comic book.** Observation and sequencing.

In most cultures (as in ours), children did some unpaid work during their school years (feeding the hens, taking care of younger children). They also helped earn the family wage, and in many countries this still happens. When not working, children played out, in mixed age groups with younger charges. They roamed out of sight of adults, made camps and formed secret societies. This is what many writers are nostalgic about.

Caring about others

A small child does not know that she can think. To know about thinking, she has to learn that her thoughts and experience are unique to her. She will also learn that other people have thoughts that she knows nothing about.

Small children do not realize that their thoughts and feelings are different from ours. They know that hitting another child on the head makes him cry – but they do not understand the concept of another person's pain because it does not hurt them. This is typical of the early pre-school years. When your child tells you about her morning at Granny's (while you were out) she talks as if you had been there. She does not explain she met a nice dog in the park, she just says, "That dog was my friend" and leaves you to work out the rest. She will talk about what she can see behind you as if you were looking at it too. This all changes between three and a half and four years, when she begins to take note of your experience and thoughts. Now she will say, "You know that girl I like to play with…, well we …", filling in the details that she knows you need to follow her story.

And then I took the bike…
It is only close to their fourth birthday that children realize that you do not share their experience if you were not there, and that they will have to explain.

Until she realizes that we can feel, hurt and experience things separately from her, she cannot develop any real concern for our hurt. She can do things because we have told her to – because we will be pleased with her if she does, or angry if she does not – but she cannot begin to have any real moral sense until she realizes her actions can hurt others. Morals are not about punishing and rewarding; they are about conforming to society's rules, about not doing things that will harm others – whether or not anybody knows about it.

How other people feel and think
Psychologists have a number of ways of testing whether children have learned that other people have thoughts and feelings. This is one you can try. Show a three-year-old a tube of Smarties (or a bag of crisps) and ask her what is inside. She will say "Smarties" because she recognizes the packet and can see the picture on the front. In fact, the tube does not contain Smarties because you have replaced them with some little plastic pigs. Now let her peep inside the tube to see the pigs. Tip them out and put them back so she is quite sure. Ask her again what is inside; she will say, "Pigs".

If you ask her what other children will think is inside the box, three-year-olds will assume that they know what she knows – that the tube has pigs in it – even though the others have not seen them. Only as she approaches her fourth birthday does she realize that they will expect Smarties.

You will see this change in the way your child understands thinking in her play, especially her pretend play. Once she knows that not everyone shares her thoughts, she realizes she has to explain what she is pretending.

Telling right from wrong

Preschool children know right from wrong. They can say something is naughty and something is good, but they tend to think the naughtiness is measured by action, not by intention – deliberately throwing one plate on the floor is not nearly as naughty as accidentally tripping and breaking five plates. The rule is: "Breaking something is naughty". It is only when a child starts to play with other children that she realizes that some rules can be bent to suit the occasion, that they are not absolutely fixed but created for the best interest of all. Once she begins to realize that intentionally disobeying a rule is naughtier than accidentally disobeying it, she can move towards a moral behaviour.

The value of helping

Moral behaviour is more than blindly following the rules. Morals allow us to do "the right thing" even when no one is watching. Adults know that it is not the behaviour which is moral but the reason for that behaviour. We can donate money to charity because we get tax relief, or because we are moved by the plight of those in need. Only the latter is a truly moral act. Children cannot learn to be moral by simply learning to obey rules. They have to develop empathy and understand how other people will be affected by their behaviour.

Stages in moral development

● **Children under four** do not understood rules. They know that good or bad

behaviour will attract their parents' attention, which they want. Rather than helping or being good because they know it is right, they behave well to gain attention or to please those they like.
● **Children aged 4–7** (and many aged 7–10) still show many of the above concerns but will begin to express concern for the physical, material and emotional needs of others, even when these conflict with their own needs. This is expressed in very simple terms by the child. Her co-operation and sharing is often manipulative (to gain approval) and not based on a sense of justice, sympathy, or compassion.
● **Some children aged 8–10** increasingly believe that good behaviour is that which maintains approval and good relations with others. Although still dependent on others for her judgments, it is their approval rather than their power which is important to your child. She has stereotyped images of good and bad people and behaviour.
● **A few children aged 8–10** (and many who are older) believe that they must blindly accept social conventions. Your child no longer conforms to her parents' or other powerful individuals' standards, but to the wider social order. Behaviour is good as long as it complies with a rigid set of rules.

TODAY

In the West, former children's jobs are done by machines. Children no longer look after younger siblings and do not learn to care for others. The woods are silent, and fewer and fewer children play out in cities. Unwilling and bored, they are not part of the cooperative world of innocent, if mischievous, gangs. Pranks are a thing of the past. Instead children slump in front of the TV, video, or computer screen.

I can help

Studies have shown that where school-age children have some responsibilities and help with household chores they grow up to be more cooperative and concerned with others.

CHAPTER THREE

The child as an individual

Although the newborn baby is immature and helpless, we see her as an individual. Just as we look at her face and discover something unique, we look at her character and see some of what she will become. It is hard to say what this is, but most parents agree that "it" exists. If they have more than one child, they know that each one is different. This uniqueness – the personality that is there from the beginning – colours your child's development as much as her position in the family.

In his genes!

Many things make up an individual: the genes he inherits from both his parents and his ancestors, the womb he develops in, how he is parented, whether the world loves him and where fate has placed him in time and space.

Happy families

Children inherit both their parents' genes, yet they may end up looking more like an aunt or uncle.

Your child is endowed with a certain potential and, as he grows, other factors influence him. His genes set broad limits, and the environment determines where within those limits he will be. The genes, for example, define the maximum height to which he will grow, but the environment (particularly his nutrition) will decide exactly how tall he will be, up to that maximum. For most physical features, these limits are fairly "tight"; the opposite is probably true for personality and behaviour. His physical and mental abilities, his intelligence, temperament, personality and his health have obvious genetic underpinnings, but the environment plays a much bigger role in all of them. He inherits a predisposition which influences how he will interact with the world, but how the world interacts with him is not always in his control.

Active and inactive genes

We might think that children of the same parents, who are brought up in the same way, would be very much alike – but clearly they are not. They may even look and behave more like an uncle than either parent. The reason for this is that all genes come in pairs. Each parent passes on one of each of their own gene pairs to their child, so the child inherits half of his genes from his mother and half from his father (but siblings will not inherit exactly the same set of genes – they share on average no more than 50 per cent of their genes).

In addition, of each pair of genes, usually only one is activated. This means that almost half the genes we carry have no influence on us at all. People may have, for example, a pair of one blue-eyed and one brown-eyed gene, but it is the brown-eyed

HIDDEN LOOKS		
	Characteristics from "active" genes	Characteristics from "inactive" genes
Eyes	Brown, hazel, or green eyes	Blue eyes
	Long lashes	Short lashes
	Astigmatism	Normal vision
	Far-sightedness	Normal vision
	Normal vision	Short-sightedness
	Normal colour vision	Colour blindness
Nose	High, hooked bridge	Straight or upturned bridge
	Narrow bridge	Broad bridge
	Flared nostrils	Narrow nostrils
	Straight tip	Upturned tip
Face	Full lips	Thin lips
	Dimpled chin	Undimpled chin
	Dimpled cheeks	Undimpled cheeks
	Normal chin	Recessive chin
	High cheekbones	Normal cheekbones
	Freckles	No freckles
	Bushy eyebrows	Normal eyebrows
Hair	Dark	Blond
	No red in hair	Red in hair
	Kinky	Curly
	Curly	Straight
	Baldness	No loss of hair
	Heavy body hair	Light body hair

Left-handedness
The predisposition to use the left instead of the right hand is inherited. In identical twins, if one twin is left-handed, there is a 50:50 chance the other one will be too.

gene which is dominant and active, while the blue-eye gene is recessive and inactive – so the person will have brown eyes.

The gene the child inherits may be the parent's active, dominant gene, but it could be the inactive, recessive one. So, although a child has 50 per cent of his mother's genes, he could share as little as 25 per cent of her active genes. The same is true of the genes he inherits from his father, and a child may end up looking more like his grandfather than his mother.

Nature and nurture

One of the oldest controversies is how much influence nature (genes) and nurture (the family and environment) have, respectively, on a child's development.

One way of looking at this is to study twins. Identical twins develop from a single egg, fertilized by a single sperm, and so they have all of their genes in common. Fraternal twins develop from two eggs and two sperms, so they are no more alike than other siblings, sharing on average about 50 per cent of their genes. A study of the differences between the two types of twins should reveal the separate influences of genes and environment. Of course, it is not

quite that simple – identical twins look alike, so they are often treated as if they were alike, while fraternal twins are usually assumed to be different.

Passing in the female line

Girls inherit two X-chromosomes – one from their mother, one from their father – both having dominant and recessive genes. Boys, however, inherit an X-chromosome from their mother and a Y-chromosome from their father. The Y-chromosome is shorter and gives the mother's recessive genes a free reign. This means that boys tend to be a little bit more like their mothers (and their mothers' families) than girls are. It also means that boys are more vulnerable to some recessive conditions (such as haemophilia and colour blindness).

Gene therapy

Advances in our understanding of how genes work may one day help us cure inherited diseases. Defective genes, or the genes responsible for a disease, could be replaced with normal genes. Fairly successful trials have already been made to cure cystic fibrosis – a virus carries "good" genes into affected lung tissue. It is possible that, in the future, the disease will be cured by a simple nasal spray.

SEE ALSO

Is everything all right?	**68–69**
Everyone is lovable	**116–117**
Every child an individual	**118–119**
Boys and girls	**130–131**

LIKELY TWINS

● The tendency to have identical twins does not usually run in families (although it may). Overall, about 1:80 births are twins, and of these about 20% are identical.

● The tendency to have fraternal, or non-identical twins, *does* run in families. Women of Afro-Caribbean origin are most likely to have fraternal twins (1:70 births) and Chinese women least likely (1:300). The European rate is about 1:86.

● Fraternal twins are no more alike than brothers or sisters. Both parents can pass the tendency to have fraternal twins on to their daughters. Fraternal twins do not "skip a generation", but the likelihood of having such twins increases with age.

So much alike
Identical twins look alike and are a similar weight and height. They also walk and develop at the same time, and go grey and wrinkly together.

Everyone is lovable

Not all children have particular talents – hidden or otherwise. Most are just average sorts of children, with average sorts of abilities. All, however, deserve their parents' unconditional love and attention.

One of the silliest things well-meaning people say to parents is that "every child is a potential winner". This is not only untrue, it is also potentially harmful. Stretching may well improve your child's abilities – but it will not necessarily make her into a high flyer. No parent should feel they need a reason to love their child. No child should have to earn love with her performance. She deserves to be loved just as much, whether she is an "average sort of girl" or the "exceptional" child we may think we desire. If she is lucky in her parents, the only exceptional thing that matters to them is that she is their child.

Escaping the average

Whatever talent we measure, the vast majority of people are average. Outstandingly talented people are very rare, which is, of course, why society values them. You cannot plan or create a child with a rare ability. You can help your child to reach her full potential, but that does not mean she can or will scale the highest peaks.

Life is not fair

Nature has no concept of fairness – the clever are often also beautiful; the dull are often plain. "She is nice, too", we say in surprise after meeting someone beautiful and talented. A child may be better at some things than others, but she will not necessarily be particularly good at anything. Most are just below average at some things and just above average at others – but no less lovable for that.

You are "the smart one"

Never label. Even "good" labels can be harmful. A label can prevent the child from seeing her real self. If she does not think she can do something, she is unlikely to try. If she thinks love comes to her because of success, she will feel insecure: love may be withdrawn if she fails. A child who is labelled as "the clever one" may never try to be a party animal, and not try her best when she is not expected to do well. She may feel that, if you try, you must win. Labels make statements about the things parents think are important. It is hard to feel good about yourself when you are always told that your abilities are more important than the person you are.

You are stupid, lazy…

Negative labels are particularly damaging. They also have a habit of becoming self-fulfilling prophecies. It is hard to keep self-control when people expect you to get into a fight, or to persevere at a task you find difficult when everyone expects you to do badly or to give up. It is hard to feel good about yourself when people are always telling you that you are bad.

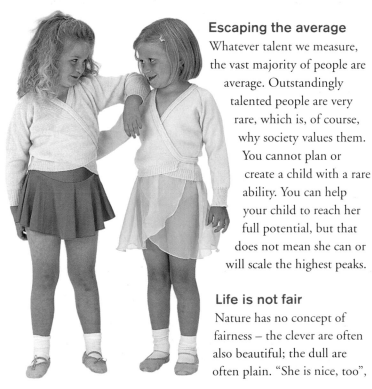

Swan lake
No matter how often your child practises her ballet steps, she will not necessarily become a great ballerina – but she may enjoy and appreciate dance more than others.

Intelligence

Although it has been a controversial subject for years, few scientists now doubt that intelligence is influenced by our genetic make-up. Fifty-two separate studies have shown that the similarities in IQ scores between family members are much higher than would be expected by chance. The IQ scores of identical twins (who have the same genes) rarely differ by more than a few points, and they also do similarly well in exactly the same areas.

The child's intelligence is, nonetheless, clearly influenced by more than her genes. Each child is born with a certain potential (her genetic endowment). For some children this endowment can be, and is, stretched to its limits. For others the stretching is minimal.

Be careful not to judge

Not all children can be clever. Once she starts school she will inevitably realize that some children can do some things better or quicker than she can. There is no way to protect her from this, but you can protect her self-esteem from being undermined by it. The more a child feels that she is loved for herself rather than for her achievements, the more secure she is in her own worth.

Helping a shy child

If you are happy out of the limelight, shyness is no problem, but it is inhibiting if you wish you were the centre of attention. You can help a shy child by being easy-going and supportive. Never force her to do things just because you think she would enjoy them. Nor should you entirely accept her withdrawal. Protect her from stressful situations and help her adjust slowly. Talk to her about her fears as you cuddle up together. Stories about shy children may help her. Shyness can be overcome – at least on some occasions.

SEE ALSO
Every child an individual **118–119**
Growing self-awareness **124–125**
Building self-esteem **126–127**
Coping with individuality **176–177**

Don't worry
Shy children may need some help in socializing. Draw them out gently, some of the time, and do not make them perform in front of others.

RUNNING IN THE FAMILY

The following types of behaviour have been suggested to run in families. Although no one has yet proved they are inherited, most of them have been shown to recur many times. They seem to form part of the child's nature and personality rather than fitting into phases of her life.

Stress reaction	Feels vulnerable and sensitive OR feels invulnerable and rarely suffers hurt feelings.
Conventional	Follows rules and authority OR deviates from rules and authority.
Attention span	Moves quickly from task to task OR persists with one task.
Persistence	Keeps trying OR gives up easily.
Distractability	Single-mindedness OR willingness to compromise.
Absorption	Imaginative OR little sense of imagination.
Intensity	Laughs or cries loudly OR with less intensity.
Fearfulness	High fear of danger or misfortune OR a love of danger and risk-taking.
Leadership	Likes to lead and be centre of attention OR prefers to follow and hide away.
Sociability	Extroverted and outgoing OR introverted and withdrawn.
Activity level	Busy, seeks lots of stimulation OR placid and content to watch.
Contact seeking	Enjoys physical contact, soothed when held OR resists physical contact and is soothed by music, rocking and other things.
Shyness	Anxious and dislikes things and people who are not familiar OR bold and outgoing.
Mood	Positive and happy OR negative, fussy and easily upset.
Rhythm	Eats, sleeps, or cries at about the same time every day OR is unpredictable.
Adaptability	Adapts easily to change OR prefers routine.

ALARM BELLS

If you (or your partner) experience any of the following signs of not loving the baby, seek help:

● Disappointed over sex of the baby

● Disappointed by health or handicap

● Concerned about a possible defect even if there is none

● Does not interact with newborn; does not show warmth

● Disgusted by the baby's normal behaviour

● Calls the baby ugly, cannot find anything to like or admire

● Does not make eye contact, talk, or play with the baby

● Picks him up as if he was an object

● Jiggles the baby roughly, does not look for feedback

● Cannot distinguish the baby's different cries; cannot judge the baby's needs

● Thinks the infant is judging him/her, and/or does not love them.

Every child an individual

We used to think of newborn babies as a jumble of reflexes who felt little pleasure or pain. We now know this is not true. Your baby may be slow to react when the nurse pricks his heel for the blood sample – but he does react.

Newborn babies face the same problem as adults: the need for emotional balance. If we become too calm, sleep follows. If we get too excited, fear is just around the corner. Normally, we can regulate our emotions while remaining interested in the world. For a baby, those things that excite him when he first sees them, will, once he knows them well, help him to calm down. A teddy initially makes him excitable, later it will make him feel secure. The completely unknown is always frightening, the relatively unknown can be exhilarating, the familiar is dull.

In the early hours it is people who give the newborn baby security. He finds the sound of a woman's voice, the intake of his carer's breath and the beat of her heart familiar and soothing. Her face, the light on her hair, the closeness of other people are novel enough to excite, but in his mother's arms there is enough that is familiar to keep him calm. When unease creeps in, we rock and enclose him as he was in the womb, and we make our own heart and lungs sound louder by holding him close to our body. Calmed in our arms, he can look out again on a world that frightened him when he was alone.

Levels of stimulation

A child needs a level of stimulation that suits his current mood. When he is awake, he wants the world to be interesting and exciting – but moderately so; too much excitement will make him afraid. When he is tired, he wants the world to be calm. Regulation has to be learned. The child has to seek the things that excite him and find the things that calm him down. Children facing pain and insecurity find regulation more difficult. It is always easier for babies whose carers mesh with their needs, than for those with less sensitive carers, but regulation is still not always possible.

Motivation and arousal

We need energy to get up and go. This is called arousal. Without it, we sink into a comatose state. If arousal rises too high, we are paralysed by panic, indecision and fear. The aim is to keep the level somewhere in the middle. The actions we take can affect

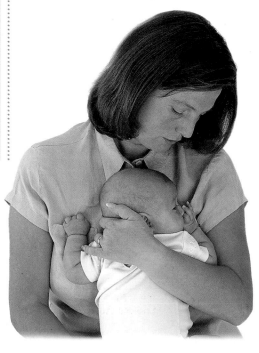

Well protected

By enclosing your baby and holding him close to your chest you create a "womb-like" environment for him and give him the reassurance he needs to face the world.

our level of arousal. We have all been in a situation where we freeze in panic, and then calm down as soon as we start to do something. Equally, we have experienced activities (dancing and sex are obvious examples) which make us more aroused.

Dips into low arousal (as in total relaxation) and into high arousal (as in riding a roller coaster) both feel good – so gauging the right level for ourselves is hard. Gauging it for our children is even more problematic. The only way we can judge what a particular baby needs, is to observe him carefully and act on what we see.

Why do babies' needs differ?

One theory suggests that individual differences are a result of very different baseline settings in the brain's arousal mechanisms. If the arousal level is set chronically low, people need lots of excitement to make them feel comfortable. These are typical rock climbers and parachute jumpers. If the baseline level is set high, even a moderate amount of excitement will be too much. These are the more timid and withdrawn among us.

Development of emotion

A newborn baby expresses disgust at an unpleasant taste or smell, and he will startle at anything unexpected, sudden, or loud. A few weeks later, he will respond with a happy smile when his face is being stroked, or to a change of arousal level in his sleep. Later, a face, a movement, a voice, or high-pitched sound will make him smile. After 12–16 weeks, he will laugh out loud at sudden noises or tickling. By 3–4 months he will show surprise. From birth, he will react to restraint with outbursts of anger, and later he will get angry when he is in pain. In toddlers, the anger may lead to tantrums. Sadness first appears in infancy, during prolonged separations, and a fear of strangers is first obvious at 6–8 months.

SEE ALSO

In his genes!	**114–115**
Temperament in babies	**122–123**
Becoming assertive	**128–129**
Aggressive children	**162–163**

ASSESSING YOUR BABY'S NEED FOR STIMULATION

	Most babies	The easily aroused	The slow-to-arouse
When hearing high-pitched sounds	Are delighted when their mother raises the pitch of her voice or shakes a rattle.	Are often upset and withdrawn when sounds are made; may shudder and cry at some sounds.	Do not always brighten when parent talks to them, even though they hear; may not respond to a rattle.
In a room with normal lighting, or when looking at an animated face	Show interest, look, kick and reach out for things you show them.	Are sometimes (or often) irritable and cry.	Often remain sombre and blank; may not respond to toys or their mother's face.
When his tummy is gently stroked	Are comforted and calmed.	Sometimes act as if stroking is unpleasant.	Show very little reaction.
When he is rocked vigorously or tossed in the air	Are happy and delighted.	Panic if tossed in the air.	Show little response to rocking; only respond to more vigorous activity.
When held upright	Prefer this position when awake.	Dislike this position; prefer a prone position.	Usually prefer this position.

Love takes time

At first your baby smiles at everyone and is happy to be passed around. Soon she will snuggle a little more closely when she gets back to you, and her face will light up.

In love with your baby

It is good to be around the people whom we love and who love us. They make us feel secure and give us the confidence to do things. Your baby will need your love in exactly the same way – as a security blanket.

From birth, babies have a strong need to be with people, but at first anyone will do. As your baby starts her third month, she begins to show interest in the special people in her life. It is around this time that she begins to know who you are, although she does not yet love you as you love her. Over the next 18 months, her love will grow, from "you're just about the nicest person to have around" (at two to three months) to "I want Mummy and no one else will do" (by the end of the year). Only at about seven or eight months do her feelings for you begin to match your own passion for her. By her first birthday it may well be as strong as yours; by her second birthday it certainly will be.

Bonding with your baby

The only difference between bonding and falling in love is that bonding happens more quickly, and the resulting love stays with us for life. There is little evidence that hormones are involved. Fathers love their children with exactly the same intensity and passion as mothers – and siblings or grandparents often do too. Love does not necessarily happen instantly, and it is not disastrous if it does not. True love grows from our knowledge of our loved ones, and love that develops with time can be just as passionate. Most parents feel passionate about their babies within the first month. If love is delayed beyond this, seek help.

My eldest son was the baby I had dreamed about, he looked like babies in my family usually look; blond, blue-eyed and very familiar. He arrived more or less on time. I loved him at first sight. I expected to feel the same second time around, but my tiny black-haired daughter was completely unfamiliar. She looked nothing like her brother, her father, or me. Before her birth I had four years of fertility treatment and one miscarriage. Looking back I suspect I was too afraid to really believe that this time my dream would come true. I was unprepared. She was three weeks early and born in the hospital waiting room after a labour of less than an hour. Six hours before I had been at work. The surge of love I felt when I first saw her brother was not there. Within the week I was back at work, her cradle on the desk beside me. I started my maternity leave when it was due – three weeks later. By then I had grown to love her just as much as I loved her brother.

Attachment

Most children (65–70 per cent) become firmly and securely attached to their parents in the first 18 months. We see the first signs of this once a baby can crawl. In a new place, or with strangers, she will crawl to you and remain close by. She will become anxious if you leave her. This anxiety reaches a peak at about 18 months.

Valuing herself

By the time your child is two, she will have begun to understand what she can expect from her care-givers. Eventually, these expectations will be used to evaluate herself: "Mummy likes me to play with my bricks: I'm good at building", or "Daddy loves me because I'm very lovable". If her parents ignore her pleas for love, she will not only try to gain their attention in other ways (by being naughty, for example), but also evaluate herself as unworthy of love. Her naughtiness can lead to bad temper in her parents, and they may call her names, which adds to her negative self-image. Warm loving from the parents plays such a crucial role in a child's development, because it has such a great influence on the way she interacts with others and the way she values herself. If a child forms a negative view of herself, it can be overcome, but the longer, more entrenched it becomes, the harder it will be to change.

Each child is unique
Once we know our child there is no way we could replace him with another. We recognize that this is a life-long and deep passion.

SEE ALSO
Everyone is lovable   116–117
Every child an individual 118–119
Building self-esteem   126–127
Providing riches   148–149

HELPING YOUR CHILD

To relate to you	To react to you	To feel secure	To reciprocate	To interact fully
● Be warm and interested in your child. ● Make her secure; if she needs to see you, stay in view. ● Be sensitive to your child's needs. ● Do not outstay your welcome. If she has had enough, let her withdraw. ● Woo her as you would woo anyone you love. ● Let her learn about love from you.	● Fine-tune your wooing. If your child is an excitable, fretful baby, be calm and soothe her into love. If she is a withdrawn baby, show emotion and draw her out of herself.	● Note what calms and what excites your child. Read her moods. ● Set aside time for pleasant and loving exchanges. ● Withdraw your attention, but never your love. Say "I love you to bits, but I do not like the way you are behaving now". ● Never undermine her view of herself. The behaviour is bad – not the child.	● Spend time with your child and do things together. ● Gain her attention, wait for her response. Interact, don't dictate. ● Smile and talk to her from across the room, and she will learn to feel secure even if you are away from her. ● Give her plenty of opportunities to hug and cuddle.	● React to your child's expressions and emotions. ● Respect your child's emotions. Help her to express what she feels. ● Help her to calm down. A child who is able to calm herself can also permit herself the freedom of over-excitement.

Temperament in babies

Parents often look back and confirm that a hint of what their children are now was there from the start. He may have progressed from a difficult baby to a temperamental child, or he was sunny from the start and still is.

Parents may say of their young scientist: "He was always filled with wonder, he always wanted to find out", and they are almost certainly right. Whether babies start as they go on, or are encouraged by others, has always been hotly disputed. There is evidence for both views. Certainly some babies are born difficult and continue on this path. Their "twos" are truly terrible; they are cranky children, moody teenagers and temperamental adults. Other babies have difficulty thrust upon them by illness and pain. Crying with chronic earache is understandable and forgivable, but for some early bad temper becomes a lifetime habit.

Babies learn to get us on their side, whether with smiles or with tears. Those who are born to smile (or whose carers make them smile) learn that smiling works. They start off smiling and they keep going. There is no reason to change tactics. Those who are born with an inclination to cry learn that tears will bring comfort and attention. When they need us, they cry and we respond. Maybe, if we ignored their tears more often, they would try smiling.

Different temperaments

When facing exactly the same situation, some of us blow up a storm, some seethe and some simply shrug their shoulders and keep their cool. For some happiness is hard

Gimmee juice!
A child will learn to scream to get his way if this is what his mother reacts to. If, however, she ignores shouting and reacts to a request, he will learn to ask quietly.

CLASSIFYING CHILDREN		
The easy child	40%	Playful, cheerful and generally happy, they adapt well to new situations and establish routines easily. Sunny babies, they fall asleep easily, are open to new impressions and rarely upset for long.
The slow-to-warm-up child	15%	Shy and withdrawn, they need time to adjust, then settle into routines. May be hard to wean, but will not be fussy. Fairly inactive, often a little negative; respond mildly rather than with enthusiasm.
The difficult child	10%	Cry a lot; generally negative. Hard to settle into routines, and easily disrupted. Will cry through the first year and not sleep as toddlers; likely to be difficult to wean and to settle into nursery/school.
The hard-to-classify child	35%	Sometimes easy, sometimes difficult; well adjusted in one situation but not in another. The sunny baby who rarely sleeps, the unhappy baby who does. Easy to put to bed; hard to wean or vice versa.

to find and invariably fleeting; for others a simple joy can colour a whole day. There are two influences here. Firstly, our "baseline" emotional tendencies can be set differently: we can blow up quickly or keep our emotions under control. Secondly, having blown up, we hold on to that mood for hours or drop back to baseline in minutes. Babies can only remember what happened from one moment to the next, so they usually react quickly and forget just as easily. However, the baseline moods of babies differ: a temper tantrum in most 18-month-olds only lasts a few minutes. Some have one or two a week, others four or five a day. By three the difference in frequency may still be there, but now some children remain upset for hours, while others still forgive and forget in minutes.

Meshing

Interaction is always a two-way street. A baby makes demands on his carers, and he also reacts to the demands they make on him. Some parental personality styles may cause meshing problems:

Withdrawn or depressed parents:
Depression is the most common reason for a parent's withdrawal. Depression can make the parent treat the baby in a mechanical way, without engaging the child's interest. An emotionally unavailable parent may fail to kindle the sparks of interest the child shows in the world. Because the baby withdraws, he fails to ignite his depressed parent's interest in him. It is a vicious circle which can influence a baby's attachment to his loved ones in the long term.

Overly subdued parents: Being subdued is not always tied to depression or active withdrawal. Some people simply do not show their emotions. They look at their babies without emotional expression, and speak to them in monotones which fails to

Sunny children
Whether sunny by nature or through careful nurture – easy-going children will find it easier to make friends in childhood and beyond.

engage the baby. An active effort is needed by the parent to overcome the tendency to hide emotion. It is impossible to change the habit of a lifetime but even half an hour a day of animated interaction will help the child. Fortunately, few people are consistently "flat"; mostly, withdrawal is a sign of temporary stress or depression – animation is easier if you are relaxed.

Excessive stimulation from parents:
Babies need engagement – but they also need calm. Too much excitement can leave the child overwrought and in need of a way out. Just as some parents are too subdued, others need to make a conscious effort to wind themselves, and their babies, down. A simple rule of thumb is that every period of excitement needs to be matched by a similar period of calm. An excitable child may well need more stimulation; a difficult or slow-to-warm-up child may need longer periods of calm. All children, whatever their basic disposition, need both: periods of excitement and of calm.

SEE ALSO
Every child an individual **118–119**
Becoming assertive **128–129**
Finding your own way **144–145**
Providing riches **148–149**

FOREVER?

We know babies inherit a tendency to respond in certain ways, because identical twins are so alike and because their behaviour is often very stable. A difficult baby can be encouraged to be less difficult, but this does not mean he will be easy. Many aspects change as the children become toddlers. Sociability, shyness, activity level and irritability are the most stable aspects of the child's temperament.

New foods
Easy-going children are open to new tastes while the more difficult child refuses the unusual.

Growing self-awareness

As adults we have a sense of identity that separates us from other people and makes us aware: "I am here and this is me". It is the stance from which we experience life. We are the heroes or heroines of our very own life stories.

We are aware of a chain of experiences, stretching back into our childhood and forward into the future. We write our life story from one central perspective – we are the "I" of our very own stories.

The heroine of the story

From the moment a child first perceives the world she views things from her own viewpoint, but at first she is unaware of this. She has neither a sense of her own body nor of a continuity of experience. If she sees an object, she believes it exists only while she can see it. If she looks away, the object disappears. If she sees it again, she thinks it is something new. Only when we see her watching her hands, and moving them to grab a toy, can we be sure that she understands her separateness from the rest of the world.

CHILDREN AND MASKS

By the time a child is four he knows that he always was and always will be "me". He still worries, however, that if he puts on a mask, he could turn into someone else. He knows he will not change, but he sees otherwise and the eyes win. If he puts on the Batman mask, he knows he is still "Joseph", but that does not stop him worrying about becoming Batman, the face he now sees instead of Joseph when he looks into the mirror. Until he is six or seven, what he sees is more important than what he knows.

Knowing there is a story

To have a real sense of a central character moving through space and time, a child must first realize that there is a "story". She must understand that there is a "before" and an "afterwards", and a place other than "here". As she sits with you, she has to realize that minutes ago she was being carried downstairs, and before that she was in her cot. A baby cannot do this – before nine months a child only recognizes things while she looks at them. When she is in her cot, the rest of the house is forgotten.

Recall and memory

Between six and 14 months two new skills emerge. The first is recall – occasionally something in your baby's environment seems to remind her of an event. Suppose you were going through the park and a dog frightened her. A five-month-old may be afraid the next time she sees a dog. A nine-month-old may feel uneasy when she gets near the park, even if there is no dog in sight. She can remember what happened there. The second change is memory – she starts to think about things even when she cannot see them. This is most obvious if she starts to miss you when you leave her, and clings to you when you try to go.

Defining yourself

By the time she can say short sentences she understands the concept of "me" and "you". She uses "I" or "me" and her own name interchangeably, and she refers to the

PICTURES OF ME

From about the age of four years, a child will begin to draw more recognizable pictures. She will, on many pictures, include a likeness of herself – she is the heroine of her own story and features in most contexts. The way she draws herself gives us several clues as to her self-image.

Is she tall or small in relation to other people and elements in the picture? Are any aspects of her body or her clothes larger than others, for example, her long red hair or her new blue shoes? All children focus on what is most important to them at any particular time in their drawings, so if she has hurt her finger, for example, that will be appear as disproportionately large.

person she is speaking to as "you" or by their name. People never address her as "me" but refer to themselves this way; it means that she can transpose what is said, and has a clear concept of what "I" means.

Besides "I", there is another, more public "me". I know this "me" as a woman, a mother, a friend. She lives in London, teaches psychology and writes books. She owns a blue car and has a pretty garden. She is untidy, optimistic and impulsive. This is who I feel myself to be, what I am, what I do, my personality, my possessions. You use many of these things that form my self-awareness to create your image of me, and I use them to construct my self-image – which can, and does, change over time.

Emerging self-awareness

A child almost certainly develops this sense of self through observing her own actions. From an early age she watches her hands as she reaches out to grab, and she adjusts her behaviour to manipulate those around her, but we have no clear evidence that she thinks of herself as "me" until she is about one-year-old. At this age a child shows more interest in a video image of herself than she does of another baby, but she will not recognize herself in it for another year.

At about two, a child begins to recognize herself in the mirror. If you place a spot of lipstick on a child's forehead and sit her in front of a mirror, a baby will rub the glass, but a two-year-old will recognize herself and rub her forehead. By three it is obvious that a child is self-aware: she defines herself by how she looks and recognizes herself in photos, she says what she likes doing and describes her possessions as "mine".

A child's self-concept

Together, the "I" (the heroine of the child's story) and the "me" (the sum total of her characteristics) form the true self. It is the child's own construction. Her self is defined by her own interpretation of her behaviour. It is coloured by her view of her own successes and failures, and how she thinks she looks. Adults or older children are able to abstract from a trivial failure to the big picture. A small child's view of herself is very black and white: she is good or bad, clever or stupid, depending on what she does at the time. We influence this view of herself. My mother's greatest gift was telling me that I was clever and beautiful and good. Not all parents are this generous.

SEE ALSO
Every child an individual **118–119**
Building self-esteem **126–127**
Becoming assertive **128–129**
Providing riches **148–149**

This is "me"

By the age of three, a child will describe herself by her looks, her likes and her activities: she is the little girl with black hair who likes playing the big, colourful xylophone.

Self-esteem is no more and no less than our love of self. We build it by assessing our worth. We judge ourselves on the things that matter most to us, and add in other people's criticisms, their praise and anger, our failings, and the way we have functioned in the roles we (and others) have set for us.

Some of these will help build a positive self-image, some a negative one. We end up with a montage of our positive and our negative aspects, as seen by ourselves and others.

Building self-esteem

A child's independence and security depend on his sense of self-worth. A child who feels good about himself does not constantly need to attract our attention. Even when we are busy doing something else, he knows that we love him.

A seven-month-old baby loves himself, and because of this he thinks others love him too. He does not separate his feelings from his actions, or his actions from yours. As long as he gets attention he feels loved. As he grows up, that feeling of being loved and lovable becomes less certain. He becomes watchful, he worries when you are not with him, he may panic when you leave. If your response to him is consistent and loving, he will gradually become able to cope with separation. He still does not like you to leave him, but at about 18 months he will feel fairly secure that you will return. Can he be sure of your love? If he is securely attached to you, the question will not cross his mind until he is 18 months. He assumes he is the centre of the world.

Feeling insecure

At some point in the second half of his second year a child's sense of his own self, and his feelings of

Daddy, don't go!

Your child will feel secure in your love until she realizes that you and her are two separate entities. Once she sees that she is her own self, she will also understand that she may be alone.

separation from his carers, increase. In many ways he knows you are separate from him, but in other ways he is less sure. Because his memory span is so short, he can only really think one thought at a time. He will assume you see what he sees because, when something captures his mind, it captures it fully and there is no room to think about you as a separate person who might be seeing something different. Sometimes he thinks of you, he checks where you are, you smile and say: "Hey, that's a nice picture you're drawing", and secure in the knowledge of your love he goes back to what he was doing.

Tantrums and smacking

The central point to remember is that a small child is desperately needy. He does not enjoy his tantrums. Lying on the floor, kicking and screaming, is a desperate and unhappy act. During a tantrum many perfectly normal children bite their arms or bang their heads until they bleed. He may know that you shout, but his need is so great that this does not deter him. In this context, a smack will just mean more pain.

From the child's perspective, what he demands as he screams in his tantrum, is not unreasonable. Now that he sees himself as separate from you, he must be reassured of your love. He simply must! He needs to know for certain what before he had just assumed to be true: that even though he is separate he is still the centre of your world. It is his growing feeling of separation from you that drives this need. In this context, clearly, what he asks of you is perfectly reasonable. His behaviour, however, is not.

He asks for attention, and if you smack you give it. At one level the smack fulfils his need. He has made you cross. He has become the focus of your attention. His tactics have worked. He is reassured that he is still the centre of your world. Next time he needs attention, he knows what to do. He has your attention, but he does not have your love. So while you reassure him on one front, his need for love gets even bigger. He remains more vigilant and watchful. Does she love me? If, after smacking him, you kiss and make up, you will stem that underlying need, but he has learned that bad behaviour pays.

Learning about himself

Once a child realizes he is separate, he begins the long process of understanding his own distinctness. He begins to look at all the ways in which people differ, and where he fits in. By three he can sort pictures into "little children" and "big children", and knows that he belongs to the "little" group. He becomes possessive. "Mine" he says, and snatches his toy from a friend. He insists on doing things for himself – even when he knows he cannot. He wants to put on his socks, he insists he can drive the car, he wants to walk up the steps when you need to use the lift. His powerful push for independence is a way of exploring himself. As he asks: "What can I do?", he is also asking: "How am I different from other people?", "Who am I and how do I compare?" By about four years, he has many of the answers. He can compare himself with other people on a whole range of dimensions and, as he compares, he will, in time, also judge.

Labelling can help or hurt

In the first two years a child's sense of security comes from the bond of love and trust he has with his family. Only if the bond is strong will he feel secure. As he develops a sense of separateness, his idea of himself as a person is increasingly based on his comparisons with others. Some are harmless: he is the boy with the blue coat whose Grandma lives at the seaside. Others are more unsettling: he is the boy who cannot run as fast, or who climbs second highest. Even a secure child learns that he is not always the best. If he believes that you love him for what he does and he does not do it well, he will feel that you love him less. The whole foundation of his security can crumble. Name calling gives him new categories to judge himself on. Say: "You are the very best Jamie in the whole wide world", and he knows on this one he is tops. But if you say: "You naughty bad boy – I'd expect that sort of stupidity from you", you will give him a much less favourable list to top.

SEE ALSO
Growing self-awareness **124–125**
Becoming assertive **128–129**
Finding your own way **144–145**
Providing riches **148–149**

I'm good at puzzles
With a developing sense of self, a child comes to define herself by what she can do. Labels can either help or destroy.

SELF-CONTROL

A child who loves himself does not need to reassure himself that he is loved by others. He knows he is loved. He does not need to reassure himself of his worth by constantly pleasing other people or by behaving badly to attract their attention. If he loves himself he can reflect back the love given to him with secure generosity. This makes him popular and lovable. There is love enough to spare for him to initiate loving. He is in control. He has self-control.

Becoming assertive

Two-year-olds can be terrible to handle, but despair not: your child's temper tantrum – and seemingly irrational behaviour – is also a sign of her growing up and separating from you. Above all, it is perfectly normal.

Unreachable rage
When your child is in mid-tantrum, there is not much you can say or do to snap her out of it. Acknowledge her feelings, then walk away to let her calm down.

While your child remained unaware that she is growing apart from you, a glance would usually reassure her. When it did not, she would crawl to you and cling to your ankles until you picked her up. As her sense of her own separate "self" increases, so does her need for reassurance.

Performing for an audience

As a child progresses into a full-scale tantrum, she will fall on the floor kicking and screaming, she will arch her back and scream. We may think she is frustrated, we usually say she is wilful, but she only has her tantrums if there is an audience, and only if that audience includes her nearest and dearest. If we walk away, she will stop. A three-year-old may be able to draw her session out longer, but at two she soon forgets what it was she needed. Either way, if we forgive and cuddle her, she will quickly recover. Once more she feels secure

in our love. From our unflinching love and support – which remains stable no matter what she gets up to – she learns that she is loved for herself, not for her actions.

Seeing both sides

We can look at the problem of the "terrible twos" from both sides. On the one hand, there is the child's need for reassurance as she discovers her separation from you. On the other hand, there is your need to deal with her totally unreasonable behaviour.

Her need for your love cannot be stopped in its tracks, nor cajoled, bullied, bribed, or punished away. Whatever you do, she will always make demands. These demands will stop, or at least become more reasonable, once she feels secure that she will remain the "apple of your eye", in spite of her separateness.

You will never be able to give her that security to last for all time – she will need continuous and ongoing reassurance. She will always need to know you love her to bits, and that nothing that she says or does will alter that, that your love is for herself and not for what she can, or cannot, do.

How to react to a tantrum

Dealing with your child's unreasonable behaviour is a completely separate matter. Remember that what she wants is your attention. She would much prefer to attract your loving attention, but failing that, any attention will do. If a child wants something, and finds a way to get it, she will, quite sensibly, use that way to get it again, the next time she wants it.

If you are ignoring her or giving her less attention than she wants (perhaps because you are concentrating on buying food for the next meal, or because you are on the telephone talking to a friend), and she can suddenly gain your full attention just by lying on the floor and kicking and screaming, then she is sure to fall to the floor again the next time the need arises. She does not have to plan this, nor even think about it. Such learning does not need awareness – we are often unaware of the little tricks we use to support our emotional needs. If we were not, most psychologists and counsellors would go out of business.

The best way to deal with the screaming child's demands is to ignore them. Keep an expressionless face, a relaxed body and walk away. If you cannot walk away, pick her up, take her out of the room and leave her in a safe place. Say nothing and do nothing that might suggest to her that you are concerned or angered in any way by what she has done.

Ways to stay sane

Power battles at meal- or bedtime, or in the middle of a shopping centre, can be intensely wearing on the parent, especially when other people give their "good advice" on how to deal with such a "bad" child. Ignore them, as much as you ignore your child's tantrums. Most of all, do not succumb to the temptation to spank.

● Start early. Defuse potential battle zones by getting your child used to different carers and surroundings from an early stage so that she will not be frustrated or worried by separation from you.

● If every answer you elicit from your child is "no", ask questions that do not permit such answers. Instead of asking her to put her clothes on, ask her: "Do you want to wear your red coat or your blue jacket?"

● If your child is very active, and her level of activity can mark the beginnings of a tantrum, make sure she has sufficient opportunities to "let off steam" before the temper has a chance to brew up.

● If your child adapts badly to new places, situations, or people, she may be better off playing in smaller groups of children, with older children or even by herself.

● If your child is easily frustrated and finds it hard to stick with one task, break tasks down into smaller bites for her. Ask her, for example, to put all her clothes into the wash basket, then to put all her pens into the box, rather than asking her to "clean up the room".

● Finally, remind yourself that this is not only a battle to gain your attention, or to separate from you, but a healthy sign that your child is growing up.

SEE ALSO

Becoming independent **164–165**
Attention seekers **172–173**
The twos and beyond **182–183**
From toddler to child **186–187**

BEST WAYS

● As much as you try, your two-year-old will not yet understand how to "share her toys" with another child. An easier way to make her do what you want is to teach her to take turns: "First you, now Jamie".

● Similarly, it is best to make her see consequences: "If you throw your food on the floor, I will take it away and you will be hungry" – but do not threaten her with something you will not do!

I can do it!

Apart from wishing to attract your attention, your child's wilful insistence is also a part of separating from you. If he wants to put his own socks on, let him at least try!

Boys and girls

Of course, little boys are not made of slugs and snails and puppy dogs' tails, nor little girls from sugar and spice and all things nice. If, however, you have parented both you may feel there is some truth in the old rhyme.

Mummies and Daddies

Even if parents attempt to bring up their children without stereotypical toys, the girls often end up playing with dolls, the boys with footballs.

GENDER TOYS

As adult sex roles have become closer, children's play has diverged further. One explanation is that small children no longer have clear adult role models. In the past, men worked to earn money, women did the housework and looked after the children.

Today, both parents wear trousers, do the same jobs, cook, do housework and look after children. The unique things about women are summed up in Barbie dolls, the unique things about men in all-action heroes.

The female gender dominates in nature. All foetuses are programmed to develop into girls unless they are "instructed" otherwise. Both egg cell and sperm carry sex chromosomes – each egg cell, formed in the woman's ovaries, has an X-chromosome, while each sperm, made by the man's testicles, may carry either an X- or a Y-chromosome. In fertilization, when two X-chromosomes meet, the child will become a girl, but when an X- and a Y-chromosome fuse, it will become a boy.

How boys develop

The Y-chromosome instructs a group of cells to become testicles – without this instruction they would become ovaries. Once the testicles develop they start to secrete the male hormone testosterone, and it is this which leads to the development of the baby's male body, with male internal and external genitals. Without testosterone, the developing baby becomes a girl, with female internal and external genitalia.

What can go wrong?

Occasionally, certain substances taken by the mother can be mistaken by the body for testosterone, and a female child will start to develop male genitalia. The same thing may happen if the mother has an overactive adrenal gland. If the baby boy's testicles secrete insufficient amounts of testosterone, he will develop incomplete male genitals. All such cases are rare and can be corrected after birth.

Gender identity

Gender identity is the feeling we all have that we belong to one gender or the other. In most cases these feelings correspond to our genitals. We look like women and we feel ourselves to be women. Occasionally, body and identity do not correspond, and some people find themselves trapped in the "wrong sort of body": men feel themselves to be women, or women feel themselves to be men. In some cases, the feeling is so strong that the person concerned will undergo a sex-change operation.

Such feelings are also sometimes present in children. No one is quite certain what causes us to feel we belong to a particular gender. It used to be thought that it was a matter of upbringing and environment, but the situation has become less clear in recent years. While some feel that gender identity can be purely learned, others suggest that this learning probably takes place against a strong predisposition to feel either male or female.

Developing an identity

As soon as a child is able to tell you whether he is a girl or a boy, he will do so, and even before he can talk there is evidence that he may be more interested in babies and children who share his gender. Although a two-year old will say he is a boy, he is by no means certain that he will grow up to be a man, or that he was once a baby boy. At two, a boy with a baby sister may assume that all babies are girls. He may also believe he will grow up to be a "Mummy". By the time he is three to four years old, he will probably have worked out that he was, and will be, male – but he may still feel that if he puts on a dress he just might become a girl. He certainly thinks this would be a very silly, and probably naughty, thing to do. By six, he is able to say that although he would not wear a dress, it is all right for other boys to do so should they wish.

Boys will be boys

There have been hundreds and thousands of studies into the differences between girls and boys, and men and women. Many differences have been found, but only a few are consistent. Men are more aggressive, they commit more violent crimes, are more likely to be in prison and to be studying engineering rather than languages. They also tend to have better spatial skills (reading maps, parking cars), but the overlap between the sexes is huge.

Men almost always hold the roles of authority in the world. Women do most work within the home. By the time they are three, children understand these gender roles. They may overstate them, saying "Mummies look after children" – even when their own parents share this role.

Girls often imitate mothering and household chores in their play, while boys imitate traditionally male, macho roles.

Sexual orientation

Gay men often say that they were clear about their sexual preferences from a very early stage in life. Some say that they knew they were different from the time they were about six or seven years old. It is not clear how true this is of all gay men. Not all boys who prefer to play with the girls, or prefer girls' toys, grow up to be effeminate men, but some do. In any case, not all gay men are effeminate.

In recent years, studies have been carried out which compared the brains of homo- and hetersosexual men, and there may be some evidence of differences in certain areas of their brains. Other studies looked at twins and the number of gay men within certain families. The results suggest a genetic predisposition towards a sexual preference, but both studies were highly controversial and not altogether clear.

The consensus of opinion is probably that there is a biological predisposition, but that this is by no means the only factor. Why some women are lesbians is even more complex, since many women do not become lesbians until quite late in life.

BOY OR GIRL?

Some years ago in the USA, identical twin boys were circumcised. In an accident the penis of one of the boys was burnt away. He had a sex-change operation and was raised as a girl.

At seven all seemed well. The boy wanted to be a fireman, the girl a doctor; the boy was rough, the girl sweet, although a little rougher than her worried mother would have liked.

At 14 problems began. The girl was called names by her peers, who said she walked like a man. No one was very surprised that she had problems.

Recently the story turned full circle. Now in his thirties the girl has reverted to being a man. He talks of a childhood in which he felt things were wrong, teenage years when he knew they were very wrong. He had another operation, and is now a married man with four adopted children.

Boys and girls at play
The differences between boys' and girls' play are marginal and there is much overlap. Generally, girls prefer to play in smaller groups of two or three, boys tend to play in larger gangs. Girls play language-based games; boys are more likely to be involved in sporty or even aggressive games.

ALWAYS

● **Seek those who will understand.** The hospital may be able to put you in touch with other parents who have gone through the same experience.

● **Communicate.** Sometimes it is easier to talk to strangers than each other. The crack in the relationship may become a chasm, with one parent escaping into a life outside the family while the other becomes engrossed in the child.

● **Give yourselves time.** It is not easy to accept that your child has problems. It is natural to feel angry and guilty.

● **Ask for help.** Most friends will want to help you, but are embarrassed to come forward, because they feel they are intruding.

● **Talk.** Find a person who will listen and talk. The answer to "Why me?" may be "Why not you?" but that will not stop you asking the question.

● **Love.** Your child needs more, not less, love.

● **Build esteem.** There will be so much to knock her down, she will need constant building up.

Not like others

The birth of a child with special needs is unexpected and traumatic. Parents will have to learn to care for a child who is different, but most of all they will have to come to terms with their own feelings of guilt and disappointment.

Some parents are so shocked by their child's disability that they avoid all contact. In some instances, the child may spend prolonged periods in hospital, which can make it difficult to bond with her. In other cases, the baby may not have long to live, but parents will find it easier to cope with loss if they have done everything they can for her, even if her time is short.

The child is not a tragedy

What has happened to the child is tragic, but she is not a tragedy and should not be treated as if she were. It is natural to mourn the child you dreamed of, but not to keep on mourning. Parents must accept the child they have. Their mood, and how they act when with the child, is important. Mothers who are happy with their babies have happier babies and bond with them more easily than those who are unhappy. When mothers are sad, babies are sad too.

Friends often do not know what to say and do. Some pretend the child does not exist; many assume that if a special-needs child dies it is a relief. Their feelings are not unkind, but complex – they feel deep sympathy, and they are relieved that this has not happened to them.

Some special-needs children are difficult to relate to because they provide very little feedback and their faces do not express their emotions. Touching may help; it also seems to have long-term positive effects on the baby who may cry less at six months than a child who has not had such contact.

Brain injury and cerebral palsy

There are literally hundreds of different types of disability, but most of them fall into two main groups: motor and mobility problems and mental retardation. Cerebral palsy, a neuro-muscular disorder, which causes a loss in motor control, is usually caused by brain damage, resulting from a complicated labour or birth. Difficult delivery positions, the early detachment of the placenta and strangulation by the umbilical cord are the most common causes. Premature babies, especially if they weigh less than 1,000 g (2 lb), may also suffer brain injury. Cerebral palsy is sometimes, but by no means always, accompanied by mental retardation and learning difficulties. Symptoms vary from mild to severe. Seizures, speech, hearing and visual problems may also occur.

Problems multiplying

Many children with cerebral palsy have problems combining their breathing with movement, as if they were always running too fast or too far. They find it hard to walk and talk at the same time, and so the children do not engage their carers in conversation while they are trying to move.

Because communication is laboured, adults often talk over the child, but this is very harmful to her self-esteem. Many cerebral palsied children find it difficult to do two things at once – such as holding a cup of juice and talking. Children without mobility depend on others to push their chairs, or carry them from place to place. Life is hard, and the inclination to help is enormous. Yet, if the child is to build her self-esteem, we must sometimes let her cope by herself. This toughness must, however, always be married with love and also with admiration for her achievements.

Down's Syndrome

Down's Syndrome is associated with delayed development, mild to moderate mental retardation and a distinct physical appearance. Babies have characteristic eyelid folds, round heads, short necks, protruding tongues and small noses. They walk with a flat-footed gait. As children, they are susceptible to heart defects and respiratory infections; as adults they age prematurely. They are affectionate, placid, cheerful and lovable, and bond strongly with their parents. Intellectual abilities are rarely severely impaired, but only a tiny minority can lead truly independent lives.

Development follows a near normal path until about six months of age, but then it slows down. Children have great difficulty with complex or subtle information, and while many start in a mainstream school, they rarely complete their education there. Children can be helped to concentrate on what they are doing by reducing the number of distractions around them.

Sensory deficits

Serious problems are usually discovered straight away, yet less severe visual and hearing problems may go unnoticed. If your child pays little visual attention, her eyes dart around unsystematically, remain crossed much of the time, or she brings things very close to her eyes to look at them, she may have impaired vision. If she does not jump at a loud noise or turn to voices, if she is often dreamy, she may have hearing problems. Get your child checked – partial impairments are hard to spot, but easier to treat in the early months.

One problem after another

Life is not fair, and a child with one problem will very often have another which may go unnoticed. A friend with a cerebral palsied child did not discover he also had an 80 per cent hearing loss until the child was eight. Look beyond the obvious and have your child checked.

SEE ALSO

Is everything all right? **68–69**

Every child an individual **118–119**

What parents worry about **142–143**

Resuscitating a child **210–211**

NEVER NEVER

● Talk of your child as if she was not there. Even if she cannot yet understand the time will come when she can. Get in the habit from the start of treating her as an individual.

● Expect disability. The more demands you make on her, the more independent she will become. There is a ceiling on her capabilities, but your aim as a parent should be to raise, not to lower it.

● Let her get away with bad behaviour. Socialization is very important for those who will always depend on others.

● Ignore your anger. Find a way to deal with it. If you do not, you may find it is all too easy to take out suppressed anger and frustration on your child.

● Ignore her anger. Find a way to help her express it.

● Isolate her from other children with disabilities. She will need friends who understand.

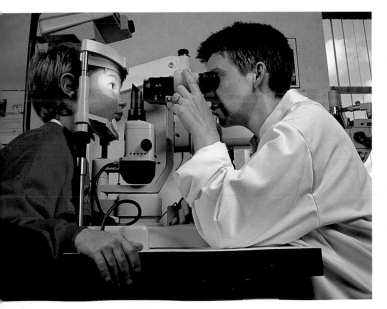

What can you see?

Both visual and hearing difficulties run in families, yet most vision- and hearing-impaired children are born into families without such problems. Never let your baby or toddler miss a developmental check so that any problems can be picked up early.

CHAPTER FOUR

Parenting skills

Few new parents have much experience of caring for children, so we take our first cues from our own parents: parenting is easy if we were fortunate enough to be well parented; it is harder, but not impossible, for those who were set a bad example. It is important to remember, though, that neither parents nor children are perfect, and that perfect parents would be a hard act to follow. If you love your children and are responsive to their needs, you will get it right most of the time.

First steps to parenting

Before you have a child it is hard to comprehend how much power he will have over you and how all-consuming his demands will be. Soon you will come to know him as the most lovable, demanding and exasperating person!

Retrace your history

Your relationship with your parents may not be the first thing you think about when you are expecting a baby, but it may reveal how you will parent your child.

It is impossible to foretell the panic a child's illness may bring, or the sheer delight of his first smile. You cannot imagine the all-engrossing nature of your obsession, or the fact that the emotions you feel for your child will never ever go away. It is the strength of these emotions that surprises us and entraps us. It is hard to explain to those without children just how it feels to know that someone will always hold the power to break your heart, or to put into words how frightening that vulnerability feels.

As you check his breathing again (and again and again), it is wise to recognize that such compulsive behaviour is our way of coming to terms with the enormity of the commitment we have made. Second babies are easier because, by the time they come along, we have accepted the potential heartbreak of parenthood and come to terms with the fact that this child will leave an indelible mark on our life.

Roots and shoots

Babies come naked into the world, but we adults carry an historical baggage of past relationships and roles: we were once the child, someone else the parent. The relationship we each had with our parents casts a long shadow over our emotional life. In our history of being parented are our earliest dealings with love, devotion, despair, anger, jealousy, pride, oppression, rejection, embarrassment, shame and a good deal more. Whether we parent in our own parents' image, or try to correct their mistakes, our own experience of being parented cannot fail to influence how we do it. We are destined to relive some of our parents' successes and failures, just as they were destined to relive some of their own

parents'. If we both had a background of good, enabling parents, the outcome is likely to be less traumatic than if we did not. It does not mean that those of us who were badly parented are destined to fail – many a child grows up determined and successful in throwing off a family history of bad parenting. It is just more difficult.

In times of stress the easiest route is to retrace our steps, to do what we know, to do to our children what was done to us. When both partners have very different backgrounds, such a reversion to "type" can lead to major disagreements.

Nailing the ghosts

Much of the turmoil of parenthood in these first weeks revolves around nailing ghosts from the past – our history of being parented and the ideas of parenthood we hold from this background.

Examine your own history: Is this how you want it to be? What changes will you make? Pregnancy prepares us for a dream. Now we have the reality. How are we going to deal with it?

Examine your partner's history: Is this how he wants parenthood to be? Do your views coincide? It is strange how little most of us discuss parenting. Yet it is the most important job we'll ever undertake.

Remember that memory is fallible: Revisit your childhood with siblings, cousins and childhood friends. Try to get a more accurate picture of what your childhood really was like. In times of stress you are likely to recreate the same patterns. It is good to know what to expect of yourself and what to try to avoid.

Beware of overcompensating: If you feel you were not loved enough as a child, it is easy to love too much and to smother your child rather than to stand back and let him grow. Too much independence, on the other side of the coin, may feel to your

child like he is being deserted. It is the middle ground you need.

Accept change in your relationship: We learned how to love by loving our parents. When we take love into a relationship, we inevitably have this model before us. In the relationship we have with our partner, each one of us is sometimes a child, sometimes a parent. How will having a child alter this aspect of our relationship? We need to suppress the feeling that being the child is inappropriate now we have our own baby.

Remember that love and relationships are complex: Our need to play the role of parent and child are part of the richness of all good relationships. Being a parent does not undermine these roles in the long run. Adjustment takes time.

Remember to be a couple: We need to be patient and to make time to reaffirm our relationships even though we are tired. Remember that you both need time to yourselves in order to accommodate the changes and time together as a couple. Get a baby-sitter and go out, even if it is only to walk around the block a few times.

Be patient: The majority of new parents do find the time to renegotiate their relationships and to redraw them with new riches. Do not rush and expect too much all at once.

Release the child in yourself: From our teenage years until the birth of a baby we are so busy growing up that we often lose sight of the child in us. It is odd to realize that you never grew up just when you first feel the full responsibilities of adulthood. Recognize that it is your child-like characteristics – the sense of wonder, of fun, your willingness to love and trust – that will make you a good parent.

Remember you will never be a perfect parent: A perfect parent would be the dullest parent on earth and an impossible role model for your children to follow.

SEE ALSO

A child is born	**12–13**
Your newborn baby	**64–65**
Active co-parenting	**140–141**
Relating to relations	**154–155**

DOS

Children do need a combination of love, understanding, security, firmness and discipline. It should always be clear to your child that there are no upper limits to your love and support for him; but he should be equally clear that there is definitely a bottom line to your tolerance and to what you will accept in his behaviour.

DONT'S

Children do not need inconsistency, insecurity, rejection, or constant criticism. Children should not feel unloved, nor ever fear the withdrawal of your love in response to their behaviour. They should not think it is impossible to please you, nor believe that they can do what they like, when they like and that they can get away with absolutely anything and everything. Set reasonable limits.

Share and share alike

Men and women have different biological roles. It is the man's role to impregnate a woman, and the woman's role to nurture the fertilized egg as it grows into a baby, and that baby while it grows into a child.

In addition to biological imperatives, there are, of course, social expectations, both contemporary and historical, of how we should act as man or woman, husband or wife, father or mother. Both biological roles and social expectations have changed drastically in the last 200 years. Women still nurture the developing foetus, but after the birth almost everything else could be different. And in another 200 years, it is likely to be very different from today.

Benefits all round

If the father shares in all childcare tasks, from nappies to night duties, he and the baby have a much better chance of bonding – and you get a much deserved rest!

Traditional parenting roles

There used to be no question about which parent cared for the children. Everyone accepted that childcare was women's work. Traditionally men provided, protected and chastised their children. They taught their sons manly things, but women provided the day-to-day care of both sons and daughters. Women combined childcare with a full programme of work. They also washed, cleaned, cooked, sewed and mended, all of which would have taken long hours in the days when families had six children or more, when household appliances were primitive and money to buy clothing was scarce.

Tasks inside the house were combined with what culture considered "women's work". In Europe this meant that women fetched water, sold fish and garden products, kept hens, milked cows, planted and weeded the vegetable garden, helped with the harvest and gathered food and kindling from the hedgerows. They also tended the sick and looked after the elderly and infirm. Tasks might differ slightly in different cultures around the world but the list was (and is) always long.

Changing times

Today such traditional role divisions have become less pronounced, and many couples expect to share household and childcare duties for most of the time. Like all voluntary codes of practice it does not always work. In theory, once women took over part of the men's role in providing for their families, the men would take over some of the childcare and the household tasks. Once the child is born there is nothing a mother can do that a father could not (except breast-feed), but tradition dies hard. Most surveys suggest that mothers still do far more of the day-to-day caring for children than fathers – the father's role is mainly restricted to playing with children.

Bones of contention

Once women return to work – as most do by the time the child starts school – this uneven distribution of tasks can easily become a major bone of contention, and disagreements are difficult to avoid. Most men know how to cook, wash clothes and do housework, yet once children arrive, they do all this less often and give less time to childcare.

● Part of the problem arises because women get a head start in hospital. They may not yet be very experienced in handling their baby, but they know more than the father because they have had some practice. All new parents worry that they could harm the baby, and many a new mother tends to "hover" over the father as he tries to do his share, which could make him feel insecure and incompetent.

● Part of the problem arises because men cannot breast-feed a baby. Most babies are comforted by the breast, and because men do not have this "comfort object" they are less able to quieten crying babies.

● Part of the problem arises because women take on extra household duties because they are not earning, during maternity leave. A man may see the increase in tiredness, the stresses and strains of having a new baby, but he does not always see that the woman has taken over some of his own chores.

WHO DOES WHAT?

Now you have a child it is time to look at the balance sheet. Which tasks do you both do? Which do you expect your partner to do? Does the list change when both of you are working? Tick the boxes below, tot up each column and discuss the outcome.

Typical baby care tasks

	Mother expects of father	Father expects of mother
Comforting the baby	☐	☐
Holding the baby	☐	☐
Changing the nappy	☐	☐
Dressing the baby	☐	☐
Bathing the baby	☐	☐
Feeding the baby	☐	☐
Preparing food	☐	☐
Putting baby to bed	☐	☐
Getting up in night	☐	☐
Taking the baby out	☐	☐
Playing with baby	☐	☐
Washing baby clothes	☐	☐
Taking to carer	☐	☐
Collecting from carer	☐	☐

Other household and family tasks

	Mother expects of father	Father expects of mother
Caring for other child	☐	☐
Taking to school	☐	☐
Taking home	☐	☐
Shopping	☐	☐
Cooking	☐	☐
Cleaning	☐	☐
Washing	☐	☐
Money management	☐	☐
Decorating	☐	☐
Social events	☐	☐
Washing up	☐	☐
Household repairs	☐	☐
Tending garden	☐	☐

SEE ALSO

A child is born	**12–13**
Sharing the care	**52–53**
First steps to parenting	**136–137**
Active co-parenting	**140–141**

AVOID DISPUTE

● Assume equal competence. Men are capable of looking after a child, but they need to learn how to do this.

● If you will return to work in the first six months, introduce your baby to a bottle in the early weeks. If left longer than this the baby may refuse a teat. The bottle allows the father to feed the baby and therefore to bond.

● Talk about the changes in work load and duties – which are temporary, which permanent? Do this before the birth, and before you return to work.

● Set up a rota. One person shops and cooks, the other does the washing. Swop the week after.

● Rotate childcare tasks – feeding, bathing, changing, dressing, comforting. Swop every week.

Regimented? Yes, but it is easier than arguing about who does what. Unless you take turns, who is to say who is doing the harder tasks?

DON'T WORRY

If you work, don't worry that:

● You are not caring for your child all day.

● He loves his carer more than you. Do not measure his love.

● He plays up when you come home. He is just testing you.

● He plays you off against the carer. All children do it. Ignore it and it will go away.

● He is deprived of mother love. Loving parents and carers are enriching.

DO WORRY

If you work, do worry about:

● The quality of the carer and that she has a warm bond with your child.

● The carer leaving. If your child loves her, he will be unhappy when she leaves. For younger children the effect is transient if all else is stable, but a rapid turnover can foster insecurity. Even babies are affected and not bond well, especially if both parents are working long hours.

Active co-parenting

Although mothers have usually been the main carers of children, they have rarely been the only ones. In the past, other female members of the family have helped bringing up a baby. Today fathers take a much more active role.

Co-parenting – or the shared caring for children – is not a new idea. What has changed in the past 50 years is who takes part in the care of the child and what is the nature of the responsibilities that the carers share. In the past, the child was cared for by the mother, but anyone who knew him felt free to chastise or comfort him and to report on him to his parents. Whoever had care had control, but today such assumptions no longer hold. Many parents now decide together who is to raise their children and how it is to be done. They expect outside carers to abide by their rules – which means, of course, that the parents have to be clear about, and agree on, their own ideas of childcare.

How to co-parent

● Do not expect others to read your mind. Tell your partner what you want and what you believe. There is no point in sulking because he has not done something he did not know you wanted him to do.

● Discuss how you want to raise your children before they are born. Try to compromise. Do not be rigid – reality has a way of undermining all our plans.

● Do not try to cling on to roles and responsibilities when shedding tasks. A father is not "Mummy's little helper".

● Dummies and bottles are wonderful inventions – use them to get a break.

● Recognize that having a small baby can be stressful for everyone, particularly if that baby is fretful and often unhappy.

● Children react to our stress and tend to be at their worst when we most need them to be good. This is natural. Our own problems undermine their security, and their feelings of insecurity lead to stress, upset and difficult behaviour.

● Recognize that in times of stress we all revert to our younger selves. Seven-year-olds revert to behaving like preschoolers, preschoolers like toddlers, toddlers like babies. Even parents lose much of their adult veneer. Be patient with yourself and with each other.

● Do not blame each other if stress makes you both act like teenagers, or if you find yourselves reverting to the sex roles which were instilled in childhood. None of us is completely immune to cultural stereotypes – even ardent feminists may suddenly wish to play "Mummies and Daddies". Fighting stereotypes takes a conscious effort. If we are tired from lack of sleep, we do not always have the energy to make that effort.

● Get things out in the open, explain the problem, then forgive and forget. Bearing a grudge takes away energy which would be better spent enjoying yourselves.

● Discuss new roles and allow each other some child-free (and also some work-free) space. If Saturday afternoon is his time off, Sunday morning should be hers. Be flexible. There will be times when one or the other will be under pressure at work and will need to temporarily shed some of their load onto the other. This is not likely to work if it is always a one-way street.

RECOGNIZING AND DEALING WITH CONFLICT ZONES

	Problem	Solution
Money	Children are expensive, and that expense is usually paired with the temporary (or long-term) loss of one income. The combination provides many opportunities for disputes.	Talk about the problems. The easiest solution is to separate money into different accounts: one for household, baby care and car expenses; one for holidays, new car, household goods and savings; two more for each partner's clothing and other essentials. Now divide what is left over down the middle and add it to your personal accounts.
Time	Babies take time. But whose time do they take and where can it be taken from? Before the baby arrived, there was time to work, to be together, relax, see friends, take exercise and talk. Now that full-time attention has to be given to the baby, something has to give. The inequality of that giving is a major source of conflict.	Talk through the problems and the solutions, taking into account the special circumstances of each partner. How can spare time be divided fairly? What are each partner's needs for social contact, for exercise of the body and the mind? There is not enough time to fill all these needs so what should be the priorities?
Sex	 During pregnancy women experience an increase in sexual desire, and sex can be very good. Birth changes all that. The constant demand of a new baby may lead to a lack of desire in the woman so she rarely initiates sex, while his desire for sex may seem like an unreasonable demand.	Balance is created over time. There is nothing wrong in occasionally giving pleasure you do not take or taking pleasure you do not give. Intercourse can be painful at first and the demands of a small child may seem endless. Men often feel rejected by the closeness between mother and child. They feel unloved, deserted and in need of the reassurance that sex can bring. No one in this situation has all right or all wrong on their side. Talking is essential.
Attention	Everyone needs to feel that they are special sometimes.	There is a time to head the queue and time to be at the back. Everyone – man, woman and child – has a right to a place at the front. Everyone has to take their time at the rear – including the baby. Sometimes he has to wait even if he cries.
Friends and relatives	Everyone wants to see the baby. If families come to stay, they should help out and try to get on with the others. But bossy, opinionated and domineering parents can be traumatic. 	Try to keep visits short and steer clear of conflict. You can avoid confrontation for a weekend, but perhaps not for a month. Problems are best addressed when you can think more clearly. It is your baby and your life. You must make your own decisions and they must abide by them.
Mixed doubles	Sometimes a whole family can do things together, at other times someone gets left out and jealousy, anger and frustration can occur. Within a family one parent must relate both across their generation and down to the child, and these two roles can lead to confusion and conflict.	Triangular relationships are always more problematic. Find time to sit down together and talk. Accept how the other feels, which does not mean that you must accept how they act on those feelings. Emotions are difficult and sometimes impossible to control. Behaviour is not.

IMMUNIZATION

- The risk of adverse reactions to oral polio vaccine is one in 8.7 million.
- After combined diphtheria, tetanus and whooping cough vaccine (DTP), pain, redness and swelling where injected, mild fever, feeling fussy or drowsy and vomiting are common.
- See the doctor if your child is very drowsy, screams with a high pitch, is unusually limp or has fits. Such symptoms indicate a brain infection which may only appear after a week. They are very, very rare and unlikely to produce long-term brain damage.

Safe sleeping

There is some evidence of increased risk of cot death in babies who sleep on their tummies, especially if they have a cold. Make sure your baby sleeps on her back.

What parents worry about

There is always something to worry about: the more you "look" the more you find. The problem is, of course, that you love your child so much and that there is no way you can protect her from all the ills of the world.

Your fears as a parent will range from the very rare childhood diseases and deformities to worries about molestation or abduction. Such worries are a reflection of the depth of your love. Face up to your fears, find out about the realities and then enjoy your baby without excessive worry.

Common worries

Cot death: Cot death or SIDS (Sudden Infant Death Syndrome) is not nearly as common as many parents believe. It seems to be less common in cultures which carry and sleep with babies. Bottle-feeding has been associated with increased levels of SIDS, but it is not clear why this is.

Baby snatchers: A typical theme in TV drama and thrillers, it is so rare in real life that we can discount it. Your baby is more likely to be struck by lightning. All cases of baby snatching make the national news. How many have been reported since you became pregnant? Relax!

Hidden problems: One in ten children are born with a minor problem; most are easily put right. Most serious problems are recognized within days of birth (deafness and autism being exceptions). If you have not been told there is a problem when you leave hospital, there probably is none.

Deep-seated fears

Accidents: Serious accidents involving small children are rare and can be minimized by child-proofing the house, strapping babies into pushchairs, using high chairs and car seats and remaining vigilant. "Near misses" are rarely as near as we think they were.

Nasty men: Abuse by strangers is very, very rare and has barely increased in the last 50 years. Paedophiles rarely molest children they do not know. Ask yourself how often a child in your neighbourhood has been abused or harmed by a stranger.

Mistreatment by someone we know: Of all the dangers your child could be exposed to, this is the one which worries us least; yet it is the one most likely to occur. Most children who are abused – whether physically or sexually – are abused by a parent, family member, neighbour, carer, or family friend. Sexual abuse of small babies and tiny children is exceedingly rare. The risk increases as children grow up, peaking in the early teenage years. Physical abuse is most likely to happen to babies, toddlers and preschool children. Unless you have reason to be suspicious, watching and waiting for sexual abuse to occur would be very disruptive to any relationship. However, if a child has repeated or unlikely injuries (such as two black eyes or bruising

which is always hidden under clothing), consider carefully whether the explanation given to you fits the facts. If a child is more knowledgeable about the mechanics of sex, or behaves in an overtly sexual way with other people, be extremely watchful.

Maltreatment at our own hands: It is only once we have experienced a baby screaming for two hours, that we can begin to understand how anyone could harm a small child. Once we have felt the frustration, worry and desperation of trying to control our uncontrollable thoughts, we will understand all too well. Luckily, the frightening desire to throw this screaming bundle out of the window has virtually nothing to do with reality. We know that in some situations we could harm a child, yet the vast majority of us never do so. Most parents have been there, but they know how to control their impulses. Very few parents and carers actually harm children. If you think you might, get help before you do.

Your child is lost: Children are more likely to get lost in crowded places, the beach, the park or when shopping than they are to wilfully run away from home. They are almost always found very quickly. If you are visiting such places, a wristband with your name, address and telephone number (particularly your mobile number) are useful. Agree a meeting place should you mislay each other.

Dangerous places: Most accidents happen in our homes or cars. How many people do you know who have had a serious accident anywhere else? How many do you know who have not? Relax. It is very, very unlikely to happen.

Immunization: In order to eradicate the diseases that once killed and maimed thousands of children, all children need to be immunized. Children can be vaccinated even if they have neurological disease,

cerebral palsy and convulsions which are not the result of neurological illness. When assessing the risk of vaccination, remember that whooping cough kills one in 100 infected children under six months.

After recent publicity, many parents worry about the combined measles, mumps and rubella vaccines (MMR). Slight reactions to it are indeed common. About one in five children develop a mild

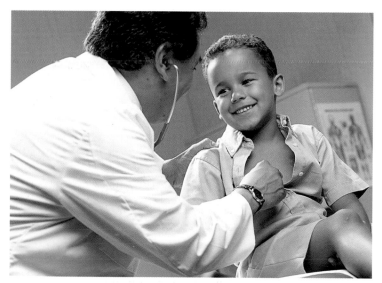

fever, about one in seven a rash or swollen glands and one in 20 aching joints which may persist for up to three weeks. There is a small possibility that MMR may cause encephalitis (brain infection), convulsions and nerve deafness, but it is extremely rare. The MMR should be delayed if your child has a cold or fever, because this makes it less effective, and clinical advice should be taken if the child has a disease or is taking drugs which lower the body's resistance to infection or is allergic to antibiotics.

Measles may have serious and sometimes fatal complications. Mumps and rubella are relatively mild, but can have serious consequences for adults. Rubella can cause birth defects, and mumps, deafness and sterility in adults. All this can be avoided through vaccination.

SEE ALSO

Is everything all right?	**68–69**
Not like others	**132–133**
Typical baby problems	**178–179**
Typical toddler problems	**180–181**

Promoting health
Every child who can safely be immunized should be. For most, the dangers of catching the disease far outweigh the dangers of immunization. Only in the case of serious illness will your doctor advise against it.

CONTROL

- Permissive parents are warm and loving but make few demands upon the child. Their children tend to be less self-reliant and self-controlled than children raised in more authoritative households.
- Authoritarian parents are cool emotionally. They tend to restrict, control and punish. They also demand unquestioning obedience. Their children are often more withdrawn, aggressive, unhappy and distrustful.
- Authoritative parents are mostly confident, warm, rational and self-correcting. They encourage their child's autonomy and curiosity but enforce rules firmly and expect a high level of achievement. Generally, their children tend to be more independent than the children of authoritarian or permissive parents.

Parents need time

Make sure your child understands from the start that, sometimes, he will have to wait while you are doing something – talking on the phone or drinking a cup of tea.

Finding your own way

Over the years, the fashions in parenting have changed from authoritarian to permissive to authoritative. There are no hard-and-fast rules. You will need to find your own style, allowing your children to thrive in a loving environment.

Most parents are strict about some things and more permissive about others. A few are strict about most things, others almost totally permissive. There is no "right" or "wrong" – provided there is consistency, mutual respect, tolerance and lots of love. Families are happier if children fit into the family style. If you hate clutter but do not mind the children staying up until midnight that is fine. If you can avert your eyes to mess but need some peace to wind down at the end of the day that is fine too. Inconsistency causes problems because it confuses your child.

How to parent a baby

- Love your children, not for what they are but for who they are, and let them know by word and deed that they are loved.
- Children under two do not understand right and wrong or good and bad

behaviour, but they can understand that one thing always leads to another. Make sure you set up the contingencies you want and avoid those you do not want. If you want your child to go off to sleep quickly, put him to bed and leave. Do not allow him to use your breast as a comfort object if you want to wean him at ten months.
- If your child demands and insists on what you have taught him to expect, he is not being wilful or unreasonable.
- Every child is an individual. You cannot stop some children being exuberant, nor others being shy or cautious. You can make small changes and help him cope with things he finds difficult, but his nature and abilities reflect the person he is, not the person you wish he was. The more you try to force him into your own mould, the more you undermine his confidence.
- Forgive him for being bad-tempered, but do not give in to that temper.
- Parents have needs too, even if it is just a conversation with each other or time to read the newspaper – your needs should sometimes come first.
- Do not make any silly rules in advance. If your baby sleeps better with a dummy, so be it. Not all principles are worth keeping.
- If you find it difficult to love and care for him, ask for help and keep asking.

How to parent a toddler

- A toddler's growing sense of self-awareness means he is able to think about what he wants and to contrast that with what his family want him to do. This inevitably leads to clashes and defiance. "Me do it" and "No!" are often heard. He wants attention and will learn how to get it. If you are concerned about his diet, tidiness, or bad language, he may play on this, doing those things that we find hardest to ignore. Our best defence is "no comment". The most effective discipline for a toddler is to withdraw attention from bad behaviour and never rise to the bait. Develop a poker face and a poker stance and walk away (or pick the child up and remove him). Allow a short cooling-off period, then return. Smile, talk, forgive and forget. If he is upset, offer comfort.

● Toddlers still do not understand rules but they can learn cause and effect. If his bad behaviour attracts your attention, he learns to be bad more often. If he gets your attention by being good, he learns to be good. He will always do a certain amount of both, but you can adjust the balance.

● Some people find that a daily session of holding the child very firmly reduces naughtiness. The technique is a bit like squeezing out the naughtiness, and it may not work for you, but it is worth a try. Gather him up, hold him tight, even if he wriggles, be still and keep on holding until he quietens, then another five or ten minutes. Relax your grip and talk to him.

● Toddlers need to let off steam. If you have a regular schedule, mixing boisterous and quiet times, you will find it easier to manage your child. Stimulation "winds him up". If you want him to sit quietly, cut the noise and excitement until you can allow him to "let go". Turn off the radio, turn down the lights and speak softly.

● Love him uniquely, and tell him: "You are the very best Dan in the whole world".

● Children are more likely to be helpful if you show them what to do. Remember that children imitate their parents.

Allow your child to grow
If he wants to help you lay the table, do not insist on doing it yourself. Show him how to do it, and that he will need to be careful, and he will quickly learn.

SEE ALSO
Every child an individual **118–119**
Building self-esteem **126–127**
Attention seekers **172–173**
Making things worse **174–175**

How to parent children over three

● As with younger children, love him, show him that love, make it unique to him.

● Give attention to good behaviour. Keep using the poker face and stance when he is behaving badly. Separate and remove yourself from him when he is naughty.

● Be tolerant. No one can always be good. Let small things pass without comment.

● Treat him as an individual and fit your expectations to the child, not to an ideal.

● Set limits that reflect your child's growing independence. His competence and responsibility will dictate how fast these expand. Remember that a child will not develop independence if he is always controlled and dominated. If you never trust him, he will never be trustworthy. Give him the structure, determine the rules, but with those rules and with that structure, give him options and choices. It is surprising how mature children can be.

SUMMING UP

● Love uniquely and show that love.

● Be consistent.

● However strict or permissive you are, try to value your child's individuality and self-expression.

● Never ask twice or threaten what you cannot deliver. Children simply ignore what they can get away with.

● If it is unimportant, do not interfere.

● Let your children sort out their own problems.

● Do not always expect all the family to do the same thing at the same time.

ENCOURAGING

● If your child is harming others and you punish or stop her without explaining what she did wrong, she will not learn how to be helpful.

● If you go away from the child when she is hurting others, or if you restrain her without explaining why you are doing so, she will tend to be less helpful.

● If you explain the consequences of a child's behaviour for the victim – "Tom's crying because you pushed him" – she is likely to be more helpful.

● If you explain to a child the emotional consequences of her wrong-doing to herself – "When you hurt Tom he does not want to be near you" – the child is more likely to intervene and offer comfort.

Raising a helpful child

A tiny baby wants something, and she will cry until she gets it. A seven-year-old may behave like this some of the time, but she will also have learned to be concerned and helpful to others rather than always making demands.

Babies are aware of their carers' moods, but they do not take their feelings into account. If you are upset, your baby is likely to be upset too and to behave accordingly. By 18 months, a child who has been praised for caring, and seen others care, will sometimes act in a concerned and helpful way, but most of the time she will still just reflect the mood of those around her. In the next 18 months she will be more and more influenced by what we do, and how we reward her for her own behaviour, and she will gradually show more concern for others and become more helpful in her activities.

One study showed that the average preschooler showed concerned helpfulness or sharing behaviour once every ten minutes. Unfortunately, not all children are so kind and helpful. Children whose every demand is being indulged by their carers learn that selfishness pays better dividends than mutual care, and a child

Some for you

A toddler will not always share his sweets with his sister, but if she falls over and grazes her knee he will almost certainly offer her one.

with selfish, self-centred parents is likely to follow in her parents' footsteps. By three and a half years, children are beginning to understand that other people have thoughts and feelings of their own, and that these are separate from hers, and this understanding will increase the empathy and sympathy they show for others.

MILESTONES IN EARLY HELPFUL BEHAVIOUR

Birth to 6 months

A baby responds positively to others, plays social games such as peek-a-boo and reacts emotionally to the distress of others (she will, for example, cry when others cry).

6–12 months

A child takes an active role in social games, starts to share things with others and displays affection to those she knows.

2 years

A child points things out to those she knows, and complies with simple requests; she understands the rules in simple co-operative games; she knows how to care for others, comforts people in distress and helps friends and family.

3 years

A child draws people's attention with words as well as actions. When she is being helpful and caring, she is so intentionally. She offers to help, or suggests that she will help, and shows evidence of knowing what "helping" entails in practice.

Helping a child to be helpful

Praise good behaviour: This is probably the most successful method with younger children and continues to be effective as the child grows up. Even as adults we still like to be appreciated.

Criticize bad behaviour: This is also effective, especially if it is combined with praising good behaviour.

Preach right and wrong: Research suggests that telling children in advance what they should do in a particular situation is not very effective – especially with younger children. It may become more effective as they get older.

Set a good example: It is far more effective to present a positive role model than to preach, especially with younger children. Studies suggest that, in children over five, parental example is by far the best way of ensuring children are helpful.

Just for you
Do not give the same thing at the same time: give your son a new jumper when he needs it, your daughter a book that she wants to read.

Reducing competitiveness

Some cultures are more competitive than others. City children are, generally, more competitive than children who grow up in the countryside, and boys tend to be more competitive than girls. Children will be less cooperative the more competitive the society is in which they grow up.

● Set an example. Children will not co-operate if everyone around them is busy competing against each other.

● If you are competitive – or you and your partner fight for supremacy within your relationship – expect your children to copy you and also be competitive.

● Create an inclusive "we" environment, encourage your children to help you and each other – not as a favour but as a matter of course, regularly.

● Do things together. Involve your children in the household (clearing up toys, cleaning, shopping), at mealtimes (laying the table, washing up, cooking) and in the garden (watering, weeding and caring for plants).

● Encourage and expect cooperation from your children. Studies suggest that those who are helpful when they are three-years-old are also likely to be helpful when they are ten-years-old.

● Show children from an early age how to help those who are less able – because they are younger, older, frail, ill

● Give according to need – not according to some rule of equality. Children can see to the last crumb which is the biggest piece of cake. If you are always trying to be even-handed, you will encourage the opposite – intense competition. If there are no opportunities for comparisons, there will be less for them to compete about.

● Love each child uniquely. Never say that you love them both the same – they will only spend their time comparing and checking to see if this is really true.

SEE ALSO
Caring about others   **110–111**
Providing riches   **148–149**
Running a family   **166–167**
The twelve golden rules **170–171**

COMPETITION

As babies grow up, they become more helpful. They copy you and others, and they are pleased with themselves when they do things for you. Problems arise because in Western society winning is rated so highly. We praise success rather than cooperation.

Traditional games of luck are being replaced by young versions of adult games (mini-rugby, mini-football), and activities like dance where trophies, exams and diplomas mark winners from losers. As they grow up, competitiveness drives out children's natural helpfulness. Most seven-year-olds are less helpful to others than they were when they started school.

UNIQUE LOVE

- Give each child unique love, not equal love.
- Give each child what he needs, not equal shares.
- Give each child the time he needs, not equal time.
- Do not ration the help you give. If Jack needs more, give it to him.
- Do not exclude. If Jack needs more help to get dressed than Gemma, concentrate on Jack – but find time to help Gemma with a puzzle if she asks.
- Allow each child to be themselves.

A friend on holiday

Ensure that your child will have something familiar on holiday to give him security in a new place. A favourite toy or book is more important than an extra T-shirt.

Providing riches

Love is the greatest wealth we can give our child but, like a well-fitting coat, that love needs to be uniquely fashioned to suit your child. It should not be a one-size-fits-all, general-purpose and all-smothering blanket.

Our love for each child needs to be unique, and it should be seen by the child to be so. Our children should be loved for themselves, judged by their own standards, spoilt, chastised, indulged and treated in unique ways. It is not the fact that you love your child uniquely that is important, but that he knows you do.

Esteem – the essential gift

It is hard to survive and prosper without esteem. For each of us the safest and most secure esteem comes from within. The best gift you can give your child is to teach him how to love himself unconditionally. Not just when he is being good and doing well, but always. Self-esteem is loving yourself because you are you. If love does not come from within, it has to be created or demanded from others. Either route is a chancy business. Success can bring esteem, but only if that success continues. We can demand from others, but they may refuse.

Protecting self-esteem

No put-downs: Make it a rule not to call each other names.

Confront those within the family who would hurt: Teach him to pause when someone says something hurtful then to say "Ouch", hiss like a snake, or ask what is wrong. The pause causes discomfort to the person being hurtful, and the question or comment wrong-foots them.

Walk away from hurt: Outside the family and close friends it is best to withdraw without comment (either word or action). Show him how to keep a poker face, ignore and simply walk away. Bullies need victims. A child who refuses to be cast in that role is less likely to be picked upon.

Providing security

A child's security comes from what is constant in his environment: his parents, his family, his home, his daily routine. This is especially important for a tiny child whose fragile memory depends on the cues in the environment around him. A one-year-old will only remember the game you played yesterday when you are sitting together in the same chair to play it today.

Fostering security

- Establish a routine and stick to it – especially in times of stress and change.
- Express your love for your child both physically and in words.
- Do not sneak out when the child is not looking. Make it clear you are leaving –

and make it clear that you have come back. Explain to an older child how long you will be away. Make a chart or draw a clock, so he can see when you are due back.

● Give him something to remember you by. A special badge that tells him you are thinking about him.

● Give him means of coping, such as a teddy to cuddle if he feels a bit sad.

Fostering independence

Independence should grow naturally, but you will need to encourage your child. If you always pick up his toys he will expect you to carry on doing this. Sooner or later you have to let go. It can be hard to accept that a child who has shared everything with you no longer wants to tell you what he is thinking or what he has been doing.

Respect his privacy: Do not expect him to tell you everything.

Respect his space: He will not learn to take responsibility for his own safety if you never allow him to do so.

Make progress: At two, lift him up to post a letter; at three, let him walk the last few yards and post it himself. By four he can buy something at the corner shop. By eight most children can go to school by themselves. By ten they could take the bus into town. Eventually, he will go out in the world, fend for himself, make his own mistakes, deal with his own problems and create his own happiness.

Creating a stimulating environment

A stimulating environment is not one that is packed with exciting things. It is one where the level of excitement is managed and where activities are presented one at a time. Small children are easily distracted. If the TV is on and the toy box overflows in the middle of the room, he will flit from one activity to the next. If he only has paper and crayons, he will draw.

Improving family relationships

For older children, formal methods can be used to regulate family relationships.

House rules: Set out clear rules stating how each person and their property should be treated, how each person can expect others to speak to him, what to do about rudeness and so on. Write the rules down, and make it clear that punishment follows if a rule is broken. "We do not hurt the cat. That is the rule. Go to your room and think why that is a bad thing to do."

Family contracts: A contract can work because children have an inherent sense of fairness. One person makes a binding agreement with another, for example: "Liam agrees not to borrow Leah's crayons without asking. Leah agrees to lend Liam her crayons when she is not using them. In exchange Liam agrees to let Leah ride his bike when he is not using it." The children sign, and the contract is placed in a box.

Family meetings: Every family member has the right to state their case while the others listen. The family then reaches a joint conclusion. Praise is given for jobs well done, and success is acknowledged. The idea of such meetings may be a little idealistic, but many of the principles are worth taking on board.

Growing independence
Acknowledge the fact that your child is growing more independent and give him his own duties and responsibilities, such as feeding or cleaning a family pet.

SEE ALSO
Building self-esteem   126–127
Becoming assertive   128–129
Becoming independent   164–165
Running a family   166–167

STAR CHARTS

The best way to change a child's behaviour is to praise him when he is "good" and ignore him when he is "bad". Star charts are an acknowledgement of effort and improvement. Start by asking very little, then gradually increase demands.

The child gets a star when he reaches a new goal. So, for example, he could start by gaining a star if he manages not to shout at his brother for half an hour, then for an hour, and so on. A full chart can be exchanged for a small present.

Talking to children

Education is based on language. A child who cannot express herself well is likely to fall behind with school work. Your child needs to learn how to speak and how to listen – and you will need to show her how to do it.

Enjoy your meal!

Make a conscious effort to eat together whenever possible, even if you get home at different times. The family table is a great forum for family chats.

A child who cannot tell you what she wants is likely to grab what she needs by behaving badly. Children do not just need help with language. They need help expressing their needs and their feelings.

How to listen to what children say
● Give a child your full attention and make sure that she knows that you have done so. Turn off the TV, face her, look her in the eye, lean in towards her and respond to what she says. "Hmm mmm" will do.
● Do not deny or reject what your child is saying. If she is frightened to go upstairs alone, acknowledge that this is true and think about ways of helping. Naming a feeling will help her to cope. Telling her not to be silly does not.
● Describe how you expect her to act. "I expect you to look after your things."
● Make sure your child is aware of and accepts your feelings. She must know that you also have certain rights.
● Do not allow her to give up.

● Accept and express what the child must feel and help her to clarify her feelings.
● Let her know you also make mistakes. Laughing at the silly things you have done helps her to come to terms with her less than perfect efforts.

Finding opportunities to talk
Small children like to look us in the eye as they talk – and this is perhaps one reason why so many children still have problems expressing themselves when they start school. Much of our children's lives is spent looking at the back of their parents' heads in the car or sitting beside them while watching TV. We need to make a conscious effort to find time to sit and talk and to sit and listen.

When boys are playing together, they tend to shout in short sentences. Girls speak more softly and use longer sentences. To help your son communicate, give him the opportunity for extra talking practice.

Talking it over – woman to boy

Some boys talk more to their fathers than their mothers. If yours does, and his Dad is often absent, make time to talk to him.

Children should be praised

There is an old sporting saying that it does not matter whether you win, only how you play the game. It is not a sentiment many people apply to life these days, but it is a good model for appreciating other family members. It is not just what they achieve that matters, it is the effort they make. Children need firm guidance, but not need every decision made for them.

Teaching by example

In the earliest months we need to train children rather as we would train a pet, rewarding them when they get it right and ignoring or punishing them when they get it wrong. As they approach their first birthday, they increasingly imitate what we do, and our example becomes ever more important. If we say one thing and do another, they follow our actions rather than our ideas, because they understand deeds better than words. As they grow up, they begin to do what they think is right and what they think will please us most.

Talking to other people

Unless your child learns the habits and skills of conversation in the home, she is bound to have difficulties communicating with others when she first enters playgroup, nursery and school.

● Always give a child time to reply. Be patient; it may be difficult for her to express herself.

● Always explain things simply. Help your child by interpreting and expanding on what she is trying to say.

● Read to her. Remember that vision dominates, and so a child who is watching TV may not be paying any attention to what she hears. One of the reasons a child looks into your face as she speaks is to cut out all the distractions.

● Encourage your child to talk to other people. Do not let unrealistic fears of abusive strangers undermine such opportunities. There is no point in telling a child that she should not talk to strangers if you do not allow her out on the streets by herself anyway. She will only remember it when you are with her, and at such times there is no danger. She will gain confidence by talking to people when she is out with you. Such conversations may be more demanding, because strangers are not as skilled at interpreting what she is trying to say. When she is old enough to go out alone, you can explain the dangers to her.

Let's read together

Read a book to your child. Listening will improve her vocabulary, and if she is sitting with you as you read, she can follow the words while looking at the pictures.

SEE ALSO

Smiling and babbling	**86–87**
Learning to speak	**96–97**
Perfecting language	**100–101**
Attention and memory	**104–105**

ALWAYS

● **Wait.** She may not find it easy to say what she wants to say, but she will need to try.

● **Give feedback.** You do not have to say anything, but you do need to show interest.

● **Interact.** Ask questions. Discuss what you read and what you watch.

● **Praise.** With praise, she will be more ready to talk.

● **Give her some independence.** Decisions she makes encourage her to think – and talk things through.

CHAPTER FIVE

A place in the family

The nuclear family is not very old – before, parents and siblings died young, mothers worked hard in home or field, and fathers went to war or work away from home. City children often lived with grandparents in the country, widowed fathers remarried, and children were often cared for by older siblings. Most of the issues that face modern families – sibling rivalry, jealousy, family break-up, care outside the home and the separation of the child from one or both parents – are not new, nor are the methods for coping with them.

Relating to relations

Most children start their lives with two parents and, while they are unlikely to have both sets of grandparents and all aunts, uncles and cousins on the doorstep, they will still gain a sense of their place within an extended family.

In Western societies, where divorces are frequent, most children still start off in a nuclear two-parent family, but for many of them the extended family will eventually also include a step-parent as well as step- and half-sisters or -brothers.

A child who grows up with one or both parents will not understand many aspects of living in a group until he starts to attend nursery school. He may not realize that adults have to share out their attention between different members of the group, or that children often have to wait until it is their turn, or that not everyone is always willing to fall in with what he wants at that point in time – as may have been the case when he was alone with his parents.

Remember me?

If a parent has to be away for a period of time, to work abroad for example, sending regular letters, photographs, or audiotapes is a good way to keep in touch.

Letting others care

If you are a first-time mother it is always difficult to believe that anyone else can care for your baby as well as you can, or that your child might be just as happy with someone else as he is with you. No one can replace you or your special relationship with him, but that does not mean that he will be unhappy with other people. Love has a way of multiplying. The more we love, the more love we receive back. The less we love, the more bereft we are of love. A baby who loves others is also beloved by them. He is likely to be happy and secure, and he will love you more, not less.

Voices and images

After my husband and I had separated, my children used to receive a weekly story tape from their father. If he was away, this would include news as well as a chapter from the current book. He read them all the classic adventure stories: *White Fang*, *Coral Island*, *Treasure Island* as well as *The Hobbit*, *Black Beauty* and many more. The children used to listen to them in bed at night, and they always gave them a topic of conversation when he phoned. These days, video tapes can be used too.

Relating to grandparents

The relationships between the older and younger generation can be very strong. Grandparents can relive many of the nicest moments of having their own children without the worries or responsibilities.

They are also often retired by the time their grandchildren arrive because today people tend to have their children much later in life, and they retire earlier.

If the grandparents live some distance away, you will need to foster your toddler's relationship with them. If he only sees them once or twice a year, a toddler probably will not remember them from one visit to the next. As he grows up, this will change, especially once he can talk to them on the telephone and know who they are, or recognize their photographs.

Keeping in touch
Put family photographs on a pinboard and point out to the child who everyone is. Initially the photographs will mean very little, but gradually he will associate the person who talks on the phone with the person in the photograph. My mother used to keep in touch by sending postcards and small gifts. It probably cost her more to post a small packet of sweets than to buy it, but the children were always delighted. Books, pocket money, toys and Christmas decorations arrived regularly from her.

Visiting the grandparents
Although relationships can be maintained over time and distances, they need to be based on contact. Ideally, children need to meet up with their grandparents at least twice a year. If the grandparents live a long way away – as they often do these days – such visits may last for weeks rather than days. This disrupts routines. Reduce the potential for friction by organizing plenty of activities and spending time away from each other. If your parents still live in your old home town there may be old friends and old haunts you could visit. If not, it may be easier to share a holiday than to stay for long periods in each other's houses.

Aunts, uncles and cousins
In the past, most people in a community would have grown up together. If they did not marry, literally, the girl-next-door, they frequently married the girl from the next street. Cousins, second cousins, childhood friends were around all of one's life. A child easily developed a sense of his place in the community and that place usually lasted for a lifetime.

Today, the closest most of us ever come to that feeling of completely belonging is when we get together with our brothers, sisters and cousins. If we grow apart from childhood friends we lose touch, but while an older generation survives our contact with cousins remains, even if we only see them at weddings and funerals. It is rare that a child likes all his cousins and, in a way, this is exactly why such extended family relationships are so important. Having to get on with those we do not like very much, and realizing that those we adore are not really that very special, are important lessons for a child to learn. It is equally important to learn how to mix with children of different ages.

Preparing and remembering
If his grandparents live some distance away, prepare your child for a visit by studying the family photo album. Afterwards, look at it again to help him connect image and person.

SEE ALSO
Sharing the care   **52–53**
Attention and memory   **104–105**
Growing self-awareness **124–125**
Divorce and remarriage **160–161**

PHOTO ALBUM

Until he is about 18 months, a child does not understand that photographs are pictures of particular people. By two years he will recognize himself and the family members he has met. He will not understand that a baby has grown up, or a big cousin was once small until he is about three, but even a child who does not recognize the people in the photo album will enjoy the photos, especially those of other children.

The second child

Once you have had one child, people will start asking you about the next, and there is a perceived wisdom about the "best" age gap between them. What is best for your family, however, only you and your partner can know.

Happy families

A larger family is a more complex social grouping, with more relationships that can go either well or badly over time.

So-called "only" children grow up to be perfectly sane individuals. Often they are also very successful; any list of "great men" – scientists, politicians, writers, or businessmen – will have more than its fair share of "only" children. Whether or not they are socially as successful, make better friends and lovers, and are happier and more fulfilled people is not on record. Personally, I would not be without my sisters and brother. Although we fought like cats and dogs as children, my sisters and I have always been very close as adults. Of course, not everyone feels about their siblings as I do.

The right age gap

You often hear it said that if you have children close together they will be good friends. Yet some of the closest sibling relationships I know are between

individuals who are quite different in age. Personality and eventual lifestyle also play a role. A bossy and domineering first child can clash horribly with a moody second, while a sunny and easy-going first child would be tolerant and supportive of her emotional sibling. The biggest clashes in childhood tend to be between children of the same sex, with boys generally more quarrelsome than girls. Those that squabble most as children often turn out to be the closest of life-long friends.

The first and second child

First children tend to be achievement-oriented. They are more often capable, conformist, strong-willed, responsible and secure than their younger siblings, and they are less likely to clash with their parents. Younger children tend to be more spontaneous, easy-going, tactful, relaxed, and have less drive than their older siblings – perhaps because they are often likely to have better social skills.

Carrying roles into adulthood

First children are the custodians of our dreams. Second children are more likely to be loved for themselves. Because they are always in competition with an older (and therefore more competent) sibling, they are used to coming second which may be why they are often less competitive. The youngest child has to learn ways to survive in unequal competitions and they can, therefore, be particularly manipulative.

Learning from brother and sister

The skills we have in deceiving, cajoling and manipulating others, in hiding our feelings and understanding others, are mostly honed in our relationships with our siblings. A parent's fallibility is easier to spot if you have seen them lose their tempers, worry, panic and have the wool pulled over their eyes by your siblings. It is not surprising that those with siblings have a more realistic view of their parents. They have a more rounded view of people in general and can be more self-confident in superficial relationships.

Getting on together

There are times when children get on with each other and times when they seem to quarrel all the time. There are age gaps which work because of the temperaments of the children concerned, and those that do not. Children develop both gradually and in leaps and bounds. Sometimes a two-year gap seems quite small, at other times very large. One child suddenly seems so much older than the other.

SEE ALSO
Caring about others   **110–111**
Growing self-awareness **124–125**
Running a family   **166–167**
Typical toddler problems **180–181**

Cats and dogs

Boys are probably more quarrelsome than girls, and it is certainly the case that same-sex children row more than those of opposite sex. Boys are more likely to come to blows than girls, who tend to argue, do mean things, scratch, kick and pull each other's hair. It goes without saying that these are over-generalizations.

My little sister
Three- and four-year-olds are generally loving to a new baby brother or sister. If you turn your back, however, they may still punch or kick.

EASY AND MORE DIFFICULT STAGES				
At 1 year	**At 2 years**	**At 3 years**	**At 4 years**	**At 5 years**
Communicating, mobile, with a new skill every week, one-year-olds are a delight, but they can also be demanding and tiring. They love their older siblings. They do not know how to play with them and need to be led. Older siblings enjoy the baby's attention, but may resent the carer's constant watchfulness.	Desperate to be independent, two-year-olds face many frustrations – they want it all now. They are also trusting and wide-eyed with wonder. A two-year-old may hug a new baby one moment and punch her the next. He loves to be with older siblings and can join in simple pretend games.	Mostly peaceable, three-year-olds relate well to school-age and baby siblings. A slightly younger sibling (at two) irritates her by smashing and grabbing, and a slightly older sibling (at four) causes problems by demanding to use the toys that she is already playing with.	Socially aware, four-year-olds need to let off steam and will quarrel if they can't. Loving to a new baby or a toddler, she can be bossy and violent with three- to six-year-olds. She may play the innocent party in a row, spoil games on purpose and make unrealistic demands.	Calmer and less demanding, this is the lull before the storm (at six). Five-year-olds can be very good with younger siblings. She wants your approval but may not behave when you look away. She often gets on well with older siblings (while they get on with her) because she wants to please.

Divorce and remarriage

In much of the Western world today, a large number of relationships end in divorce or separation. Having young children will not prevent this from happening – on the contrary, it probably makes it more likely.

REMARRIAGE

● About 75–80 per cent of divorcees will remarry and 25 per cent of children will spend some time with a step-parent. More than half of remarried parents will divorce again – leading to very complicated families.

● Remarriage is not easy. Often, younger children accept it, older ones do not. Older girls have a particular problem accepting a mother's or father's new partner, younger boys a mother's.

● Do not foist your new relationship on your children. Give them time to get used to the idea of the divorce first. A resentful or unhappy child can be very disruptive.

● Do not be gleeful if your ex-partner is having problems in a new relationship. A parent's happiness filters down to the child. Their hearts can break, especially if they felt close to a new partner.

Time together
Your children will need time with each parent, especially in the early weeks. Go out alone together, without a new partner tagging along.

Children have little say in the break-up of their parents' relationship but they often feel that they are a contributing factor. Such feelings are reinforced by the fact that the stress of separation can make us distracted and bad-tempered.

How children cope
Children have no control over who they live with, where they live, their parents' new partners, or whether both parents and extended families remain in contact with them. The very heart of their emotional security can be ripped apart by separation, divorce and remarriage.

In some countries in the West, half of all marriages end in divorce, and in many of these marriages there are young children. It is a very stressful time for all those involved. Stress makes us all behave unreasonably and this is doubly the case with children. Be prepared for sleeping and eating problems, a reversion to babyish behaviour, bed wetting, withdrawal, unhappiness and bad behaviour at school, perhaps even stealing, destructiveness, fights with siblings and many, many tears.

Children have a right to be angry about their parents' separation and to be given a (simplified) explanation of why it happened. Make this factual, but do not denigrate or blame your ex-partner. It may be more his fault than yours, but children have a right to feel respect and love for both their parents even if it is difficult for us to encourage such feelings. You may wish that your "ex" would disappear from your life, but it would not be good for your children if he did.

Stay in touch
It is difficult for the parent who has the care and control to see through the fog of hurt to the needs of the children. It is even harder for the parent who no longer lives with the children to bear the pain of brief meetings and tearful departures. Many do not cope. Over a third of all fathers (and mothers) who separate from their children lose touch with them. Many of their ex-partners have directly or indirectly

encouraged this breakdown. It is the duty of both parents to make the contact between the children and the non-custodial parent as straightforward and unemotional as possible. If this is tough on you and your new partner, too bad.

Grown-ups should behave like grown-ups. Children should not have to pay for their childish behaviour. It does not matter whose fault it was, or what they did or did not do. They are the child's parent. To the child this is what matters, and as parents what matters to the child should matter to us. Sensible adults will be able to ignore the bad behaviour and attention-seeking of other adults, just as they ignore such behaviour in children.

Pandering to the childish jealousies of a new (or old) partner puts us in the role of parent to a spoiled "child". Think not of the difficulties, remember instead that contact between the child and the non-custodial parent will offer a break from childcare for the custodial parent.

Helping your children

Tell them: Let them hear what is happening in your relationship from you, not from friends, family, neighbours, or listening behind the door. Do not let them overhear you talking to friends before they know what is happening.

Reassure them: Many children feel that they are the ones to blame for their parents' separation because they have often been the cause of their parents' worries, anger and stress. The withdrawal and distraction of their parents only reinforces these feelings of guilt.

Allow feelings: Let the children express their anger and sadness: do not cover it up with platitudes.

Hold your tongue: He may be a selfish brute and a rotten, no-good, two-timing so-and-so, but he is also their beloved father and you should not let them hear you running him down.

They are not spies: Of course you want to know what he is up to, but you must resist the temptation to ask your children.

Only one Daddy: A new partner is not a new Daddy or another Mummy. Children have only one mother and father. Hearing your child refer to another woman as "Mummy" or another man as "Daddy" will cause unnecessary hurt.

Settle out of court: The sooner the fighting is over, the sooner everyone's lives can be rebuilt. Do all in your power to make the relationship between your children and your ex a good one, however painful it may seem. Happy, stable children enrich your life and unstable ones bring heartbreak. Being pleasant to him may be hard in the beginning but in the long run it is the least painful way.

SEE ALSO

Talking to children   **150–151**
Coping with family stress **158–159**
Jealousy and loss   **188–189**
"Naughty" behaviour   **192–193**

STEPCHILDREN

● Children would probably prefer to be without step-parents. There is no reason for them to like them, let alone love them, nor for them to like their new stepbrothers and -sisters. It is unrealistic to think you will be a big happy family.

● Expect jealousy. Both sets of stepchildren have been through a difficult time – it is not the easiest circumstance for a new friendship.

● Listen to your child's complaints, but encourage her to make friends.

● Give in fantasy what she cannot have in reality. "You wish Daddy still lived here. I understand that. Do you want to draw a picture of us all together?"

Give it time

In most cases, new step-families learn to live together. There is nothing you can do to make one person like another, but you can demand civility.

Aggressive children

A certain amount of aggression is a good thing. Without aggression a child could never hold a "cold war" truce with his friends and foes. Some children, though, fight incessantly with all their friends, and especially with their siblings.

When they are fighting, children are learning to control and use anger – those who quarrel most often become the best of friends in later life. This knowledge, however, does not help the hassled parent deal with their angry, fighting children.

Stop it, boys

From an early age, boys are more aggressive than girls, and they are likely to remain so throughout life. Even so, only intervene if physical fighting breaks out.

Angry young children at home

Small children direct most of their anger towards themselves or their parents. They shout at parents, they are naughty and rude, they may kick and spit. Their aim is to seek our attention, and the more we give it, the more they act up. Turning a blind eye and walking away in silence is often the best way to deal with such behaviour.

Children also show anger and jealousy towards brothers and sisters. They snatch back toys and, occasionally, they thump their siblings or push them over. If you consistently punish the aggressor and comfort the victim, you set up a scenario which both can use to gain your attention: the bully uses aggression, the victim manipulation and crocodile tears.

Anger outside the home

Preschoolers often come to blows because they cannot deal with equals. He tries to treat his peers as he treats you; when it does not work, he loses control. Angry preschoolers do not use hurtful words – they spit, kick, bite, scratch and punch. He boils over easily, but he calms down just as quickly.

Angry older children

At home, brothers and sisters fight because they enjoy fighting, because they feel unloved, in order to take control, or to redress a wrong. They also fight because it gets our attention. Same-sex children are the worst, and boys are worse than girls. Children sometimes deliberately and systematically annoy each other. They do it even though they know it gets out of hand and upsets them. Most fights take place when children are tired and hot, bored, ill, or upset. In most cases the best thing to do is to let them get on with it.

As children grow up, their aggression becomes more controlled. It flares up quickly, but it can also build up fairly slowly. The older they get, however, the more likely are they also to bear grudges and remember earlier wrongs.

Avoiding conflict

Once they have reached school age, most children come to blows less frequently because they have learned how to control their anger. Many will have learned to read the signs of impending trouble and know how to walk away from the situation. By the time they are seven or eight, most children are able to judge another person's aggressive intent, especially if they have honed their skills at home on their own brothers and sisters. Being able to predict what other children might do next, even if that guess is not always accurate, makes it easier for them to take avoiding action.

The role of the family

Most parents do not set out to teach their children to be aggressive, but the way they discipline them may play a major role in the level of the child's aggression. Brutality breeds brutality. While there is no evidence that the occasional slap turns a child into a bully, there is little doubt that frequent corporal punishment, especially if it is inconstant, erratic and severe, will do so. Most bullies in the school playground – as in life – are, or were, the victims of bullying parents. Research suggests that some children actively elicit punishment. In a world where attention is hard to find, aggression and bad behaviour become the easiest way to get it.

How to react to fighting

- Don't interfere unless really necessary.
- Don't judge. This is bound to make one of them think it is unfair and to become even angrier (and vindictive).
- Don't protect the younger child. This will only encourage him to irritate his brother into fighting.
- Don't blame the older child. A child who is called a bully often becomes one.
- Clarify: "Is this a real fight?"; describe what you see: "I see two very bad-tempered children". Remind them of the house rules: "In this house we do not hit each other."
- Separate the children: "To your rooms, both of you."
- Tell the children how to close their rows. "You can come back into the living room when you have both decided to calm down."
- Don't shout. It raises the overall temperature.
- Don't hit. The children are likely to copy you – and fight all the more.

Violence on television

By the time he reaches 16, the average American child has spent more time watching TV than he has spent in school, and has witnessed 13,000 violent TV murders. TV violence in the USA occurs at an astonishing 17.6 per hour in daytime children's TV. The rates are lower in Britain and other parts of Europe – a "watershed" often keeps the more violent programmes out of daytime and early evening viewing.

Studies (in Britain, Finland, Poland, Australia and the USA) suggest that watching aggression on TV leads children to believe that this is an acceptable and effective way of solving conflicts. They also suggest that it increases the level of violent play and that regular viewers show less emotional reaction to violence. Our experience of TV aggression has probably also influenced our perception of the level of violence on the streets, and makes us afraid of letting our children play out doors.

SEE ALSO
Building self-esteem   **126–127**
Brothers and sisters   **190–191**
"Naughty" behaviour   **192–193**
Friendship problems   **194–195**

QUARRELS

- Only intervene if it comes to blows. If not, keep a poker face and walk out.
- If the battle is more serious, acknowledge their anger: "You both seem very cross." Let them explain; say you're confident that they can sort it out themselves.
- If it happens again, talk to each child separately. Suggest strategies: "If you turn your chair round you won't see Joe." Again, tell them you know that they can sort it out.
- Never shout, never ask who started it (this encourages blaming the other), or what it is all about (it does not matter).
- Never accuse them of always fighting or pretend it is making you ill.

Separate the children
Send your children to separate rooms if they are fighting. Do not allow them to apportion blame, but give them help in overcoming their quarrels and to return to "normal".

Off to school

Your child may be sunny and cheerful at home, but untypically withdrawn or aggressive at school.

NAUGHTINESS

Her growing sense of independence enables her to think about what she wants and how this differs from what other people want of her. She also learns that she can affect your feelings by the way she acts. She can deliberately worry, punish and irritate you. If people find it hard to love her (or if they have not tried very hard to do so), naughtiness may become a permanent way of life for her.

Becoming independent

As she grows up, your child will become more independent. It is up to you to lead her there gently, when she is ready, competent and secure. If you deny her this freedom, she will demand and take it anyway.

Start in small ways. By five a child should not be communicating every action nor always play underfoot. You should not intervene in every quarrel, and not expect her to explain her every thought and feeling to you. On all fronts you need to start the long process of letting go. Sooner or later you will have to do it.

Starting school

These days starting school is rarely a major landmark. Most children have been to day-care, preschool or nursery beforehand, and schools are today a good deal more welcoming than they used to be.

● Make sure your child understands that she has to go to school every day.

● She will be happier at school if she has learned to sit still, concentrate and wait her turn. This does not come automatically to a small child. It needs practice.

● She needs to know that you will not be there in person. Give her a little button to touch when she feels she needs you. Tell her that "when you touch the button I will be thinking of you". If she has a pocket put the special button in her pocket.

● Do not expect her to tell you everything she does and do not worry if she does not. Sometimes she is too tired, sometimes there are other, more interesting things to talk about at home.

● If she always tells you about her day but one day just stops, ask the school if they have noticed any problems. It is the change of habit which is important here.

Making friends

Between the age of one and two, children become more and more social but they do not play together until they are about two. Until then they engage in parallel play: sitting next to each other, watching,

LACK OF FRIENDS

Some people never seem to attract any friends. This is not at all unusual. About one in five children do not to have a "best friend" or are frequently left out.

● Find the problem. Does your child know how to make friends? Would it help to join an after-school club or activity? Does she irritate other children and could you help her to change this?

● Talk to the teacher or supervisor. They may see why the problem occurs – children often act very differently at home and at school.

● Let the child decide on the friends that suit her, then invite them over. Ask the teacher to recommend another "outsider" that your child might befriend.

Good at sports

Children who are bright at school or good at a skill such as gymnastics tend to be more popular with their peers.

exchanging toys and the odd word. The more time children spend together, the sooner they progress. Some time around the age of three, children begin to engage in cooperative play and to form friendships. As they play together opportunities for both conflict and cooperation increase. What begins as a mild interest in each other at two becomes a firm friendship by three. At this age children begin to have special or "best" friends. Such friendships may not be as long-lasting or as intense as they will be in later years but they are nonetheless important.

On the outside

Some people seem to have a natural ability to attract friends. Others spend their days on the outside. As children grow up their lives centre more and more on friendship, and those without friends can become isolated and very unhappy.

• Watch her with other children. Is she being deliberately excluded at someone else's behest? Is this her fault or someone else's? Are there any bullies in her class, or is she too bossy or dominating? Is she aggressive or does she pick on other children? If so, address these problems.

• Help her through role-playing. In such games she can sometimes play herself, and sometimes watch you playing her role. Help her to play through the solutions.

• Does she listen when others talk – or just talk? Make sure she learns to listen and to comment on what is being said. These are problems you can tackle by encouraging her to play with other children. You can also practise give and take within the family (with the child learning to do more of the giving). Self-centred people are never very popular.

• She may be frightened of crowds, especially if she is an "only" child. Practise playing with older children, and spending

time in public places such as a swimming pool or playground may help her overcome her fears. Take her to a shopping centre, using public transport, and make your outing exciting and part of a treat.

SEE ALSO

Building self-esteem 126–127
Each child an individual 176–177
From toddler to child 186–187
Friendship problems 194–195

My best friend

Between about four and six, children will begin to have a "best friend". They will enjoy spending as much time as possible together, and disappear into a world of their own.

WHAT MAKES A CHILD POPULAR?	
Friendliness	The friendlier a child is to other children the more popular she is likely to be.
Being outgoing	Gregarious children are more popular than withdrawn children.
Success	She does not need to be top of the class, but popular children tend to be academically successful.
Family position	Youngest children are usually more popular than first-borns.
Physical size	Tall children and those of average build tend to be more popular than smaller children.
Physical attraction	The more attractive the child, the more friends she is likely to have. A currently popular name also adds to the child's popularity.
Special abilities	Children who are good at sports or some other valued task tend to be popular.

CHAPTER SIX

Ask the expert

Six basic principles sum up the best way to cope with most problems – one: if behaviour is rewarded it will be repeated, if it is ignored it won't; two: children need, and respond to, clear rules and consistent boundaries; three: children demand attention – they would rather have you in a bad temper than ignoring them; four: all children want to be treated uniquely, and every child deserves love that is special; five: self-esteem anchors the child and protects him through storms; and six: believing something about yourself – whether good or bad – will make it come true.

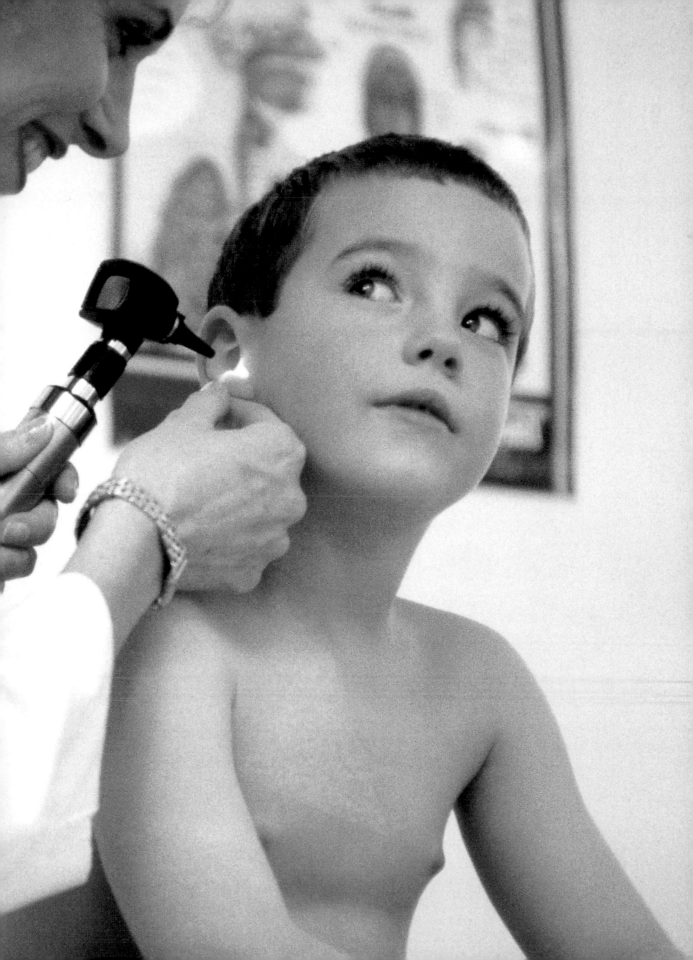

The twelve golden rules

There are different ways of bringing up a child, and children will differ from each other in their needs and temperaments. However, the following twelve maxims apply to virtually all of them.

Knowing how a child will react and why she does so will help you gauge your own response and hopefully avoid the worst of the problems.

The first thing to remember

A preschool child can only think about one thing at a time, and the sights, sounds and actions of the moment dominate. The more excited she becomes, the more her thoughts are backgrounded. She does not see that two steps along the way danger looms. It is this inability to look ahead when she is excited, not foolhardiness, that stops her taking into account that ice could break. Nor does she correctly predict our response to what she does. This failure to look ahead makes her vulnerable to distraction. As a baby she completely forgets what she was doing once she looks away. As she grows up she can hold on to ideas for longer, but this is not always easy for her, especially if the distractions are very loud, colourful, or exciting. What is happening at that moment dominates, even at the age of five.

Boisterous play

"Letting off steam" is fun and makes a child more manageable. It may also stop him being hyperactive and easily distracted.

The second thing to remember

Children are a bit like pressure cookers. Sooner or later they have to let off steam. A child who has "a head of steam" will fidget and fiddle, and be easily distracted. To let off steam she needs company: a parent to chase her or playmates who will rough and tumble with her. Most small animals engage in this exuberant play. Those who are deprived will be hyperactive and easily distracted.

The third thing to remember

The younger the child, the more she thinks she should be first in the queue for your attention. Except when she is engrossed in her own activities, a child wants her parents and carers to be with her and attending to her all the time. The very last thing she would wish for is to be ignored. Keep this in mind – if she cannot get your smiles, she will engineer your shouts.

The fourth thing to remember

Children always keep an eye on their place in the queue for love and attention. Behind many of the things they do is the simple question: "Does she/he love me best of all?" This is not a foolish question if we think of it as: "Whom will she save first in an emergency, or whom will she give the last crust to in times of hunger?" Remember that it is not so many generations ago that our ancestors would have come across wolves, bears, or other large predators as they gathered food and firewood, or as they tended cattle and faced the hardships of poor harvests without food reserves.

The fifth thing to remember

It is impossible to be fair, at least from the receiver's point of view. You cannot love equally because you love uniquely. The skill is to convey the uniqueness of your love to each of your children.

The sixth thing to remember

A child with a strong sense of self-esteem is likely to be better behaved and to create fewer behavioural problems than one who has low self-esteem. Try to avoid criticizing the child – it undermines self-esteem.

The seventh thing to remember

It is a basic principle of learning that we will avoid actions that are punished (by taking from us what we like), and repeat actions that are rewarded (by giving us what we desire). We will repeat our actions the next time we feel a desire for the same reward. The more predictably certain actions lead to specific rewards, the more likely they are to be repeated. What young children desire most is our undivided attention. If naughtiness, disruptiveness, or meanness become more reliable ways of attracting our attention, these behaviours will be repeated.

The eighth thing to remember

If we withhold rewards when the child does something we do not wish her to do, she is less likely to do it again.

The ninth thing to remember

Children copy their carers. If you shout at them, they are more likely to shout at their siblings. If you quarrel with your partner, they are likely to be quarrelsome. If you bully your partner or hit him, they are likely to be aggressive and bullying too.

The tenth thing to remember

Children must develop independence. Many of the problems of childhood arise because we do not negotiate this very well. We can never do it to a small child's satisfaction – sometimes the child wants more independence than we can allow and, at other times, less than we would wish. Negotiating the middle ground is extremely difficult. In recent years we have become over-cautious about playing out or walking home from school alone, but we allow the child to decide what she eats, wears, or watches on TV.

The eleventh thing to remember

We cannot help the way we feel, but we can help the way we act on those feelings. Accept that she is angry. Let her show you how angry she is, but never accept the behaviour that arises from that anger. She can be cross if her sister uses her toys. She cannot thump her if she does.

The twelfth thing to remember

People have a habit of growing into labels. Whether they are bad labels such as "bully", or good labels such as "clever girl" – labels are ultimately limiting.

SEE ALSO

Building self-esteem **126–127**
Providing riches **148–149**
Becoming independent **164–165**
Running a family **166–167**

You've got more!

It is best not even to attempt to be completely fair and to divide equally – one slice of cake will always seem bigger, and it will always be the one she didn't get.

NEVER NEVER

● Criticize a child or belittle her.

● Label a child, especially if the labels undermine her competence.

● Tell a child not to feel. Feelings cannot be helped, but whether we act on those feelings is our responsibility.

● Make threats. Warn and then act. Threats are empty if they are not carried out. If you always ask three times, she will wait to act until the third time.

● Provide an audience for bad behaviour.

● Ignore cruelty or violent behaviour.

● Give in to her bad behaviour.

● Force a child to fight your battles. Children are great conformists.

● The best way to deal with attention-seekers is to refuse to give them your attention – just walk out of the room. Don't make a fuss about it. Simply get up, put on a poker face and walk out. A poker face should not reflect emotions – nor should your body language. If the child follows, ignore him. Wait a few minutes, then explain why you left, briefly and simply: "I don't like being in the room when you are swearing."

● If it is impossible to leave the child (in the middle of a TV programme, or while cooking), simply pick him up, without any comment, and remove him from the room, then return to what you were doing. When he comes back, say: "I see you have decided not to be silly. I am glad. When I have finished, I will read you a story."

● If you are outside (for example, in a shop), pick him up and hold him very tightly. Look directly at him with a totally expressionless face, or look away. He will certainly struggle but you should hold on tight until after he has stopped.

Attention seekers

Children cannot be good and compliant all of the time, nor would any reasonable person expect them to be. Even as adults, we are often selfish and self-centred, so we can hardly expect more from a young child.

No child is trouble-free, but some are certainly more problematic than others – more argumentative, disobedient and troublesome. There is a big difference between a child who is sometimes naughty and defiant and one who is constantly difficult and badly behaved.

Not all of these children have been badly parented or were born difficult, nor have their behavioural problems been made worse by parents and other carers. It is usually a mixture of all of these things, together with the child's chance discovery of what pulls our strings. Children grow and change throughout childhood – the way we treat them today will not be appropriate next year. Sometimes we expect too much of them, sometimes too little. If you get this entirely right, you will be the first parent to do so.

Testing the limits

When a child throws her toys to the floor, she is trying to attract your attention, and she will want to see if you carry out your threats. She will also be asserting herself.

Why children seek attention

Many parents unintentionally encourage attention-seeking by giving more attention to bad behaviour than to good. It is easy to do – parents need a respite, and the easiest time to take it is when the child is being good. Depression makes things worse. We find it hard to engage with the child, except when he is at his most demanding or naughty. Children learn to do what most easily brings them attention. The same sort of problem can arise at school for a child with learning difficulties: because he is rarely praised for his competence, he learns that he gains attention from the teacher and other children by being naughty, cheeky, or disruptive.

How children seek attention

Temper tantrums: All tantrums have an element of attention-seeking. Children virtually never have tantrums when their main carer is absent, and tantrums are more likely to occur when the carer is busy (for example, when she is shopping or talking to someone) which temporarily excludes the child. Obviously, there are other factors involved. Withdrawing your attention from the tantrum is always the best way to deal with it.

Food fussiness: Like tantrums, the underlying behaviour has other causes, but it is aggravated by the ease with which children gain attention by refusing "wholesome" food and the readiness with which they consume the "empty calories" of processed foods. Diet is a modern obsession. It is wise to remember that if toddlers and preschoolers were fed "naturally", they would be breast-fed until their second teeth started to erupt. Preschoolers' natural food – breast milk – is sloppy, contains no fibre and is fatty and sweet. It it is a good idea to instil the right eating habits from an early age, yet, as long as they have plenty of milk, preschoolers do not need lots of fresh vegetables and fibre-rich foods.

Once a child is labelled a "fussy eater", he knows that he can gain attention by refusing food. In my experience, when left to their own devices, most children grow out of their fussiness by the time they are teenagers. Studies have shown that children will always select a balanced diet for themselves, because not doing so makes them ill. Of course, children will still eat too many sweet and fatty foods – you can control this if you stop buying them.

Silliness, swearing, rudeness: This type of behaviour requires an audience. Hard as it is to ignore, it is more likely to disappear if we do. This does not mean that we have to grin and bear it.

Nose picking, farting, belching and other embarrassing behaviours: Again, although the root cause may sometimes lie elsewhere, this type of behaviour is clearly made worse if children learn that they can draw our active disapproval.

Playing with the genitals

"There is nothing wrong with masturbation in private, but it is not something we do in public." This is the message we need to give children. Even small children can learn it. They do, after all, learn to go to the toilet. Ignore private masturbation, or suggest the child moves to a more private place. The easiest way to deal with public masturbation is to point out to the child

that, while we can do this in bed, it is not something we do in public. Be perfectly matter-of-fact, then distract the child so that he does not return to the activity.

When children play sexual games

Do not scold, lecture, give undue attention, or cause embarrassment. Explain the distinction between self and others: children are allowed to touch their own genitals, but should wait until they are grown up before they touch other people's, or let others touch theirs. Be firm and avoid any repetition of this sexual play by keeping a close eye on them. Tell them that sex is something adults do, and children do not (like going to work). Discuss what has happened with the other child's parents. They will need to talk to their child. If you catch them again, tell them you are disappointed and ask them to stop at once.

Being firm is not going to make children sexually repressed. One or two games are natural, but frequent games (or games with older children) should sound alarm bells. Precocious sexuality may be a sign that a child has been sexually abused. Parents should take it very seriously – most children are abused by friends and family.

Diet of choice

A child who is active, fit, growing normally and rarely ill, eats all he needs – even from cartons.

SEE ALSO

Making things worse   **174–175**
Typical toddler problems **180–181**
From toddler to child   **186–187**
"Naughty" behaviour   **192–193**

WARNINGS

If you threaten a child repeatedly, he will quickly learn how long it takes before you act. Instead:

● State the facts: "I do not like toys to be thrown in the lounge. You could break something and it is dangerous."

● Give a choice: "You can throw a ball in your bedroom, or you can play in the lounge without throwing."

● If he throws again, send him upstairs.

● When he comes down, make sure he knows he cannot throw in the lounge: "I see you have chosen not to throw. I'm glad, because I missed you."

Making things worse

Sometimes, with the best will in the world, we hinder rather than help our children's development with the ways we relate to them. But a critical look at what we say and do, will show us how to improve.

Good girl, bad girl

Even "positive" labels can influence your child negatively, restricting her options in life. "Negative" labels seriously damage her chances to develop her full potential.

It is important for us as parents to stand back and try to see things from our child's point of view. Self-observation, however, is not easy – some parents will be too critical of themselves, others will be too lenient.

Saying the wrong things

• Don't say: "You can't do it"; say: "That is so hard, I'm amazed you could even try to do it. Tell me if you need some help."

• It is frustrating when she makes a mess, but making her worry about this makes it harder for her to succeed. Instead of scolding, say: "What a mess, I'll get the mop and we can clear it up." And never send her to preschool in her best clothes.
• Never call her stupid. Behaviour can be stupid but the child is not. If she is careless address the problem without undermining her. "Julia, you have forgotten to put the cloth down. It will be easier to clear up if there is something to catch the bits." If she is still careless, say: "I know you can do this carefully. I trust you to try your best."
• Do not label her. Instead, describe what you see: "I know you are angry with Tom, but we do not hit even when we are angry. That is the rule." Give her confidence: "I know you can be nice to your brother"; and ask her for what you want: "I am trusting you both to sort this out without fighting." Accept children's anger: "I know how angry you must feel. Do you want to kick the cushions to show me? That much? Tom must have really annoyed you." Expect her to sort things out without resorting to blows and praise her for doing so: "Julia, I was really proud of the way you handled that."

Problems with lack of self-esteem

Children need to be loved and they need attention. A child who is confident in her own abilities does not need to behave foolishly to attract your attention. She can try, even if things are difficult, because she knows that any failure will only dent her self-esteem, not flatten it. Lack of esteem makes children give up easily and behave in silly, attention-seeking ways. It also makes them vulnerable to being led into trouble by other children. Children who have low opinions of themselves, find it more difficult to make good friends: if she does not like herself very much it is hard for her to see how others could love her.

Helping her self-esteem

● Teach confidence. Outlaw put-downs. A good technique is to say "Ouch" or to hiss like a snake when others put her down.
● Teach her to pause, then ask if something is wrong when others are unkind.
● Teach her to make a light but meaningful comment if someone calls her names: "That says more about you than me."
● Teach her to withdraw if people are being unkind. Bullies need a victim. If she refuses to play they will have to find someone else.

Labelling children

Why be good if everyone thinks you are naughty? Why try if no one ever notices? If everyone thinks you are stupid, is it not better to act that way than try hard, fail and prove them right?

Even if we do not consciously act on our labels they can have a compelling effect on behaviour. In one study, men who were told (in error) that they had heart disease had become invalids three months later. Parents and teachers label children every day of the year. Always make sure children are labelled as "competent" – the words you need are: "I know you can."

A distracting environment

A child who is surrounded by temptations and distractions generally finds it hard to concentrate on the task in hand. She just "skims the surface" and is easily bored.

Because she has never been able to concentrate on "quiet activities" she thinks she cannot do them and will not enjoy them. So she opts out. The older she gets the more problematic it becomes, especially at school.

Things are made worse if she cannot "let off steam". She becomes restless and fidgets. Any task which requires sitting still, sustained attention, and the ability to work from start to finish is affected. As the child's confidence is undermined, the problems escalate in a downward spiral.

While some children are hyperactive before they start school, some only develop problems after they start to fail. Do not risk this – it is so easy to help her. Start by structuring her environment and her day. Put away toys she is not playing with, turn off the TV and the radio, face her when you talk. Make sure she has frequent opportunities to let off steam and, after she has done so, slot in a short quiet activity. Reading to her is a good start. Once she has learned to sit still while you read, move on to other activities such as drawing, cutting up paper, or building. Keep outside stimulation to a minimum.

Tiptoeing around children

Some children are certainly more difficult than others, but parents who tiptoe around them enhance such difficulties. If you allow children to control you with their tempers, you may unwittingly set a strategy for life – bad-tempered children often grow into bad-tempered adults. Difficult children are not usually difficult all day. It may be harder to reinforce their good behaviour than to ignore the bad, but it is not impossible.

SEE ALSO
Everyone is lovable   116–117
Building self-esteem   126–127
Providing riches   148–149
Attention seekers   172–173

Wild boys
Often, boys are at a disadvantage because they are not taught to play quietly. Show your son how to let off steam by kicking a cushion, then let him be calm and work in concentration.

Each child an individual

All children should be treated as individuals, and this becomes more important as they get older. You can help your child to develop a sense of himself as a separate person, and to cope with the pains of separation.

The way a child relates to his parents or other carers will affect how he interacts with the rest of the world, for the rest of his life. Until he is about two, he does not see himself as an individual, but by the time he is four he knows that his thoughts and feelings are separate from those of his carers and that he is quite distinct from anyone else.

How to develop his individuality

- Refer to him by name and status: "My big boy Jack"; "My special boy Jamie".
- Give him a word of encouragement when he looks to you for reassurance: "Yes, Jack, you can have the ball."
- Let him know you understand what he is trying to communicate. Name what he asks for so he knows that you know.
- Name his emotions and respond to them: "Joseph, I can see that you are very sad; come here and have a cuddle."

A present just for you

Give your child a present when he needs one or you see one that suits him. Do not try to give all children the same thing at the same time – treat them separately and individually.

Feeling safe in love

Research suggests that poor attachment lies at the root of a wide range of behavioural problems. Children who do not bond tend to be less curious, less integrated with their peers and are more likely to be dependent. They seek constant approval and affection from adults. Feeling loved, and being secure in that feeling, helps the child to develop self-confidence and self-control. Being judged for yourself, not for what you manage to achieve, gives a child the confidence to try his best, and to try again if he fails. Love and security form the basis of his good behaviour in later life.

Growing pains

The transition from feeling part of us to feeling separate from us inevitably brings difficulties. Most of the problems we call "the terrible twos" arise from this transition. The understanding of his separateness drives a child to greater independence, yet he clings to the dependency of babyhood at the same time. Because he cannot yet judge his own abilities or plan his actions he is inevitably frustrated.

Understanding separate feelings

At about 21 months to two years, children start to see themselves as separate from us; by 3½ years they understand that their thoughts, feelings and perceptions are separate from ours. This learning is made easier if we treat the child as an individual. As children become self-aware they will also become more critical of themselves. Three-year-olds comment on how they look, what they own and what they can do. Parents help them by referring to the child by name, by commenting on his behaviour and by placing him in roles (brother, friend, cousin, schoolboy). Children under six are supremely confident in their abilities, but it is all too easy for parents and carers to crush this confidence.

Growing independence

● Remember that even though his actions are deliberate they are "of the moment": he does not plan to hurt people or make you cross, he is just playing with dependency.

The only feelings he understands are his own. Always forgive him, try to forget as quickly as he does and comfort him. Deep feelings are frightening.

● If you react to his behaviour by giving it your attention he will likely behave this way more often. This is true whether you "reward" (smiling, praising, laughing) or "punish" (shouting, smacking).

When children are stressed

Love, security and esteem act as a buffer to the stresses that undermine his security. If he feels insecure he will lack confidence, seek attention, bully, or play victim. Children are stressed by being different from other children, failing in school and by family changes such as divorce, the birth of a sibling, moving house, or the loss of a loved one. If the groundwork is firm and you continue to demonstrate your love of this unique child, such problems will be temporary. If he feels insecure, they can have devastating, long-term effects.

SEE ALSO

Growing self-awareness **124–125**

Building self-esteem   **126–127**

Providing riches   **148–149**

Coping with family stress **158–159**

Let's pretend

Make your child step into someone else's shoes, perhaps by playing nurse and patient – she will learn the difference between people and feelings of empathy.

WAYS OF DEALING WITH GROWING INDEPENDENCE

A sense of himself	Beginning to separate	Avoiding competition
Once a child develops a sense of himself as a separate individual, your love needs to be demonstrably given to that unique person. This is what you say:	As he begins to separate he needs to know that you love him still.	Undermine competition between children by treating them uniquely.
● "You are my one very special boy."	● Not "You naughty boy", but "That was a very naughty thing to do." His behaviour is bad but he is good.	● Not equal time: give to each according to their need.
● "Jenny loves her big brother."	● "People can be very unkind. I know you better than they do and I know they are wrong."	● Not equal love: unique love. Never say "I love you just as much", always "I love you for who you are…My special Jamie. My special Jenny."
● "There is no one in the whole world who hugs like you do."	● "I am so proud of you. It was very difficult and you tried so very hard."	● Find special times when each child's needs come first.
● "Jamie, you are my very best boy, and Jenny, you are my very best girl."	● "You must feel very angry."	● Ignore children who try to grab attention from those whose turn it is at the front of the queue.
● "I love you because you are such a special person."	● "That must have frightened you."	● Expect children to fall out, and also expect them to sort out their problems for themselves. Intervene as infrequently as you can. Remember that problems can be solved – battles over your attention cannot.
● "What could be more wonderful than seeing your smiling face?"	● "I know you can sort this out by yourself and I expect you to try."	
	● "You have behaved in a silly way, but you are a good sensible boy and I can see that you're sorry. Let's forgive and make up. I like it when we are friends."	

Typical baby problems

Even if your baby is as good as gold, you are likely to encounter some difficulties at one stage or another – colic, crying, sleep problems and problems with weaning are the most typical examples.

Babies and very small children depend on stimuli to learn. This means that your reactions to their behaviour and their problems have a significant influence. The associations babies make between the place they sleep and feeling sleepy, or the people, places and things that are around when they feel secure, are important.

Endless crying

A baby who cries on and off during the day is unhappy. She will have a reason: she may be hungry, in pain, lonely, or afraid. Some babies, however, are certainly more prone to unhappiness than others.

● Keep a record of when she cries. What have you eaten? What has she eaten? Does anything make it worse?

● Is she at a stage when she is growing and changing very quickly? Growth is a painful business, change is frightening. All babies are more difficult at such times. If she is in pain, an analgesic will help to soothe her.

● Crying can become a habit. If she always cries in the same place, move her.

● Sometimes babies just need company. If you cannot keep her on your body, give her your sweater to cuddle.

● If there is nothing wrong and she cries every time you put her down and stops when you pick her up, you are rewarding her for crying. If everything is OK leave her to it. Pick her up when she stops and give her lots of attention whenever she is happy and smiling.

Happy eating

If you have recently introduced solid foods, check that this is not what upsets her. Generally speaking, baby rice and potatoes tend to be unproblematic.

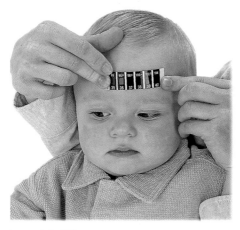

Is your baby ill?

If your baby does not normally cry, and cannot be soothed, she may be ill. If she has a fever and her ears are red, take her to the doctor.

Babies cannot tell us what they want. If we react to their tears rather than their smiles, we may land ourselves with a crybaby.

Crying from colic

No one knows why some babies have colic. All babies cry more between 6–12 weeks, and in the evening. Colic exaggerates this tendency. Crying occurs at the same time each day, most often in the early evening, and can last for an hour or more.

● If you are breast-feeding check your diet. Try replacing cow's milk with sheep's or goat's milk or soya milk products. Leave other products out in turn and see if this improves matters. Then reintroduce them and see if the problem returns.

● Carrying babies is thought by some to reduce the problem. Although it does not work for all babies it is worth trying this. Swaddling, holding, rocking and rhythmic sounds also soothe them.

- Simethicone, a treatment for indigestion, helps some babies. Your doctor can prescribe it. It is not absorbed and so is completely safe. Gripe water may also help.
- Take it in turns to care for her. Accept that there is often little that you can do. If things get too much, close the door on her for a few minutes while you calm yourself.

Weaning problems

People have an in-built tendency to avoid new foods, and this is particularly strong in young children. This protective strategy can lead to future fussiness.

- A child who is inclined to vomit may associate feeling nauseous with a certain food. If you have tried to override this, you may have made her more cautious overall.
- You have tried to wean the baby on to a variety of foods and this has produced a general rejection of all new foods.
- You are overly concerned about diet and the child plays on this. This is not a serious problem, but it can start a trend.
- The child does not like the feel of food in her mouth. This is more likely to be a problem for a breast-fed baby. If she is not ready, wait. Once a child starts to explore objects with her tongue, lips and gums she will find eating from a spoon much easier.

Successful weaning

Find the right time: Breast-fed babies may not be ready for solids before about 7–8 months. If you start weaning before six months do not use wheat-based foods.
Introduce foods very gradually: Mix very little of a new food with an old and loved food. Gradually increase the amount.
If she is ill: Avoid any new foods you have introduced just before she became ill. Try them again in a month or so.

Sleep problems

Some people – and some babies – sleep more than others, some less. Lack of sleep is rarely a problem for the child, she will always catch up. You cannot. There are two basic solutions.

Quick and easy night-time feeds: Get a large bed and put the cradle beside it. When she wakes, lift her immediately, put her to the breast and feed her lying on your side. Do not try to stay awake. Do not even think about burping or changing her. If you are bottle-feeding, take two bottles to bed with you and leave them beside the bed, one with milk powder, the other with warm sterile water. Add the water to the powder. Feed her, doze as much as you can and if you are still awake when she finishes, return her to her cot. If you find that she sleeps better if she remains in bed with you, let her sleep in your bed.

Teach her to fall asleep: Learning to put herself to sleep without your help is the key to your sleeping through because she will not cry for you when she wakes in the middle of the night. Make the sleeping room so dull that she has no alternative but sleep if she wakes. Remove all toys. A completely dark room is the best place to sleep. Remove lights, which are bad for the eyes, and line the curtains. If she knows how to go to sleep by herself, and finds nothing to distract her from sleep, she is much more likely to sleep through.

SEE ALSO

Sleepless babies   **36–37**
Crying babies   **38–39**
Establishing a routine **40–41**
Weaning from the breast **46–47**

CONDITIONING

You can teach a dog to beg for a bone – just follow an arbitrary action (the dog sitting up on the hind legs) with a desired reward (food or a pat). In the same way you can condition a child so that her action (having a tantrum) leads to a desired consequence (some chocolate).

You can train her to scream to bring you into the room, or to spit out food to stop you talking to your partner at table. Or you could teach her to say "please" if she wants something, laugh and smile and shake her head "no" as she hands you the chocolate in such a cute way that you buy her a bar.

Sleepy baby

Teach your baby to go to sleep by herself. Put her to bed and say good-night, then go. She will protest if she is not used to it, but she will learn in just a few nights.

The twos and beyond

While the twos can be terrible (as is obvious in many a supermarket queue), two-year olds are also a great delight. They are warm and loving, always delighted to see us, vocal and increasingly organized and helpful.

Your two-year-old's behaviour and the things she says generate a fund of funny and endearing stories, some of which will stay with you all your life. On the downside, she will need constant attention. She can no longer be left safely strapped in a chair. Because she does not understand the consequence of her actions she will do things that are dangerous, such as carrying a large toy downstairs or throwing things into the fire.

She is becoming more independent, and "Me do it" and "No!" are two of her favourite phrases. At the same time she remains dependent. If she could tell us what she wanted, it would probably be fine for her to do her own thing

when she feels like it, and for us to help her when she feels she needs us. It is a transition we can never get right all the time. Clashes with two-year-olds are inevitable and impossible to avoid.

Reducing the clashes

Clashes are most likely to happen when our needs conflict: we are busy and the children are tired. They commonly occur when we confine the child (such as putting her in a car seat), and during dressing, shopping and such activities that must fit our timetable rather than hers.

● **Avoid flash points** such as shopping when she is tired or hot.

● **Letting off steam** before confining her in the car can reduce problems. On wet days go out and stamp in puddles. Try to find a child-centred activity to intersperse with shopping trips. Her growing body needs frequent meals – take a drink and some food with you in case you are held up.

● **Distract her** since her memory is short. Promise her that you will see a cat, and keep talking about it – it will enable you to slip on her shoes without her noticing.

● **Select easy clothes** such as socks without heels, pull up trousers and skirts, sweaters and easy necklines that she can put on by herself.

Growing independence

Like a plant, your child grows best in fertile ground. If she has a good and strong attachment to her parents she will easily

Cool your child down
Overheating makes us all cross. So if your child feels hot and agitated, sponge him down with a tepid flannel or put him in a tepid bath or shower to calm tempers.

make the transition to independence. Attachment is easiest if her carers are able to express their feelings and emotions openly, and show physical warmth. She does not always know what she needs and will often depend upon them to interpret her feelings for her. It is difficult for a child to form an attachment to a carer who dislikes physical contact, withholds her emotions and feelings, and is withdrawn and unavailable.

Beginning to let go

- Start to encourage choice.
- Never say: "You cannnot do that". If it is too difficult tell her it is very, very hard and she can ask for help when she needs it.
- By the age of three you can offer her choices as you discipline her: "You can play quietly in here, or you can go outside and make a noise in the hallway."
- Show respect for her efforts: "You nearly did it and it is so hard. I didn't think that anyone under three could do that."
- Always believe that she can.
- Stand back and leave her to try. Do not rush in too soon with help or answers. Let her try to work it out.
- Let her post the letter. Watch her while she walks to the gate. Independence has small beginnings but should progress. Walking to the corner to post a letter will lead to walking the last 200 yards to school alone. Independence should unfold gradually. That way it goes hand in hand with responsibility.

Impulsive children

Some children – and some adults – always leap before they look. Most of them probably started out as impulsive babies and will grow up to be impulsive adults. Children who act on impulse get used to making mistakes. They are more likely to pick themselves up and start again because

SEE ALSO
Becoming assertive   **128–129**
Becoming independent **164–165**
Attention seekers   **172–173**
Typical toddler problems **180–181**

I can ring the bell
Let your child develop her independence. If she wants to ring the doorbell or press the button for the traffic light to change, let her try. She will soon learn, and be very proud of her independence!

of it. Compared with other children, they need rather more physical rough and tumble, and rather less stimulation. Do not put a brake on their enthusiasm. Let them find out for themselves what works and what does not. Do teach them to slow down, though, to count "one, two, three" before they rush in. This way you may be able to prevent physical and mental hurt.

TANTRUMS

Between 60 and 80 per cent of all children have tantrums, beginning between 18 and 24 months and continuing for about 18 months. The average child has three to seven a week. The later they start, the fewer tantrums they are likely to have. Most are brief, but can be violent: children fall to the floor, arch their backs, kick and scream. Some hurt themselves intentionally, banging their heads, or inducing fits. It is hard to believe but such violent behaviour is a normal part of growing up!

- Children use tantrums to manipulate and to gain attention. If you give in to their demands and give the attention they crave, you encourage them to use tantrums more often to get their own way.

- Tantrums occur when emotions get out of control, something we all find frightening. Evidence suggests that comforting and cuddling the child after a tantrum reduces their incidence.

- Parents can often tell that a tantrum is brewing, and may be able to head it off. Once it has started, walk away and leave the child. If this is not possible hold her very tightly until she stops struggling.

- Reports from over 1,000 families show that smacking makes matters worse: smacked children have longer and more frequent tantrums.

Accepting differences

Some children are born easy, and some difficult. Although we can build on and modify these basic temperaments, something of that birth endowment remains, and we will have to find ways of accepting it.

Variations in temperament are often easier to see in a large and close family: the personalities of some relatives, like their looks, may be mirrored in other family members. As well as recognizing Grandma's nose in one child, we can see her quick temper in another.

The shy child

It is not altogether clear why some children are shy. One suggestion is that they are born with an overactive arousal system. Introverted children are relatively highly aroused, and are thus easily pushed into levels that make him avoid others. Since social behaviour increases arousal in unpredictable ways, they are cautious in social situations. Extroverted children are exactly the opposite. Chronically under-aroused, they seek excitement. Unfortunately, this theory is unlikely to tell the whole story. Some shy children become actors and rock climbers – activities that would push most of us over the top.

Helping a shy child

Children do not have to be the life and soul of the party, but they do need friends.
- Build your child's confidence. Let him know he is special – say so and act so. If others label him as "shy", relabel him in a positive way: "not shy, just very self-contained."

- Don't push him into situations. Allow him time and accept his refusal: "You can stand with me and watch." Express his feelings for him: "I understand you feel a bit frightened", and accept them: "I know you will join in when you feel ready."
- Help him to gain courage: "Shall we whisper the courage words? Are you holding your courage sleeve?" As he grows older encourage the power of the positive inner voice: "Just keep saying I can."
- Help him to resist fear: "Don't listen to the voice that says you cannot do it. Just say 'I'm not going to listen'."
- Children tend to think things are black and white. Encourage him to think about the shades of grey that are in between. He did not talk to anyone today but he did sit at the same table. That's a pretty good grey.
- Encourage him to interact in every way you can: let him pay in shops, invite children around to play. He will find it easiest on a one-to-one basis.
- Pretend: if there is something he cannot do, pretend he can. Play a pretend-game a few times, and he may feel confident enough to try it for real.

Irritable children

There are many factors which feed into irritability – stress, pain, tiredness, illness and, of course, habit and example. Those who gain attention by flying off the handle are likely to be more irritable. Yet we are not all born the same: some children find it much harder to control their tempers.

Hiding away

Your child may hide behind activities, for example, by fussing with his shoelaces, in order to escape the attention of others in social situations. Help him to gain courage gradually.

Gaining confidence
Shy children can "come out of themselves" by attending classes with others which allow them to follow an activity on their own, for example, horse riding or swimming.

Helping an irritable child

- If a baby is unhappy and irritable check that he is not in pain. Those who suffer from frequent illnesses as babies often grow up to be irritable adults.
- Children copy us. If we display temper, they are more likely to do so.
- Do not reward a child's bad temper with your attention, but do let him know you understand why he feels the way he does.
- Separate out the feelings from the action. Expect him to learn to control his temper. A child who thinks he cannot do it will not learn. One who is told he can will try.
- Always forgive the child after he has calmed down. Praise his efforts.
- Teach him strategies such as taking a deep breath, saying a magic word, distracting himself by thinking about his moving fingers which will keep him calm for longer. Often one moment is enough.
- Teach him how to release stress, how to be active and how to relax.

Distractable and hyper-active

All young children are fairly active, have short attention spans and are easily distracted, but as they grow up, they learn to concentrate and sit still.

- Surprisingly, boys only start to be more active than girls once they are seven or eight. However, more boys encounter problems settling down at school.
- Small children are easily distracted. By keeping music, TV, competing toys and activities at a low level we will help our children learn to concentrate better.
- All behaviours increase in frequency if they are reinforced. If you pay attention to him he will carry on. Learn to keep calm.
- Expect problems when he is stressed or tired, and find activities for him to let off steam, such as jumping off the stairs or shouting. Follow this with calmness.

Games and competitiveness

Most children under five can only play games of chance. They cannot plan ahead and have no strategies. They do not always remember the rules and will usually need to play with adults.

- Cooperative or team games are the easiest games to play with small children.
- Most games can be adapted so you can play them in pairs.

   Some children always have to win; if they don't win, they sulk. Letting one child win brings cries of "not fair" from others. Letting him lose brings tantrums.
- Play down competition. Compete for the lowest score. "Not as low as me, I'm still the winner of the losers."
- Don't compare a child with better behaved children if he sulks. (Some parents are just as bad, and innocent games quickly turn into rows.)
- Competitiveness runs in families. You'll have to grin and bear it.

SEE ALSO
Aggressive children   162–163
Becoming independent 164–165
Attention seekers   172–173
Attention problems   200–201

Let's all have a break
If your child loses control when playing a game, let him cool off. Take a break and make a drink for everyone so he can creep back in "unnoticed" before you start again.

From toddler to child

It is hard to say exactly when a child stops being a toddler, but it has certainly happened by the time she is three and a half. She no longer has the flat-footed gait of a toddler – she now walks with a spring in her step.

We obey house rules
If a young child breaks one of the house rules that you all agreed on, he will need to be punished.

WIND-UPS

● **Don't blow up.** She is trying to annoy you – don't let her succeed.

● **Don't intervene.** If she is winding other people up, let them sort it out.

● **Never act as a referee.** Refereeing is a thankless task once you start.

● **Let it go.** Getting to the bottom of each misdemeanour is pointless: your leisure is more valuable than this.

By five she will run and jump, stop and start, skip and walk up and down stairs with alternate feet. She will talk in sentences, about the past and the future, and about her likes, dislikes, needs, feelings and dreams. She knows how to be naughty (and how to be good) and can be quite sanctimonious about others. Her idea of naughtiness is still primitive – she does not yet understand that it makes a difference whether you mean to be naughty or not.

Discipline for 3–5-year-olds

There should be no upper limit to your love at this age, but there should be a bottom-line for your tolerance. Children of this age divide the world into black and white, good and bad, friend and foe. Complete freedom of choice leaves them uncertain – they need firm and consistent rules which are set against a background of love and tolerance, where trying one's best is more important than success and where, although bad behaviour is not tolerated, it is quickly forgiven and forgotten.

Set limits: Limits should reflect her growing competence. She cannot learn if she is always controlled. She needs independence which unfolds gradually within a firm structure. She cannot always think ahead to the consequences of her actions, but she should be made aware of them. Mistakes should be acknowledged but not harped upon, effort valued as much as success.

Set house rules: Make these suit your lifestyle. Breaking the house rules is an offence and should be punished. The most important rules concern the way family members interact: "We do not call each other names"; "We discuss problems, we do not punch"; "We do not hurt people, pets, or things"; "Even small people should help"; "People can say how their belongings are to be used". Such rules need no explanation. They are the black-and-white house rules which everyone in the household must obey. Whether or not a child calls another names, or breaks her brother's crayons, is non-negotiable.

Other rules are more flexible. You can expect the children to change their shoes at the door, never to race about in the lounge and to ask before they get down from the table. On the other hand, you may feel all such rules are restrictive. It is your choice.

Time out and cooling off: Removing the child from the scene and other ways of withdrawing attention from her bad behaviour are still the major discipline tools. Expect apologies and once they are given, forgive and forget. If the child is upset, offer her comfort. Use cooling-off positively: "I think you need to cool off; come back when you have calmed down"; "I need time to cool off because I feel angry", as you walk out and leave her.

Teach them how to behave: As she grows up, reasons become more important as do expectations. Warn her and act on those warnings: "If you sit quietly in the car we will stop at the station on our way home and watch the trains, but if you behave like a naughty girl we will go straight home. I will leave you to choose." Be positive and try to control things before they get out of hand: "Come here and let me turn your volume down"; "I see angry children; I think we need to stop and calm down."

Offer more choices: "You need to clear up by the time the big hand is on the six. You can do it now or you can wait until the big hand is on the five. I will let you know when, but you will have to be very quick if you wait until then."

Avoid situations which spark conflict

Stand back from squabbles: Unless things are seriously getting out of hand it is always better for children to sort out their own problems.

Award gold stars: Star charts can be effective in moulding behaviour. The child gains a star for every day (or morning or afternoon) in which she behaves in the desired manner or in which she does not behave in the undesirable manner. At the end of the week, she can exchange stars she has gained for a small gift.

Making her do what you want

Don't nag: If it is unimportant let it pass.

Don't dictate: Give her some say in what she does. Decide which points are negotiable and which are not. Give choices where this is possible.

Tell her what you expect. When she is behaving badly describe what you see and give information: "The crayons are all over the floor; they will make a mess if anyone treads on them." Say what you expect: "I expect you to pick them up."

Be reasonable: In some cases it is reasonable to wait before she has to start picking things up: "We'll be eating soon; if you want to finish the drawing, we can leave clearing up until later." If she often uses delaying tactics to avoid clearing up announce a sanction: "If you do not clear

up later, I will put the crayons away until Thursday." Then remind her with one word when supper is finished. If she fails to pick them up, keep your word.

Listening, asking and refusing

If children can express the way they feel and ask for what they want, there is less need for battles between child and carer, and this gives an easier context for learning to control emotions. Children who can talk freely about their feelings will have less need to fight because they can get our attention without misbehaving.

Don't judge: Respect her views even if you do not agree with her. Try to see things from her point of view. Give her your answer after she has finished, do not barge in with your views while she speaks.

Read between her words: Verbalize what she is trying to say but cannot.

Play conversational "tennis": You can give her your attention as a gift and reinforce her for her conversation. The only valid interruptions in mid-sentence are friendly noises of encouragement.

Reflect on her feelings: She will still find it difficult to express these accurately. Even if you disagree, or are annoyed by her, respect what she feels.

SEE ALSO
Becoming independent **164–165**
The twelve golden rules **170–171**
Typical toddler problems **180–181**
"Naughty" behaviour **192–193**

Gold stars

Children can chart their own behaviour if you award stars for good days. The reward for a full chart on Sunday is worth the effort!

RUDENESS

- Ignore her if she wants attention.
- If she has gone too far describe the situation: "I hear a child who is rude."
- State what you feel: "That makes me feel angry."
- Accept her anger: "I know that having to put away your toys just now makes you feel angry."
- State any rules: "We are not rude to each other."
- And what you expect: "I expect you to apologize."
- Add sanctions: "Go to your room until you feel calm and can apologize."
- Forgive her.
- A persistently rude child may need bigger sanctions. Discuss these with her, impose and enforce them. Don't lose your temper.

Jealousy and loss

Powerful emotions such as jealousy or envy make sensible adults do things that are quite out of character. What else could make us want to hurt someone or damage their belongings? And children are so much more vulnerable.

Most of us manage to control the worst excesses of jealousy, but this is only so because we are rational and can envisage the consequences of our actions. Small children do not have recourse to either rational thought or the ability to imagine the future as we can.

As parents we know that loving a second child does not stop us loving the first, or that forming a new relationship does not affect how we feel about our children, but there is no reason why our children should see it that way. There are, after all, many situations when we would not be able to "forgive and forget" easily ourselves. A brief affair, for example, may have meant nothing to the partner who had it, but we are unlikely to see it that way ourselves. A former partner (especially if they are more attractive or successful than we are) can haunt us for years. If all the novels in the library which touched on jealousy were removed, the shelves would be half-empty. It is jealousy which makes violence and murder primarily a family affair.

Change and vulnerability

Change makes adults vulnerable to stress, and stress makes it hard to control our emotions. Even those things we want and look forward to, such as a holiday, may be stressful. Similarly, our first child may be looking forward to the new baby, or he likes your new partner, yet the change in his life makes it harder for him to control what he feels. We may move to a bigger house before the birth, or when we start to cohabit, and the child has to cope with a whole range of new experiences – a new baby, a new home, new surroundings and even a new play group or school. Each change increases the stress.

Coping with change

● Read the script from his point of view. It might seem a good idea for him to start nursery or to change carers once you have a new baby, but such changes produce extra stress. Make them before the baby arrives so that he is settled and happy by the time he has to cope with a new sibling.
● Be tolerant. Stress makes us all revert to more childish behaviour. Turn a blind eye to minor lapses and babyish behaviour.
● Be loving. Stress makes us needy. He needs extra time, and time when he can be assured that he is first in the queue.

All new

Moving house may seem like the right time to redecorate a child's new room. Do so cautiously. There is so much that is new in his life – leave him something familiar.

• Be demonstrative. Jealousy makes us blind to the love we have, a jealous child needs lots and lots of reassurance.

• Make it clear that he has love which can never be stolen from him: "You are my own very special Liam; there is not another Liam in the whole wide world who could be as special to anyone as you are to me."

A new baby

For most children a new baby brings mixed emotions. There is his fascination with the baby and his growing love for her. There is also the jealousy of all the attention the baby receives, and insecurity about his new role in the family.

• Find times when he comes first and the baby has to take second place.

• Accept his frustrations. Put his feelings into words: "I know that sometimes you wish we did not have Abbi."

• Put his wishes into words: "I bet you wish sometimes that we could send her back. Show me how much. That much? That's a big wish." Give him those wishes in fantasy: "Let's pretend there is just you and me, and no one else."

• Remind him of the good moments he has with the baby: "No one makes her laugh as much as you do, I think she loves you best of all. That doesn't stop her being a pest sometimes though, does it?"

• Avoid telling him things which are patently not true. The baby may be a good friend and playmate in years to come, but she is clearly not one now.

Moving house

• A child under four does not understand change. However clearly you explain things he may still expect to return "home".

• Prepare him. Show him his new home, the shop where he can spend his money, the park and his new school or play group.

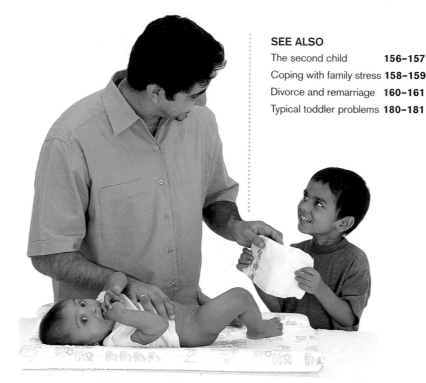

SEE ALSO
The second child   **156–157**
Coping with family stress **158–159**
Divorce and remarriage   **160–161**
Typical toddler problems **180–181**

• Tell him someone else will live in your home. Children are often shocked to find someone measuring up their bedroom or to see the removal van waiting to unload new furniture as you leave. Reassure the child that all your things (and especially his things) will be moving to the new house.

• Tell him that people will move out of the new house and take all their things with them. A friend tells of his disappointment on finding, after he moved house as a child, that the previous owner's bike was no longer in the shed. His excitement was completely tied up with having a bike.

• Expect him to cling, be afraid, sleep badly, come into your bed.

• Put him at the top of the list. What does it matter if it takes twice the time to get straight? He needs you more than you need to change the wallpaper.

• Give in fantasy what he wants in reality: "You wish you could go back to the old house. Shall we pretend we are still living there? What shall we do first?"

Help your little sister

Children are more likely to help if we show them how. Let him fetch the nappy. Show your appreciation. Being involved in the care of a new baby will make him less jealous.

Brothers and sisters

Siblings know each other only too well. They know exactly how to please their brother or sister, but they also know how to wind each other up, hurt, irritate and undermine. And, inevitably, they will do all these things to each other.

Many of the emotional skills we have acquired – for example, for hiding or expressing feelings, understanding others, for manipulating, deceiving and cajoling – are learned by interacting with our siblings. Siblings move the focus of the family away from the parents, which is one reason why we find sibling difficulties so hard.

Good times, bad times

There are times when children get on with each other and times when they do not, age gaps that do work and age gaps that do not. The good news is that, if it is bad, it will get better. The bad news is that, if it is good, it will not always be as good because children grow up in leaps and bounds. A two-year age gap can put children into the same developmental stage – for example, if they are aged three and five, or seven and nine – or into a different developmental stage – for example, if they are aged four and six, or 12 and 14 ,respectively.

Children who are passing through a period of growth and change are often very difficult; in a stable phase, however, they can be surprisingly pleasant and easy. A child in a period of change can be aggressive and spiteful to her siblings because we have the tendency to give more attention to her easy-going brothers or sisters.

How to reduce rivalry

Children within competitive families are bound to be competitive themselves. It is impossible for a small child to take on the message: "I want you to succeed", without wanting to compete. A brother or sister is the natural person for a small child to hone her competitive skills on, and we often encourage this. We get them to run races, play board games and eat up all their dinners. The more competitive our family, the more likely the children are to quarrel.

● Treat children uniquely, not equally. Siblings look for advantage in everything. They will see it, even when it is not there. You cannot give equal shares – so stop trying and give each according to need.

● A child who is passing through a period of change needs more attention than one who is in a state of relative stability. Stop trying to divide your time equally and give what is needed.

● Do not compare one child's behaviour or ability with the other's.

● Play down competition and try to leave your own competitiveness at the door.

● Competitive parents have competitive children, competitive cultures produce competitive children. If you want her to claw her way to the top of the pile, you will have to grin and bear her behaviour.

● Do not label children.

● Do not make roles for your children. She is not the sweet, good-tempered one. She is Hannah. Like all children she has a right to be foul-tempered and unpleasant.

Your toys, my toys
Give each child a box to store their toys in. If you label the boxes, there will be less need for children to quarrel about which toy belongs to whom, or who has not cleared away their toys.

Tania

James

Alex

Do not get drawn into quarrels

● Avoid getting involved in minor quarrels. If you start playing the referee, you will find yourself with a full-time job.

● The way the problem presents itself may seem silly; look beyond the package. You should say: "I have confidence you can sort this out", not: "Stop being silly."

● Start by describing what you see. Do not make judgements: "I see two very angry children." Listen to each child without comment: "Jamie you need the scissors to cut your paper; Jenny you need the scissors to cut your string." Do not impose a solution, instead acknowledge the problem but express confidence they will solve it: "That is a difficult problem, but I am sure you can sort it out."

● Always acknowledge a child's feeling: "I know you feel angry." Remember children cannot easily sort out problems once their emotions are deeply involved. If one or both children are very upset, you may need to impose a cooling-off period. If you think that simply listening to both sides will calm them down, do this and help them to find a solution that is acceptable to both, without imposing your own.

● Discuss each child's point of view: "Jenny was using your crayons and you wanted them back"; "Jamie wasn't using his crayons so you borrowed them."

● Now remind them of the rules if they apply: "Jenny you should ask Jamie if you want to borrow his things; that is the rule."

● Do not excuse the way they act: "I know you are upset, but it was wrong to rip up Jenny's drawing." After your intervention, express confidence that they can sort it out.

Encourage helpful behaviour

● All children should have daily chores – laying the table, washing the dishes, taking the dirty clothes to the washing basket. It

does not have to be arduous – the point is to emphasize that, within a family, we are helpful and do things for each other.

● Counterbalancing competitiveness with cooperation can reduce rivalry. Children should be encouraged to help each other. Ask an older child to help the younger with her shoes; ask the younger to hang up her brother's coat. Such things undermine the self-centred attitude which can develop in families when we make everyone responsible only for their own things.

● If children cannot sort out quarrels, reserve the right to confiscate or ban the cause of the argument. Set time limits (use the kitchen timer) to sort out problems. If they have not found a solution by the time the bell rings, the cause of the argument (the toy, TV, video) will be banned. Switch off the TV, or put the toy away for a day.

● Ban name calling.

● Notice when fights occur and try to head them off. Go out with your children and jog down to the corner shop together, go to the park and feed the ducks, or read a story. Encourage the children to let off steam, if they are tired or showing signs of bad temper. Put cushions at the bottom of the stairs and let them jump down.

SEE ALSO

The second child   **156–157**
Coping with family stress **158–159**
Typical toddler problems **180–181**
Jealousy and loss   **188–189**

Cats and dogs
Siblings fight for all sorts of reasons, but many of them are to do with seeking their parents' love and attracting their attention.

QUARRELFREE

● Make rules about when and where quarrels can occur. For example, we do not quarrel in the car, the sitting room, or at meal times.

● Each child has the right to say who may use their things.

● Each child has his or her own space – a room or the corner of a room – and can determine who comes in to it.

● Each child has a cupboard or box with a lock for their special things.

THE BULLY

- Never call a child a bully. Emphasize his kindness and cooperation.
- Do not let him or the victim gain by bullying, or both children will stick to their roles.
- Let him overhear how well he has behaved, especially towards his victims.
- Let him see himself differently.
- Teach him that he can get what he wants in other ways.
- Set a good example. Children mimic our behaviour.
- Show that you are even-handed.

Present choices

Explain to your child that he cannot have it all – he may need to choose between one big or several small presents.

"Naughty" behaviour

Once children leave the house, they put a public face on our parenting which may not always be very flattering: few children get through childhood entirely without a period of swearing, spitting, stealing, or worse.

Most parents are shocked to find that their child has deliberately stolen from their purse or has been caught spitting at another child, and they will be horrified when it happens again and again.

Dealing with constant demands

Small children can simply be told "no"; they will soon forget. Older children may just keep on nagging. The first question here is to ask how much you can afford, or feel you should spend on the child. Add it up, and include Christmas, birthdays, holiday spending money, pocket money and treats. Explain to the child that this can all be blown on special treats at Christmas, or that he can use some of it at other times. Children do not need the huge array of treats we give them at Christmas; treats through the year are usually appreciated and enjoyed more.

- The child should understand that the budget is limited, that – once spent – money will not be replenished. If he wants an expensive item for Christmas, he cannot also have the home and away football strips and special trainers. It is his choice.
- Encourage him to save his pocket money. Give him a bonus if he does.
- If your child has reached school age, you can explain family finances in a simplified way. Show him a pile of sweets and three pots. Each sweet represents a unit of money. Start with the monthly income, the amount you have left after tax, pensions, major savings and investments have been deducted. Now put everything that goes on basics (food, rent, mortgage, electricity, telephone, car, heating and so on) into the "spent" pot. Work out how much money you spend on clothes in a year, divide this by 12 and add it to the "spent" pot.

Now add the money you need to save for holidays, birthdays, Christmas, a new car, furnishings and emergencies. Put this into the "savings" pot. Explain to your child that this pot needs to have enough money in it to cope with small emergencies like the washing machine breaking, and bigger ones like being ill or not being able to work for a while. What is left over, goes into the "treats" pot. You should not paint too gloomy a picture, nor should you make it seem as if there were vast amounts of money for every whim. The idea is to show him that the overall amount is limited and that money needs to be managed properly for it not to run out.

- Explain that this is private. This is for our family to know and discuss. It is not something to tell other people.
- Explain rich and poor. Not all parents have the same. Some people have their cars paid for by their jobs. Some have rich grandfathers who can help. Some people lose their jobs and have very little money. Some people have nothing and may need help from others.

Dealing with a child who steals

● Before the age of four, a child cannot put himself in another child's shoes. Although he seems to have grasped the idea of "mine" and "yours", what he really sees is that something is currently in someone's possession. He thinks that, by taking it, it becomes his. It will be easier to explain to him that he is making the other child sad.

● Be patient, keep face and do not accuse him. Labelling does not help.

● Do not ask him if he took it when you know he did. If he sees you are angry, he will want to lie. Don't make him lie.

● Explain simply: "This car belongs in Liam's house. We must take it back."

● Pre-empt: "Remember what we talked about. School toys must stay in school."

● Explain how others will feel: "Liam will be sad when he looks for his car and cannot find it."

Instilling good table manners

● Family meals are for all the family. The sooner the children sit up at table with you, the sooner will they come to learn and appreciate the culture of the table.

● Table talk should include everyone. If parents have things that they want to discuss privately, they should do so over coffee, when the children have got down from the table.

● Be reasonable. If there is a long pause between courses, it is reasonable to let children get down. They should not be expected to sit quietly for a long meal, nor to eat everything that comes to the table. Show them how to spit things out discreetly, using a paper napkin or a cup.

● Rules are the bottom line. They need no explanation: "Jenny we do not touch every piece of bread before we choose one that is right. If you cannot stick to that rule I will have to choose your bread for you."

Raising polite children

● Children should never be made to hug or kiss people unless they want to.

● Children should only be rude if people tell them to do things that are wrong.

● Children should not be expected to be better mannered than their parents.

● Teach them to be assertive, not rude. Explain that manners are about asking and asserting without being unkind.

● Explain to children that what is thought of as polite in one house may not be considered polite in another: "Visitors to our family keep our house rules; when we visit their house we have to keep theirs."

THE STUBBORN (OR OVER-ASSERTIVE) CHILD

Stubbornness and wilfulness are very close to assertiveness. We might say they are assertive behaviour that we do not want.

Situation unimportant	Just ignore it. Give in gracefully.

Situation negotiable	
Identify his feelings	"You want to wear your wellingtons."
Give information	"It's hot. I think your feet will get too hot."
Offer solutions	"Perhaps you could grin and bear it if your feet get hot."
	"Perhaps we could carry your sandals in the bag."

Situation non-negotiable	
Identify his feelings	"You don't want to wear your raincoat."
Give reasons	"Clothes get wet in the rain."
Describe your feelings	"I will be worried that you might get ill."
Offer a choice	"You can wear the raincoat and we will go to the park, or you can stay home. It is your choice."

Situation absolutely non-negotiable	
Identify feelings, give reasons and insist	"You must go to the child minder. You can get dressed or you can go in your pyjamas; it is your choice." Follow through. Put him in the buggy in his pyjamas and take his clothes in a bag.

SPITTING

- A common and annoying habit, spitting is also a foolproof way of getting attention.
- Put on a poker face, pick the child up and take her out of the room.
- Talk about what happened; remind her of the rules.
- Accept her feelings but insist she must behave.
- If she spits when frustrated, distract her beforehand.
- Prepare her: "Leah is coming to play. Remember the rule about spitting?" Remind her with a "secret" word.
- Give choices. "You can play with Leah, but if you spit you must come home." If she spits, take her.
- Praise effort: "I am pleased you did not spit at all today."
- Let her spit when it is harmless.
- If spitting persists, make a star chart – one star for each day without spitting.

I'm feeding the rabbit

Caring for a pet will make your child feel responsible and confident. If she has a real "job", she will not need to brag about invented ones.

Friendship problems

Not all children find it equally easy to make friends. Some behaviours are generally disliked by other children and their parents, and you may need to help your child overcome any antisocial tendencies.

When a child first interacts with others, she may automatically act like a bossy child, or she may be unwilling to share her toys. You can help her.

A child with few friends

Help a child with few friends by showing how much you like her for herself. Tell her to praise herself for her efforts, not just her successes. It helps if you praise her too.

- Teach her not to put herself down. Self-criticism can become a bad habit. No-one should say things about themselves that they would not say to a friend's face.
- Tell the child to pay attention to her own strengths, to judge herself by her own standards, rather than to compare.
- Shyness is a major stumbling block. Give the child the courage to overcome it. Give her a magic button, collar, or cuff that she can touch whenever she needs courage.
- Suggest she starts conversations by asking for help: "I don't know how to do this"; or "Where do these go?"
- Suggest she uses an old standard: "Look at that rain"; or flatters: "I like your dress".

The bragging child

We all embellish the truth. The ability to know the acceptable "height" of a tall story is part of the art of good conversation. Life would be dull if everyone always stuck to the bare facts, but there is a huge difference between a funny story and a constant stream of bragging. Bragging is a symptom of the teller's need for attention, insecurity and often low self-esteem.

- Build self-love and self-esteem. Praise the child's efforts, love her for herself.
- Show her how to think positively about herself. Teach her to say: "That's not like me", rather than "I've messed that up."
- Never do things for her that she can do for herself, except as an occasional treat. Let her reciprocate.
- Give her independence and trust her.
- Don't reward her bragging. Ignore it. Make no comment. Change the subject.

The spiteful child

Children learn to be spiteful because their behaviour is being reinforced.

- Do not label; correct others if they do: "Your sister also knows how to be kind."
- Acknowledge feelings. Then use time out and best poker face to deal with her.
- Tell the child who is being spiteful that you are confident they can and will behave well.
- Attend to the injured party if they have been wronged. Do not blame the spiteful child.

● Keep a keen eye on the victim, and make sure she will not egg on the aggressive child into more spiteful behaviour.

● Check for causes. Stress, unhappiness at school, illness and the spiteful behaviour of others can suddenly cause this behaviour.

The possessive child

● If friends are visiting, negotiate with the child which toys are to be shared and which not. If she will find it difficult, choose a secret word to remind her.

● Describe the situation, understand her feelings and offer advice. Keep visits short.

● Play games that do not use her favourite toys. She'll feel less possessive about them.

RUDE NOISES

Deliberately belching or passing wind are particularly irritating ways of showing off. They never fail to get attention.

● Say nothing, just act. When she farts or belches, leave the room without comment. If you are with someone, or it is more convenient, pick her up, walk to her bedroom, put her inside and close the door. Say nothing.

● If she belches at the table, simply put your meal on a tray and eat elsewhere. During a family meal, pick her up and take her to her room. Warn children who laugh that next time they too will go to their rooms. Do not warn again – act.

● If you are in public, quickly and calmly remove your child. Keep a poker face and when you are away from the audience say: "You can choose to go back, or you can choose to go home. If you belch again I will know you have chosen to go home." Then return. If she belches again, pick her up and leave.

● If she is belching because she wants to go home tell her she can go on belching but that you are counting, and that she will spend three minutes per belch in her room when you get home. Do not make this an empty threat. Act exactly as you predicted you would.

The bossy child

Elder children are often bossy; so are those who are not used to playing with others.

● Ignore bossy behaviour whenever you can. Discuss her bossiness with the child. Tell her when she is using her bossy voice – but do so discreetly. Play being bossy and being bossed around by her.

● Encourage leadership rather than bossiness. Ask other adults if they think you are too bossy. Change your own attitude, and model less bossy behaviour.

The child who tries to buy friends

● If your child is trying to buy friends, check that she is not unhappy for some reason. Build up her self-esteem.

● Check that she is not being bullied. Talk to the school about it. The teacher may be able to advise you on how you can help her.

● Role-play can help a child break the ice.

● Make sure she "fits in". Is she wearing the same clothes? Does she watch the same TV programmes? When children meet, they need common ground to talk.

SEE ALSO
Aggressive children   **162–163**
Becoming independent **164–165**
"Naughty" behaviour   **192–193**
From toddler to child   **186–187**

Let's play together
Ask if there are children your child would like to play with, and invite them around. The teacher may also be able to tell you which children could come to your house.

Passing problems

If your child encounters problems in his development, try to find the causes and address them. You may need professional help, but many problems are just passing ones, and your child will soon grow out of them.

Often, problems such as bed-wetting or immature behaviour are caused by family stress. Shaming and blaming the child does not help here, but reassurance or a system of rewards may do.

Bed-wetting

Bed-wetting tends to run in families. If you or your partner were still wetting the bed at five, it is very likely that at least one of your children will do so too.

- Most 3–5 year-olds occasionally wet the bed; one in four children still do aged 4–6 years, but half of these will have stopped by 6–8 years. Only one in 20 children still has a problem by the time he is ten. More girls than boys have problems at all ages.

- Children continuously wet their beds if they have never fully learned to control their bladders at night. They wet their beds occasionally if they have learned bladder control, but developed problems later.

- If the child's bladder control mechanisms mature slowly, this is likely to cause continuous bed-wetting.

- Give a child less to drink in the evening and ensure he goes to the toilet just before he goes to bed. Lift him a couple of hours after he has gone to sleep, and again when you go to bed. The emptier his bladder, the easier it is to get through the night.

- Star charts work well with occasional bed-wetting. The child gets a star to stick on the chart for each night he is dry. He can exchange a certain number of stars for a small gift or treat.

- Help boys to increase muscle control: put a tennis ball in the lavatory and let him aim, stop, then aim again.

- Train the child to retain urine. Encourage him to wait until his bladder is really full. Once the child can retain half a pint of urine, the problem will disappear. Work gradually towards this goal – slowly increase the time between lavatory visits and ask him to wait for five, then for ten minutes after he feels "he wants to go".

- If you know when he wets the bed, you can wake him up just beforehand. Use an alarm clock. If he wets the bed three hours after going to bed set the alarm for 2½ hours. Put a pot by the bed, or leave the bathroom light on, so he can go to the toilet easily. After a week of dry nights, set the alarm for two hours. After a further

Reassure your child
Stroke your child gently and cuddle him before he goes to bed. It will lower his stress levels, reduce his fears and may avoid bed-wetting.

week of dry nights set it to 1½ hours. Continue until it is no longer needed. Progress in smaller steps if necessary.
● The bell-and-pad method works well, especially with older children. It trains the child to recognize the signs that he is about to empty his bladder. A special training pad is placed under the child. When it is moistened, it rings a bell and turns on a light. The child is woken as he starts to pee, and on waking he gains control and stops.

Unwarranted fears

Never laugh at or belittle a child's fears. To him they are serious. Fears are not always logical, even when we are adults. If a child is afraid, the first thing you need to do is calm him down. He can do nothing to control his fear while he is afraid. Sit him on your lap, hold him tight and talk about the things that frighten him. Read books about the frightening things, play games, draw pictures. If he can feel happy and relaxed while thinking about those things that frighten him, the fear disappears.

Immature behaviour

Sometimes immaturity is late development on one front. At other times it is a reaction to stress or a call for help. The most likely causes for sudden "childishness" (such as wetting his pants or reverting to having tantrums) are stress, anxiety, or possibly illness. A child may also be inadvertently encouraged by parents who do not allow him to grow up – it is easier to dress a child than to let him attempt it himself.
● Look for any stresses in your child's life: a new baby, the depression of a parent, difficulties between parents, starting school, problems at school. Address the cause of the stress. If you are worried about something, it is usually better to explain to him in simple terms what worries you than to pretend that everything is fine.
● Be aware that stress may produce long-term problems if it persists.
● Regressing to immature behaviour is very common. If you criticize the child, you may make it worse. Ignore the behaviour, comfort the child and deal with the stress.

Empathize with the child
If your child is frightened or unduly anxious, tell her of any fears you may have had yourself as a child. Tell her how you overcame them and give her ideas for doing so.

SEE ALSO
Coping with family stress **158–159**
Divorce and remarriage **160–161**
Typical toddler problems **180–181**
Jealousy and loss **188–189**

ANXIETIES

Anxious parents tend to have anxious children but there are things you can do to help.

● **Encourage.** A positive self-image.

● **Give choices.** It will make the child more confident.

● **Praise effort.** Tell the child he has been brave.

● **Acknowledge his feelings.** Never tell the child he is silly.

● **Be consistent.** If he does not know how you will react, it may worry him.

● **Structure his life.** Give him a diary with symbols so he knows what will happen every day.

● **Set limits.** Being too permissive feeds insecurity.

● **Reduce anxiety.** Let him achieve within his own limits.

Problems with speech

Most children will learn to speak sooner or later, and probably by the time they are two. If your child has problems with speech, you may be able to deal with it yourself, but you may need professional help.

Speaking problems, such as late speech or stuttering, are much more apparent than hearing problems (notoriously hard to spot), but the two may be linked. Some problems will pass by themselves, some can be treated at home, by the parents or carers, others will require professional help.

No parent should ever feel embarrassed because they need help. We accept that some illnesses and some household jobs are too difficult for us to deal with on our own, and the same is true of parenting. Some children may need professional help. Childhood is short, and problems are more easily solved if they are caught early. By delaying matters you could be making things more difficult for the child – and for yourself – in the long run.

Late speech

A number of different factors influence the age at which your child will start to speak. If she has been late reaching all the other milestones, her late speech may simply reflect the fact that her development is generally delayed (as may be the case with a premature baby, for example).

Late speech could also reflect poor hearing. It could, of course, reflect both a late development and hearing problems. All babies should have their hearing tested in the first year, and all those children who are not saying anything by the age of 14 months should be re-tested. Speech is often delayed in families where dyslexia is common: although the child understands words, she has difficulties producing the little sounds which make up each word.

Stuttering

Speech requires very precise timing, and therefore any disruption in the sequence if the little sounds within a word can cause a child to stutter. Some children stutter while their timing mechanisms are not yet fully mature. Others stutter because they listen too closely to the sounds of their own speech, and there is a delay between uttering something and hearing it. Most of us stutter if we hear our voices with a delay

Breathe hard

If your child stutters, encourage her to breathe from the belly instead of the chest. Use a mirror or a waistband to make her aware how her navel rises.

(as can occasionally happen if there is an echo on the telephone line). It is assumed that the child who stutters always hears an echo of her speech. All children who stutter need help and reassurance. The difficulties they have in communication can make them withdrawn.

● Benign stuttering begins at about 6–8 years, and lasts for about two years.
● Persistent stuttering begins between three and eight years, and in some cases – but not all – it persists into adulthood. Four per cent of children stutter before they start school, but most of them grow out of it. Only one per cent of the adult population are known to stutter.
● Secondary stuttering, which can be recognized by a serious struggle to speak, facial grimacing, arm and leg movements and irregular breathing, needs immediate attention. Consult your doctor at once – this form of stuttering may be the expression of another problem.

Relating to a child who stutters

● Always let your child try to say what she wants to say, without rushing her.
● Be patient. Do not interrupt the child to finish her sentences for her.
● Reduce stressful situations for the child. Stress makes it harder for her to speak without stuttering.
● Look the child in the eyes. Concentrate on her face and what she is saying. This will give her encouragement. Do not read or watch television while she is trying so hard to speak to you.
● Build up the child's self-esteem. Other children can be cruel and call her names. Give her the means to cope with teasing. Show her that stuttering has nothing to do with intelligence or good looks.
● Many people who stutter do not stutter when they sing. Use this fact and make her sing, to enhance her confidence.

Helping a child who stutters

Accept the child for who she is: Remember that the stutter will get worse if the child (or you) are self-conscious about it. Never talk for her or over her head.

Adjust your family style: The child needs a relaxed atmosphere in order to cope. Calm words and safe routines should ground her day. She cannot easily join in arguments, but you can make sure she is included when everyone makes up.

Keep calm: Stress makes everything worse. There is a very good chance the child will grow out of stuttering. Be warm and supportive to her without being over-protective. She must learn to cope alone. Consciously aim for a happy medium in the attention you give her.

Promote adequacy: Be especially vigilant about any behaviour which will make the child unpopular. Use role-play to help her. Practise having a relaxed chat.

Arrange for speech therapy.

Professional methods at home

To help a stuttering child, try the following for short periods. If one of the methods helps, continue; if not, try another.

● Encourage the child to slow her speech, and to start each sentence in a whisper. Use a candle to practise this.
● Encourage the child to inhale and exhale once from the abdomen before she starts to speak, and then to do so again between her sentences.
● Encourage her to breathe from her abdomen while she is speaking. Practise it.

SEE ALSO

Learning to speak	96–97
Perfecting language	100-101
Talking to children	150–151
Attention problems	200–201

Candle tricks
Stuttering is often diminished if the child whispers. Teach her to speak into a candle, so the flame moves but is not blown out.

Attention problems

All young children are sometimes hyperactive and inattentive. Attention deficit hyperactivity disorder, or ADHD, however, describes those children who are persistently so and experience problems because of it.

Children with ADHD make up between five and ten per cent of the early school-age population in the USA, although much lower percentages prevail elsewhere. Such children lack, or appear to lack, the ability to sit still or to concentrate, and they have short attention spans. Children with ADHD do not do things that other children do not do; they just do them more often and continue doing them when they are much older.

Causes of ADHD

Not all children with ADHD display all the symptoms, and it is unlikely that children who are said to have ADHD all have the same type of problems. This is confirmed by the fact that the disorder is apparently less common in some countries than in others. The underlying causes are unknown. Many believe that they are biological. While this may be the case for some children, it is not the case for all of them. Some children, for example, do not show any symptoms of ADHD until they start to fail at school.

Many of the things we know about disruptive and attention-seeking behaviour in children would suggest that similar processes are involved in cases of ADHD. It is unlikely that the explanation is ever going to be simple. The fact that

ADHD children are often especially sensitive to the disrupting influences of noise would suggest, for example, that they are generally more easily distracted by outside over-stimulation.

Symptoms of ADHD

Children who are diagnosed as suffering from ADHD typically display one or more of the following symptoms:

Poor attention: The child is a poor listener and forgets or ignores instructions. He is visually inattentive and easily distracted. He is inclined to flit between activities, and may forget what he is saying in mid-sentence.

Impulsivity: The child does not plan anything in advance, he speaks before he thinks, and he is easily led.

Hyperactivity: The child is irritable and disruptive, he fidgets and is affected by noise, he is tense in crowds.

Clumsiness: The child is clumsy and accident-prone.

Disorganization: The child has problems sequencing his actions. He finds dressing or stringing actions together difficult.

Aggression: When aggression and ADHD are combined, the prognosis for a child is particularly poor.

Social ineptitude: The child has a low tolerance of failure. He acts the fool, and does not know how to mix. He speaks without thinking or listening.

Poor self-esteem.

Specific learning problems: Problems, such as dyslexia are more common.

Hyperactive children

Children with ADHD who are hyperactive, impulsive and inattentive are highly visible. They are loud, always on the go and talk back to adults. They are also likely to take risks.

Professional ADHD treatments

In the USA, the treatment of choice is the administration of Ritalin or any similar amphetamine-based drugs, and they are now increasingly used in Europe, too. These drugs increase the child's attention span and reduce his activity. One per cent of all children in the USA now take such drugs on a daily basis, and as many as ten per cent will have been treated at some time in their lives. It cannot be denied that the drugs have some benefits. However, reliance on them is almost certainly too heavy and they should not be seen as a cure-all. Always get medical advice on whether drugs would suit your child.

Part of the benefit of drug treatment arises from the fact that the children lose their "labels", and that people begin to have different expectations of them. The same benefits could also be reaped without giving the child a powerful stimulant. The success of behaviour modification (which rewards children for appropriate behaviour and ignores them when they are behaving inappropriately) attests to this.

Helping your hyperactive child

Turn off the radio and TV: Speak more softly. If your child is pushed "over the top" by extraneous stimulation, reduce that stimulation to help him.

Put away the toys: If one of your child's problems is concentrating on what he is currently doing, distractions will make this more difficult for him.

Allow the child to let off steam frequently: Intersperse his day with frequent raucous activities.

Build self-esteem: Some of the child's behaviour may stem from his own frustrations at being hyperactive and unable to focus. Help him achieve little successes by breaking tasks into smaller, more achievable portions.

Help him to relax: Cuddle your child and stroke his forehead as you read to him. Keep the lights low.

Help him sleep: To sleep we need to relax, and to do that we need to push aside distractions. Your child will sleep better in a totally dark room.

Change his diet: The Feingold Diet is an additive-free diet which is claimed to reduce hyperactivity. Although many find it helps in the short term (as all treatments do), there is no evidence that it has anything more than a placebo effect. It helps, because the parents, teachers and particularly the child believe it will.

Stop labelling: Children have a habit of living up to the labels they have been given – too wild, cannot concentrate, never finishes anything, etc. Help him explore his strengths instead of his weaknesses.

Start expecting good behaviour: Structure and organize your child's life. Introduce routines, rules and expectations. Reward effort. Star charts can work. Make a chart for the following week and set a target for improvement. Make each step small. Set a standard for the day which is just a tiny bit harder than the day before. Praise his attempts and ignore his failures. If you believe in him, you will be surprised what can be achieved.

Get down to his level: Remember that attention is difficult and distraction easy. Vision dominates in small children – look him straight in the eye. There is evidence that ADHD children are especially sensitive to noise – speak softly.

Reduce tension: Stress almost certainly makes the situation worse. Let him know when routines change. Turn a blind eye to his bad behaviour and praise the good.

Adapt the environment: Keep the television and the radio out of the dining room; make sure the telephone does not interrupt his or your concentrated work.

SEE ALSO

Building self-esteem	**126–127**
Becoming assertive	**128–129**
Aggressive children	**162–163**
Attention seekers	**172–173**

Calm your child down
Hot baths, dimmed light and cuddles will help him relax and reduce the level of tension he feels. You could also try gentle music, played softly in the background.

CHAPTER SEVEN

Safety and first aid

Accidents happen. We can organize our homes so they are less likely, and we can limit their severity, but our homes will never be perfectly "childproof". Knowing what to do in an emergency can literally mean the difference between life and death. This chapter can be referred to whenever you need it, but you should know straight away what to do in an emergency. By the time you have looked up how to give artificial respiration, the damage could be done. If you are unsure how to act in an emergency, make sure you commit this section to memory.

THE KITCHEN

- Use the back burners for cooking. When using the front burners, point pan handles away from the front. Never use deep-fat fryers or large pots of boiling water on the front of the stove. Fit a guard if this is possible.

- Keep electrical flexes out of reach. Switch off sockets at the mains and unplug appliances when not in use.

- Do not leave hot coffee- or teapots where a child can reach them.

- Fit child-proof catches to drawers and cupboards. Self-closing doors can trap fingers. Use safety film on any glass doors.

- Arrange a safe play area within (view of) the kitchen. Make sure you do not have a child under foot when you are cooking.

- Clean out pets' bowls right after use, and pick them up from the floor.

- Do not leave anything near the edge of a work surface. Keep high chairs out of reach of work surfaces .

- Keep sharp tools and knives, empty bottles and tins in a safe place.

Making indoors safe

However hard we try to child-proof our homes, our efforts are never foolproof and dangers remain. We must always be vigilant, but we must also balance the child's need for protection with her need for independence.

A child who depends entirely on her parents to make her world safe is a potential danger to herself. Providing for her safety has three aspects: training the child to think about her own safety; structuring the environment to make it safe; and eternal vigilance on our part.

Be aware of the dangers

- There are times when you can relax a little and times when you must be vigilant.
- Cleaning products, medicines, electric appliances, cigarettes, alcohol, power tools, knives and garden products are hazardous for mobile babies and toddlers.
- Know what to do if things go wrong. You cannot always prevent accidents but quick actions can make a potentially serious accident less serious.
- Babies and toddlers cannot think ahead or judge dangers. They need careful supervision at all times.
- It is hard to be attentive when you are worried or stressed. Be aware that you need to be particularly vigilant not to leave matches, cigarettes, or hot drinks within the child's reach.
- Avoid hovering over her. The child will never learn to be safety-conscious if you are always there on hand.

Set up a playpen

Once your baby is mobile, a playpen is ideal. If the doorbell rings or you are cooking, you can pop her in and she'll be safe – although possibly frustrated!

Children learn by their mistakes, but we can try to make these less serious. Children need physical play and active rough-and-tumble. They need to climb, balance, jump and race about. We cannot hold their hands and smoothe their paths for ever. There is a happy medium. Find it.

- Set a good example. Children imitate what we do. Explain to your child why you do things in a safe way, point out the dangers even if she is still too young to be responsible for her own safety.
- Never leave a mobile baby or young toddler alone in a room or with a preschool child – they are not old enough to realize the consequences of their actions.

Keeping homes safe

Fireplaces, heaters, radiators: Put a protective grill around these and warn the child. Cover very hot radiators in corridors and near doors with a blanket or thick towel. Always guard naked flames.

Electrical cables: Make sure that there are no loops for the child to pull the cable. Make sure that the cable passes behind shelves and secure loose cables. Never leave an appliance cord which is separated from that appliance (such as one for a kettle) plugged in at the mains.

Sockets: Put socket shields on all easily accessible outlets and switch sockets off. Ensure the system is earthed.

Lights, lamps and fittings: Keep low voltage lights in the hallway and a light in the bathroom so that the child can go to the toilet in safety. Research suggests that night-lights in bedrooms may damage eyes. Do not place lamps where a child could touch hot bulbs or pull the base on top of her. Do not leave lamps without bulbs.

Video recorders, TV: Keep recorders out of reach or install a guard. Place TVs on stable surfaces.

Floors and stairs: Keep floors clean and clear. Children fall frequently, but they rarely hurt themselves because they break their falls. Problems arise when they fall onto or into an object. Use non-slip polish. Fix loose carpets, especially on stairs. Do not place rugs on slippery floors or where they can be tripped over. Check that stair banisters are less than 10 cm (4 in) apart. Make sure children cannot climb on horizontal rails. Gate the stairs at the top and bottom for children under two.

Choking hazards: Always keep small objects out of reach of toddlers and mobile babies. Make sure older children do not leave toys lying around that are unsuitable for under-threes (small pieces can get stuck in the throat). Small children use their mouths to explore – you can't teach them not to put things into the mouth. Even for older children it is hard: it is comforting to suck and chew. Do not let them run about with lollipops in their mouths.

Furniture: Make sure that furniture is stable, especially when babies start pulling themselves up. There should be no sharp edges, especially on low tables – the child may fall onto them. Make sure that the flaps of desks and drawers at head height are closed as they may run into these. Ensure bookcases are either fixed to the wall or blocked by other furniture.

Locks: Keep a double lock on the door (or fix a chain or bolt, especially if you live on a busy road).

Emergency numbers: Always keep the number of a local cab company and the taxi fare to the local hospital to hand. Call an ambulance if a child is badly injured. You can drive to the casualty department, if she needs a stitch or two, but there may be situations when she needs you to comfort her, or you feel too upset to drive. If you are going to the hospital with a relatively minor injury, take a few books. Although children are usually given priority, you may have a long wait.

Check a friend's room: if you are visiting, ask them to remove dangerous objects.

Safe houseplants

Some houseplants – such as dieffenbachia (dumb cane), philodendron (sweetheart plant), daffodil and hyacinth bulbs – are dangerous. Once a child is mobile, check the plants in your house. Move dangerous ones out of reach. If this is impossible, take them into work or give them to friends until the children are old enough to understand the dangers. Check the care labels or ask a good florist or plant centre. Teach your child the difference between food and plants that look pretty but make you poorly. Warn them about getting poison on their fingers. Ban those plants which can be dangerous to touch (such as dumb cane) until children are about seven.

SEE ALSO

Crawling and walking 90–91
Reaching and grasping 94–95
What parents worry about 142–143
Making outdoors safe 206–207

BATHROOMS

- Keep medicines out of reach.
- Keep all cleaning liquids, especially bleach, lavatory cleaner and other corrosives, out of reach. They are safer in a wall cupboard fitted with a child-proof lock than under the sink.
- Do not leave cleaning fluid in the lavatory pan. Clean and then flush three times. Family germs are much less dangerous than cleaning fluid.
- Floors should be non-slip and any spillage cleared. It is easy to slip when holding a child in one arm.
- Do not leave the razor lying around.

Making outdoors safe

Once your child is mobile, it is not sufficient to child-proof only inside your home, you will also need to pay close attention to the outside of the house, the garden and various openings that let him get from one to the other.

A child who understands dangers knows how to avoid them. We could not rely on such learning to protect the youngest children, but will have to rely on it for older children. The sooner we start teaching, the better protected they will be.

Teaching about safety

● Instil a respect for his own safety even before your child understands what you say. Spotting dangers and modelling good safety habits becomes second nature if we do it often enough.

● Build and use a vocabulary to indicate danger: "ouch", "hot", "sharp", "nasty", "hurt", "make you cry", "careful", "don't touch"; "no" by itself can mean too many different things. Teach your child the difference between naughty and dangerous.

● Toddlers can learn that sharp and pointy things are dangerous. Remind the child when you use scissors, knives, razors, or any other sharp implement. Touch the sharp point and say "ouch".

● Teach a one-year-old that "hot" means "do not touch": make him touch the outside of a coffee cup, a hot tap, or a radiator (but not hot enough to burn). Continue reinforcing this.

● Teach children to go up and down stairs as soon as they become mobile. Keep toys and other objects off the stairs at all times. Carpet provides a non-slippery surface, but you need to make sure it is well secured. It will also reduce the injury from falls. Show a baby how to turn and go down stairs feet

first. Babies over seven months do not attempt to crawl down face first. Once they want to walk up and down stairs, show toddlers how to hold on to the rail. Most children will usually be safe, providing they do not get distracted and they can see what they are doing. Danger arises when they stop to do something half-way down or carry something that blocks their view.

● Never keep a gun in the house, unless this is absolutely unavoidable. Guns and ammunition should be kept in separate locked cupboards.

Safe ways to get out

Doors: Fit a chain or child-proof lock to the street door. If you live on a busy street, use the double lock at all times. Make sure that the glass in doors is special safety glass, or cover it with safety film, particularly for internal doors. Children running down passageways can easily fall and put an arm through a pane of glass.

Windows: Fix window locks to all windows above ground level. Attach the key to the curtain rail in upstairs rooms so that the window can be used in case of fire. Make sure windows in upstairs rooms, which open at window cill height, are kept closed and locked, and that there is nothing the child can drag to the window to climb onto the cill. Windows which only open at the top are safer. Windows which come down to floor level should be made from safety glass or covered in safety

PLANTS

Poisonous plants
The following list is not exhaustive: azaleas, belladonna, bleeding heart, bryony, buttercup, Christmas rose, crocus, daffodil and narcissus bulbs, daphne, foxglove, holly, hyacinth bulbs, hydrangeas, iris rhizomes, ivy, laburnum, Japanese yew seeds, Jack-in-the-pulpit, larkspur, laurel, lily, lily-of-the-valley, mistletoe, morning glory seeds, oleander, poison ivy, poison oak, privet, rhododendron, rhubarb leaves, sweet pea, tomato plant leaves, wisteria pods, yew.

Toadstools/fungi
Pull these up as soon as they appear.

Hazardous plants
Fruit and seeds are hazardous as small children may use these as pretend food. Bulbs (which look like onions) run a close second. Explain that certain fruits and seeds are poisonous and should never be used for games. Always warn them not to touch plants after they have been sprayed. We rarely eat flower petals, so children must not try to do so. Show them which ones are safe (roses, nasturtiums).

film. If it is difficult or impossible to keep windows closed, fit window guards. Tie curtain and blind chords out of reach so that children do not get entangled in them.

Balconies: Make sure that balcony restraints cannot be climbed by the child, or that a small child could not squeeze between the bars. Never leave chairs or tables on the balcony when a child has access to it and could climb on them.

Painted surfaces: Modern paints are lead-free, but in old houses flaking paint can expose earlier paints which contained lead, and lead may also be present in any flakes of paint which peel from walls that have been painted over. If you cannot strip back years of paint, paint and paper over the cracks. Lead is safe as long as it stays on the wall. If your paint is peeling, and you suspect there may be lead paint underneath the modern layers, clean toys, floors, carpets and hands frequently – flakes cling.

Lead in old houses: Although mains water supplies no longer use lead, the pipes in early 20th-century (and older) houses may do. This can be checked by your water board. They should be replaced.

The safe garden

● **Empty ponds** or pools, or fence and cover them with strong mesh netting. Tell the children they must not play near them. If you have a pool which is unguarded, never leave the child alone.

● **Chemical sprays** can stick to the skin. Teach children to wash their hands, particularly before eating.

● **Most garden chemicals** are poisonous, some are lethal. Buy them in small quantities to minimize storage, and safely dispose of any that you will not use in the next weeks. Keep them in a locked toolbox, and return them to that box immediately after use. Keep the box out of reach. Be cautious when in use.

SEE ALSO
Crawling and walking   **90–91**
Reaching and grasping   **94–95**
What parents worry about **142–143**
Making indoors safe   **204–205**

Stay away from water
Encourage a healthy respect for water in your child. Teach him that he must never go near a river, stream, or pond without an adult, however tempting it may seem.

● **Garden stakes** should be taller than the children and capped. Keep hedge cutters, garden shears and other sharp gardening tools out of reach. Store rakes and hoes so they cannot swing up and hit the child if he accidentally steps on them.

● **Cover sandpits** so they cannot be used as latrines by the local cats. Clear up after pets. Keep rubbish sacks out of reach.

● **Put up deckchairs** and folding furniture yourself so that small fingers cannot get trapped. Keep ladders out of reach, and keep garden sheds locked.

● **Attach child-proof locks** to gates and ensure the child cannot escape through breaks in the fence or gaps in the hedge.

● **Cover drains** with wire mesh and any water collecting device with a closed lid.

Nursing a sick child

If your child is ill, you will need to take her temperature and you may have to administer medication. It may also be necessary to stop her becoming dehydrated, especially if she has a fever or diarrhoea, or has been vomiting.

Giving a child medicine

Using a spoon: Hold a small child in your arm. If she will not open her mouth, gently pull down her chin (ask for help). Place the spoon on her lower lip, raise it and let the liquid flow in. If she refuses to swallow, stroke her throat gently.

Using a dropper: A dropper is useful for administering medicine directly into the mouth of a small baby. Alternatively, place a tube or syringe on her lower lip.

Using a finger: If none of these methods work, dip a clean finger into the medicine and let the baby suck it from your finger.

If your child hates medicine

- Get another adult to help.
- Wrap a baby or small child in a blanket and hold her firmly to stop struggling.
- Put only a tiny portion of the medicine in the mouth at any one time.
- Ask another adult to hold her mouth open while you pour the medicine in. Follow this with a quick squirt of water from a syringe, then with a drink.
- To an older child, suggest that she hold her nose; for a younger child hold it yourself. It lessens the taste and encourages swallowing.
  - Mix the medicine with a fluid she likes, a spoonful at a time. Do not mix it into a drink as the medicine will sink to the bottom. Bribe her with a sweet treat or chocolate, but help her to clean her teeth afterwards.

Medicine in a syringe
Place the tip of the syringe in your child's mouth so it points towards the cheek, then slowly press the plunger. Do not aim it directly at her throat – it could cause choking.

FIRST AID BOX

- Antiseptic liquid, to be used in a diluted form to clean cuts. Antiseptic wipes are even more convenient
- Bandages – stretchy crepe bandages when firm pressure is needed, tubular finger bandages and a couple of general purpose rolls of bandage
- Plasters – the best "heal-all" for all children's ills
- Scissors – to cut bandages and plasters to size, if necessary
- Sterile strips – to close wounds
- Sterile dressings
- Sterile cotton wool
- A sling – for injuries to the arm
- Adhesive tape – to hold wound dressings in place
- Tweezers – to remove splinters
- An eye bath and eye wash
- Paracetamol syrup for pain relief and to reduce fever
- Thermometer – a forehead thermometer is the easiest to use
- Medicine spoon to measure doses accurately
- Medical dropper or syringe for giving medicines to very young children
- Tongue depressors
- Hot water bottle
- Calamine lotion for bites and rashes
- Re-hydration fluid
- Sunscreen and after-sun cream
- Petroleum jelly
- Antiseptic ointment
- An unopened bottle of mineral water (which is sterile)

Medicine in a dropper
Comfort your child, while gently pulling down her chin. Take a measured amount of liquid into the dropper, place it in the corner of the child's mouth, then release the fluid a drop at a time.

Taking a child's temperature

Measuring a fever accurately is not usually important: a child with a fever is hot to the touch; a child with a high fever is burning to the touch. A child who is "felled" with fever is inert, dazed, very hot, withdrawn and "not herself". She probably has a racing pulse and is clearly and obviously very ill. This needs immediate attention.

Temperature discs: Best for babies. Easy to use, but not very accurate. Place the disc on the forehead, leave for 15 seconds. Read once the numbers have come to rest.

Rectal thermometers: Accurate. Shake the thermometer to lower the mercury, lubricate it with baby oil. Lay the baby or child on her back and lift up her legs, or lay an older child face down over your knee. Gently ease the thermometer 2.5 cm (1 in) into the rectum. Remove after two minutes, read, then wash the thermometer.

Ear thermometers: A reading can be taken in less than two seconds, while the baby is asleep. Accurate, but expensive for home use.

Oral thermometers: For older children. Place bulb of the thermometer under the child's tongue. Tell her to keep the tip of her tongue firmly behind her lower teeth and to close her lips (not her teeth) over the thermometer. Read after two minutes.

Dangerous fevers

A mild fever is not serious, but a high fever can become so. Fever causes sweating, and this can result in fluid loss. If fluid is not replenished, the child's blood pressure will fall which could lead to heart failure. It is vital to treat dehydration, especially if it is accompanied by diarrhoea and vomiting.

What to do: In all cases, the priority is to reduce fever – cool the child by sponging, showering, or bathing with tepid water and give paracetamol.

● Give a feverish child plenty of fluids. Water is fine for mild fever, but for high fever use re-hydration fluids to reinstate lost sugar and salts (see p. 218).

Call the doctor if: a raised temperature (above 38°C/100.4°F) is combined with any of the following:

● She is less than three months old.
● She is vomiting or has diarrhoea.
● She cries or moans for no reason.
● She is unusually drowsy or lethargic.
● She is not feeding.

SEE ALSO
Keeping your baby warm **16–17**
Keeping your baby cool **18–19**
The recovery position **212–213**
Heat exhaustion **218–219**

Forehead temperature
Hold the temperature strip against the child's forehead with both hands. Keep your fingers clear and make sure it is flat against the head. Read after 15 seconds.

Armpit temperature
Sit the child on your lap. Shake the thermometer, then place it into her armpit, lower the child's arm and hold in place. Read after two minutes.

Resuscitating a child

Stopping breathing is the main cause of heart failure in a child. Different ways of resuscitating him should be used for different ages. Below are the steps for a child aged one to eight years; opposite, those for a baby under one.

If you suspect that a child has something in his mouth or throat, turn his head to one side and carefully run your index finger around his mouth. Remove what you find. Liquids are more easily removed if you cover your finger with your shirt or skirt. Be very careful not to push objects into the throat, particularly in a small baby, since the mouth is so shallow. If you think he has something stuck in his throat, place him head down across your knee and slap the upper part of his back. Continue until the object is cleared. Support a baby on your forearm with his head down. Slap between the shoulder blades.

If a child is not breathing

1 Lay the child on a firm surface. Place one hand on his forehead and put the other under the back of his neck to immobilize the cervical spine. Press very gently on the forehead and gently tilt the head back. The chin should be parallel to the floor or slightly tilted towards the ceiling. Place two fingers on the bony part of the chin and lift this so it juts forward. The tongue will come forward with the jaw.

2 If he is breathing, his chest will move and you hear and feel breath on your face. If not, pinch his nose; place your mouth around his; breathe deeply 5 times, until his chest rises.

3 Using two fingers, check for the pulse in his neck, between windpipe and large muscle. If you cannot find it, start chest compression.

4 Place one hand two fingers' width below the end of the breastbone. Press down firmly to a third of the depth of the chest, 5 times in 3 seconds. Give one breath (step 2). Repeat.

If a baby is not breathing

To find out if the baby is conscious, talk to him and gently tap or agitate his feet. Never shake a baby by the shoulders.

If the baby does not respond, start to resuscitate him. Place the child on a firm, flat surface such as a table. The basic breathing technique used for resuscitating a small baby is the same as that for older children, but because the baby is so small you will find it easier to seal your mouth over both his mouth and nose at the same time.

CAUTION: Do not tilt the baby's head back too far, because his neck and airways are still more fragile than an adult's. Do not breathe too hard – the air can get into the baby's stomach, forcing its contents into the lungs.

1 Place an index finger on the chin and the other hand on the baby's forehead. Tilt the head back to open the airway. Look inside the mouth to see if anything is blocking the airway. Use a hooked index finger to remove it.

2 Look for a rising chest and listen for breathing. Place your cheek close to the baby's mouth to feel for breath. If he is not breathing after 5 seconds, start artificial respiration. Make a tight seal by completely covering the baby's mouth and nose with your mouth.

3 Breathe deeply enough to make the baby's chest rise. Give five breaths, taking your mouth off after each one. Check the pulse, using two fingers on the inside of the arm, midway between the elbow and the shoulder. If there is no pulse, start chest compression.

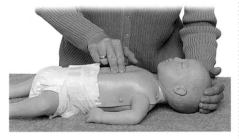

4 Place two fingers on the baby's chest, a finger's width below his nipple line. Press the chest down 2 cm (3/4 in), 5 times in 3 seconds. Give one breath. Repeat until help arrives or the heartbeat returns and the baby is breathing. Place him in the recovery position.

SEE ALSO

Nursing a sick child	**208–209**
The recovery position	**212–213**
Shock	**214–215**
Poisoning	**218–219**

SEQUENCE CHECKLIST

- If a child is unconscious, open the airway and check for breathing. Be careful not to push an object farther down his throat.
- If you suspect head or neck injury, move around to the head end of the child's body, kneel down and tilt his head with your fingers, firmly holding his lower jaw at the junction of upper and lower jaw, while another person supports the neck on both sides.
- If there are no signs of breathing, give artificial respiration.
- If there is a pulse, continue artificial respiration. Check the pulse every tenth breaths
- If the chest does not rise after two breaths, check how you opened the airway and give artificial respiration. If three more breaths fail, check for an obstruction (see opposite).
- If there is no pulse or sign of recovery, begin chest compression (see step 4 above), combined with artificial respiration.
- If the child's breathing returns, put him in the recovery position (p.212).

The recovery position

If your child is unconscious but breathing, place her in the recovery position while you are waiting for help. It will allow her to breathe freely, and promote good circulation while supporting her body in a comfortable position.

Recovery position for children

1 Lay the child flat on the ground and kneel next to her, by her side. Turn the child's head towards you, tilting it back slightly to keep the airways clear. Place the arm nearest you by her side or stretched away from her body and your knees.

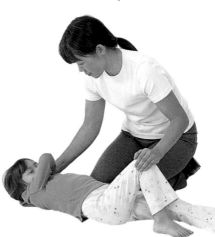

2 With your right hand, lay the child's other arm across her chest, pulling it towards you. With your left hand, pull up the knee of the leg that is farthest from you. Cross this leg over the one nearest to you at the ankles.

RECOVERY POSITION FOR A BABY

If the baby is unconscious, shout for help.

- Check if the baby is breathing. You should be able to see the rise and fall of her chest. If you place your head next to her mouth, you should hear and feel her breath.

- If the baby is breathing naturally, her heart will also be beating. Place the baby in the recovery position. Sit down and place her on your lap. Hold the baby with her feet pointing towards your abdomen and her head tilted downward. Hold your arms stretched out either side of the baby and securely support her head with your hands.

- If the baby is not breathing, open the airways and begin mouth-to-mouth resuscitation (see pp.210–211). This is your first priority because permanent brain damage can occur after only three minutes.

3 Supporting the child's head, grasp the hip farthest from you; gently roll her towards you. Bend her arm and leg to stop her rolling onto her face. Make sure the head is tilted back.

In an emergency

Children are accident prone. They also find it hard to think ahead and this can be a dangerous combination. Fortunately most accidents are minor, but quick action can literally mean the difference between life and death.

SEE ALSO
Making indoors safe   **204–205**
Making outdoors safe   **206–207**
Resuscitating a child   **210–211**
Bleeding   **214–215**

Broken arm

1 While your child holds onto the broken arm, slip a three-sided arm sling or a folded scarf under the arm, with the point past the elbow.

2 Take both ends of the long base of the triangle around his neck, one behind the injured arm, the other in front of it.

3 Tie the ends together , using a reef knot: bring the left end over and under the right one, then the right end over and under the left one.

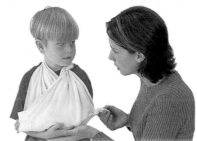

4 Secure the elbow end of the sling with a safety pin, or twist it and safely tuck it inside the sling. Tuck in any extra fabric.

5 If the upper arm, shoulder, or collar bone are injured, secure the sling with a strip of cloth tied horizontally around the arm and chest.

Supporting the arm
If you suspect that a child may have broken his arm, apply a sling or hold the arm in position and take him to hospital.

APPLYING TRACTION

If it seems that a child may have broken his legs, you can reduce both bleeding from any wounds and the child's pain by appplying traction.

● Make sure the child lies flat on a hard, straight surface, with both legs stretched out.

● Gently but steadily pull on the foot, following the same line as the broken bone, if the child can bear it.

● Place a blanket on the child if he is cold, and try to distract him from his pain, always making sure he will not move his legs.

MINOR CUTS

Most small cuts and grazes can be dealt with at home. Hold the cut under the cold tap to clean the wound, or wash it with plenty of water. Pat dry and dress with a plaster or dressing pad and a clean bandage.

Bleeding

Heavy bleeding is particularly serious for small children because they only have a relatively small volume of blood. A fall in the volume of blood may cause shock, and eventually heart failure.

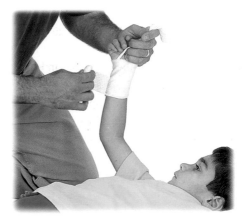

Severe bleeding

1 If the child is not already lying down, help him into a lying position. Apply pressure directly to the cut area. At the same time, raise the affected body part higher than the rest of the child's body. Maintain an even pressure.

2 If available, apply a wound dressing to the wound. Alternatively, use any clean, non-fluffy material, such as a paper nappy, tea towel or sanitary pad, and secure it with a scarf.

3 Maintain pressure on the wound by tying the ends of the bandage directly over the pad. If the bleeding persists, add a second pad, but do not remove the first dressing.

DO'S AND DON'TS

- Get the child to the casualty department as soon as possible.
- Do not place anything other than the dressing on to the wound.
- Do not remove foreign bodies. They may well be stemming the bleeding. Apply pressure either side of the object.
- Puncture wounds may carry infection into lymph areas. Soak a small puncture wound in hot soapy water for 15 minutes. Watch the area carefully. If the infection is spreading or swelling, go to casualty.

Watch carefully

Lie the child on a flat surface, raise his legs so they are higher than his heart, and prop them up with several pillows.

Shock

Clinical shock is not caused by surprise or fright – it is the body's response to severe loss of blood pressure or heart failure. It can also be caused by a severe allergic reaction to medicines or insect stings.

Watch a child if he is bleeding severely, is dehydrated, or has severe burns, even if there is no sign of shock. It can be fatal.

Possible symptoms: Cold, clammy and pale bluish/grey skin; rapid, weak pulse; shallow and fast breathing; sweating; agitation; dizziness; blurred vision; thirst.
What to do: Treat the possible causes (such as severe bleeding or burns). Raise the child's legs (see left). Loosen any tight clothing. Turn his head to one side. Cover him and keep him comfortably warm, but be careful that he does not overheat – this could move blood towards the skin and away from his vital organs. Watch him carefully – if he stops breathing, start mouth-to-mouth resuscitation (see p.210).

Choking

Call for help: if a child continues to cough for 2–3 minutes.

Act immediately: if the cough becomes silent, the child is struggling for breath or turning blue; if he makes high-pitched sounds or is unable to speak or cry; if he is sick (he may have a swelling in the throat).

If someone else is present: or you do not know what to do, call 999. If no one else is there, act first and call for help later.

SEE ALSO

Making indoors safe　**204–205**
Making outdoors safe　**206–207**
Resuscitating a child　**210–211**
The recovery position　**212–213**

If the child is unconscious

1 Lay the child on his side and give him five back slaps. Turn him face upwards and check his mouth for an object. If he is not breathing, give five breaths of mouth-to-mouth resuscitation (see pp.210–11). Using the heel of one hand on his lower breastbone, give 5 sharp inward thrusts, one-third of the depth of his chest, once every 3 seconds.

For a child aged one to eight years

1 Hold the child from behind. Make a fist, put it against the lower breastbone and grasp it with your other hand. Press into chest 5 times with a sharp inward thrust every 3 seconds.

2 If choking continues, grasp your fist on the child's abdomen, under the rib cage and above the navel. Press with a sharp upward thrust up to 5 times. Continue until help arrives.

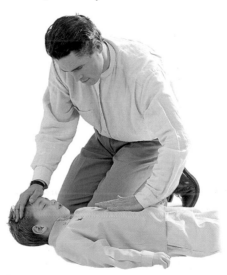

2 If the obstruction has not been cleared, put the heel of your hand halfway between his navel and breastbone. Give up to 5 firm upward thrusts. Check his mouth again for any object that may have become dislodged. Continue until help arrives. Put the child into the recovery position (see p. 212) as soon as he starts breathing.

CHOKING BABY

● Hold a baby face down, supporting his chest with your arm and his chin with your hand. Slap firmly between shoulder blades 5 times. Turn the baby over and check his mouth.

● If the object was not dislodged, hold the baby on your knee, head lower than chest. Press two fingers firmly on his chest, just below the nipple line, 5 times. Check the mouth.

Drowning

You can only help your child if you are safe yourself. Do not jump into the water if you can reach her from the shore. If she is in a fast current, try to get her further down stream. Very young children can go into a state of suspended animation and hold their breath underwater for a surprisingly long time.

- **If your child is conscious**, get her out of the water as quickly as possible and cover her with dry clothing. Take her into shelter as quickly as possible. Carry her, head lower than body, to drain any water from her mouth and throat.
- **If your child is unconscious**, check if she is breathing. If she is not, start mouth-to-mouth resuscitation (see pp.210–11). If you can stand in the water, start mouth-to-mouth breathing as you carry her ashore. Support her head with one hand, take a breath and place your open mouth so that it covers both her nose and mouth. Blow gently into her lungs, watch her chest rise. Remove your mouth and repeat. Lay her on the shore and continue.
- **If she is unconscious but breathing**, put her in the recovery position (see p.212) and cover her. Do not remove wet clothes. Keep checking breathing and pulse.
- **Wait for the ambulance or**, if it is quicker and you have another adult with you, drive directly to casualty. Turn the child on one side if you suspect she is trying to vomit.

Safety first

You can help no one if you also receive a shock. Don't let the current pass through your body.

Electric shock

Switch off the power source or break electrical contact before you touch the child. If you cannot switch off the fuse, use a wooden or plastic broom handle to push the electric source away from the child. Do not use metal. Make sure your hands are dry, and do not stand on a wet or metal surface.

- **Once the contact is broken**, examine the child carefully. Check for burns. Call an ambulance. Comfort him and treat him for shock (see p. 214) while you are waiting for help.
- **If he is unconscious,** check that he is breathing. If not, apply mouth-to-mouth resuscitation immediately (see pp.210–11), checking his pulse after one minute. If he is unconscious but breathing, put him into the recovery position (see p.212).

CONVULSIONS

Symptoms. Falling over, eyes rolling, foaming at the mouth, stiffening of the body, followed by uncontrolled jerking movements and drowsiness.

Causes. Brief convulsions are not uncommon in very high fevers, and some children are prone to these. All first-time seizures should be reported to your doctor. Other possible causes are illness, brain damage, infection and epilepsy. Convulsions may sometimes be caused by taking prescription medicines. It is important that you inform the hospital if this is the case.

Treatment. Clear the area around the child, or move her to an uncluttered area. Loosen the clothing around her neck and middle. Put the child on her side, with head lower than hips (use a pillow to raise the legs). If she stops breathing, resuscitate. Call an ambulance. If you are alone, wait until she breathes again before calling for help. Always call 999 if a seizure lasts more than 2–3 minutes, or is particularly severe, or if seizures occur in rapid succession.

Burns

All but the most minor burns need professional treatment. Call the doctor immediately if a burn is larger than a child's hand, looks raw and blistered (2nd degree), charred or white (3rd degree).

Cool the affected area as fast as possible, to stop the burn reaching deeper tissues. Serious burns produce shock and fluid loss, and this should also be treated. If a burn gets worse, call the doctor at once.

1 Cool the burns by putting the affected area under cool running water for as long as the child can stand it, but at least for 10–20 minutes. Call an ambulance. Use tepid, not ice-cold water. If a large area is involved, put the child into a cool bath or under a tepid shower (about 10–15°C/50–60°F), then cover her with cool, wet sheets. Use smooth (not brushed) cotton or linen sheets, and keep them wet.

CHEMICAL BURNS

Put the affected part of the body in cold water as quickly as possible. Leave it in the water for as long as the child can tolerate it. Hold your child in a position that allows the contaminated water to drain away directly – do not let the chemical run down her body. Carefully remove all contaminated clothing, but do not try to slip it over her head.

2 Carefully cut away clothing. Only undress the child if you are certain the area is not affected, so you do not pull the skin off with the clothing. Leave areas where clothing has stuck to the skin, but bath to arrest the burn.

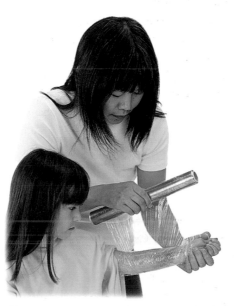

3 To prevent the burned area becoming infected, cover it with cling film, aluminium foil, or a plastic bag, or with any other non-fluffy material such as a clean bandage or a pillowcase. Secure the covering with a plaster wrapped around the film or bag; do not stick the plaster onto your child's skin. Take your child to the hospital or call an ambulance.

SEE ALSO

Making indoors safe	**204–205**
Making outdoors safe	**206–207**
Resuscitating a child	**210–211**
The recovery position	**212–213**

DO'S & DON'TS

- If the limbs are burned, raise them above the rest of the body.

- Do not put any fats or ointments on burns. Do not break blisters. Do not cover with anything which could stick to the injury. Take care when immersing children in cold water. It can cause hypothermia.

- Check regularly. If burns you are treating at home start to get worse, call the doctor immediately or go to casualty.

- Providing a child is conscious and does not have any burns to the mouth, give her sips of water or of a re-hydration liquid.

Poisoning

Symptoms. Your child may have burns to the mouth, convulsions and/or diarrhoea, and he may vomit, lose consciousness, or have a seizure. Look for an empty bottle nearby, or leaves or berries in his hand, and keep these. If the poison is known, an antidote can be given.

What to do. Ask him gently what he has swallowed. Tell him you are not angry but insist that he tells you. Act quickly – it's possible that he

Avoid danger

If you need to resuscitate an unconscious child, be sure you will not ingest the poison yourself.

could lose consciousness. Keep a sample or the medicine bottle, even if it is empty.

● **If he has taken a corrosive poison,** such as bleach, lavatory cleaner, or weedkiller, do not try to make him sick. Anything that burns on the way down will burn on the way up. Give cold milk to cool the burns. Get him to hospital. If you know he has not taken a corrosive poison, give him a glass of salty water and tickle the back of his throat with your finger until he starts to gag.

● **Never make an unconscious child sick.** Place him in the recovery position (see p. 212). Call the hospital immediately. Check his breathing. Before giving mouth-to-mouth resuscitation (see pp. 210–11), wipe his mouth. If necessary, close his mouth and breathe through his nose.

Heat exhaustion and heat stroke

Heat exhaustion results from overheating from excess sun or exercise. Mild heat exhaustion is not serious, but should be treated without delay. Heat stroke, a progression, can be fatal if left untreated.

● **Symptoms of heat exhaustion.** Temperature over 38°C (100.4°F), rapid

Keeping cool

Wrap the child in a wet towel, and have more wet towels ready to replace it once it has become too warm. Cool his head with a wet, tepid sponge or a towel.

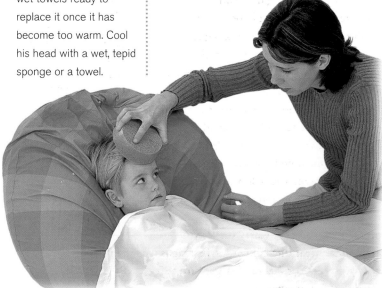

pulse, pale and clammy skin, nausea, dizziness, muscle cramps, headache.

● **Symptoms of heat stroke.** Temperature over 40°C (104°F), rapid pulse, hot, dry skin, no sweat, drowsy, confusion followed by unconsciousness.

● **What to do.** Call for help immediately if your child seems to be drifting towards unconsciousness, or take him to casualty.

● **Give the child liquid** and reduce his temperature, then get help.

● **At home,** undress him immediately and put him under a tepid shower or bath. Do not use cold water. On the beach, get him into the warmer shallow water, immerse his body and splash water over his head.

● Wrap him loosely in a wet towel before you take him to hospital. Cover the head with it. Take water to pour over his head.

● **Rehydration formula:** use rehydration crystals; or a solution of 6 tsp sugar and 1 tsp salt to 1 litre water; or dilute cola 50:50 with water; or dilute fruit juice or squash. Add 1/2 tsp salt to 1 litre. Make him sip continuously unless he loses consciousness.

Hypothermia

Symptoms. Severe shivering, very cold, pale blue skin, drowsiness, and confusion, slurred speech, loss of consciousness.

What to do. Wrap something dry around the child, over any wet clothes. Carry him to shelter, close to your body. In the warm, remove wet clothes. Hold him close, wrap in a blanket and call the doctor. Put an older child in a bath of water that is just warm to your elbow. Give warm (not hot) sweet drinks. If his temperature does not rise, or he drifts into unconsciousness, get him to hospital immediately.

Important. It is important that the core of the body warms first. He must warm up gradually. If his skin warms too quickly, the blood will move to the surface and the core will warm more slowly.

Cold babies

Very young babies are in great danger of hypothermia. If he feels cold to the touch, is drowsy and floppy, put him against your body or wrap a blanket around you. Call for help.

SEE ALSO
Keeping your baby warm **16–17**
Keeping your baby cool **18–19**
Making indoors safe **204–205**
Making outdoors safe **206–207**

Head injury

If your child has had a blow to the head, and shows any of the following symptoms, take him to casualty immediately.

Symptoms. Stunned or dazed, drowsy, periods of unconsciousness, irritable, vomiting, discharge of blood or straw-coloured fluid from the ears or nose.

What to do. See a doctor. Even if he loses consciousness for a few moments only, he needs to be checked by a doctor.

● **If he complains of a sore bump** and a headache, let him sit down for an hour, preferably in a dark room. Watch him. If he develops any of the above symptoms, take him to hospital.

● **Press a clean pad onto the wound** until the bleeding stops. Clean with soap and water, then dress. If the wound is jagged and long, he may need stitching. Dress with steri-strips and go to casualty.

● **If there is a discharge from the ears** or nose, let it flow. Absorb it on a pad. Take him to casualty immediately.

Severe allergic reaction

A severe allergic reaction or anaphylactic shock is a rare, life-threatening reaction to an insect sting, an injected drug or, less commonly, a food or drug taken orally.

Symptoms. Swelling of the face, tongue and the back of the throat, which may cause severe breathing difficulties; blood pressure may drop rapidly because the small blood vessels near the skin quickly dilate, drawing blood away from the core of the body; the heart rate increases to try to compensate for this.

What to do. Emergency treatment is needed immediately. Get the child to hospital. He will be given an adrenaline injection, which will quickly reverse the allergic response. You will probably also be issued with an injection or aerosol spray to take away, which you can use if the problem arises again. Carry these with you at all times, treat the child at the first signs of any problem or, failing this, get him to the hospital immediately.

ASTHMA

● If an asthma attack does not respond to the usual medication, urgent treatment with steroids, broncho-dilators and oxygen is needed.

● If treatment is given early, you can to do this at home, especially if you have a nebulizer.

● If the attack becomes worse, consult your doctor.

● Very young children do not always respond to the drugs and may need to go to hospital. Remember: children may die from asthma.

● If the attack seems much more serious than usual, go to casualty, especially if your child is having serious difficulty breathing, is getting very tired and if he is is looking rather grey or blue.

Index

Acknowledgments

If the publishers have unwittingly infringed copyright in any illustration reproduced, they would pay an appropriate fee on being satisfied to the owner's title.

Picture credits
The author and the publishers greatly acknowledge the invaluable contribution made by Mike Good who took all the photographs in this book except:

l=left; *r*=right; *t*=top; *b*=bottom; *c*=centre.
p.2*l* Adrian Weinbrecht, **2***r* gettyone Stone/ John Fortunato; **3***l* Telegraph Colour Library/ Spencer Rowell, **3***r* gettyone Stone/ Charles Thatcher; **6***r* The Stock Market; **7***l* and **c** SuperStock; **12** Laura Wickenden; **13** gettyone Stone/ Tim Brown; **18** gettyone Stone/ John Fortunato; **20** Adrian Weinbrecht; **22** Andrew Sydenham; **36** Bubbles/ Jennie Woodcock; **37** Adrian Weinbrecht; **38** Robert Harding Picture Library/ Jim Trois/ Explorer; **40** The Image Bank; **43** Bubbles/ Frans Rombout; **50***t* gettyone Stone/ Camille Tokerud, **50***b* John Freeman; **51** Bubbles/ Jacqui Farrow; **54** Bubbles/ Pauline Cutler; **56** The Image Bank/ Tom Hussey; **58** Bubbles/ Ian West; **64** gettyone Stone/ Bruce Ayers; **65** Bubbles/ Moose Azim; Telegraph Colour Library/ Spencer Rowell; **68** Robert Harding Picture Library/ Brad Nelson/ Phototake NYC; **71** Bubbles/ Frans Rombojt; **78** Adrian Weinbrecht; **84** Telegraph Colour Library/ Mel Yates; **86** gettyone Stone/ Camille Tokerud; **109***t* Robert Harding Picture Library; **112/113** The Stock Market/ Bill Miles; **115** The Stock Market; **120** The Stock Market/ Jose L. Pelaez; **123***t* gettyone Stone/ Bob Thomas; **124** John Barlow; **125** Laura Wickenden; **128** Camera Press; **131***l* The Photographers Library, **135** ZEFA-Stockmarket; **131***r* Powerstock/ Zefa/ Norman; **132** The Photographers Library; **136** Bubbles; **143** gettyone Stone/ Charles Thatcher; **147***r* The Photographers Library; **150** Laura Wickenden; **152/53** SuperStock; **156** gettyone Stone/ Roger Ellis; **160** Bubbles/ Loisjoy Thurstun; **164** Bubbles/ Elizabeth Carter; **168/69** SuperStock; **185***t* Telegraph Colour Library; **188** The Stock Market; **191** Bubbles/ Richard Yard; **201** gettyone Stone/ Roy Gumpel; **204** Retna/ Sandra Lousada; **207** Corbis/ Macduff Everton; **210** Iain Bagwell; **211** Andrew Sydenham; **212** John Freeman; **204** *tl*, *bl*, *tr*, *bc* Iain Bagwell, *br* Andrew Sydenham

Charts
The charts on pages **70** and **73** are reproduced with with the permission of the Child Growth Foundation 1996/1

First aid
The publishers acknowledge the assistance of St John Ambulance in the photography for the first aid chapter.